# Duelling in a New World

## *By Ann Birch*

BWL Publishing Print 9780228600497

*BWL Publishing Inc.*

*Books we love to write ...*
*Authors around the world.*

http://bwlpublishing.ca

# Dedication

*To Frances, Claire, and Lee—with love*

# Acknowledgements

I began my long journey researching this book by looking at archival documents. Many thanks to the archivists at the Law Society of Upper Canada in Toronto and the National Archives in Ottawa who supplied me with boxes of John White's letters and his diaries. I also thank the archivists of the Baldwin Collection at the Toronto Reference Library for facilitating my reading of the letters and journals of Elizabeth Russell, most of which were first drafts scribbled on scraps of paper.

Many books enabled me to recreate the world that John White was part of. I am especially thankful for these historical accounts: *Murder Among Gentlemen* by Hugh Halliday; *Muddy York: A History of Toronto Until 1834* by Richard Fiennes-Clinton; *Crime and Punishment in Upper Canada* by Janice Nickerson; *The Colonial Century,* ed. by A.J. M. Smith; *Spadina* by Austin Seton Thompson; *The Diary of Mrs. John Graves Simcoe,* ed. with notes by John Ross Robertson; *The Capital Years: Niagara-on-the-Lake 1792-1796,* ed. by Richard Merritt, Nancy Butler, and Michael Power; *The Town of York 1793-1815* by Edith Firth; *Elizabeth Postuma Simcoe 1762-1850* by Mary Beacock Fryer; *A Cooking Legacy* by Virginia T. Elverson and Mary Ann McLanahan; *Empire Fashion* by Tom Tierney; and *$18^{th}$ Century Clothing* by Bobbie Kalman.

I am grateful to the people who stayed with me for the many years leading to  publication. Novelist Barbara Kyle offered wise advice and intensive editing.  My husband Nicholas and sons John and Hugh gave support at all times. Carolyn Thompson helped with nitpicking details. She even went through the tailors' bills for White's fine clothes!

Finally, I thank the amazing folk at Books We Love Publishing Ltd, especially Nancy Bell, Michelle Lee, and Judith Pittman. They moved me through the process of publishing this book with skill, speed, and wisdom.

# Chapter One

*Near London, England, September 1791*

John White's boots pinch, but the stink of London bothered him more. On his long trek north through the city, he hopped over clumps of shit, and he could not avoid the piss. He stopped several times to let herds of cattle and sheep find their way across the street to the stench of slaughterhouses and tanneries. An hour ago, in the thick of London traffic, he narrowly missed having the contents of a chamberpot dumped on his head from the second storey of a row house.

Now the countryside opens before him, green fields and the occasional flock of sheep, tended by shepherds sitting nearby. How he envies them, as he plods onwards. Looming before him now is a steep hill. There's a pub just ahead, thank God, and he's tempted to have a pint and an hour's rest with his boots off. But will it make him late for his appointment with the pastor? He reaches the pub and stands by the door, mulling it over. Then he hears the clatter of a cart.

Salvation, though perhaps of a temporary nature, not the eternal sort the pastor might pray for. He gestures to the driver.

"Give ye a ride, matey?"

"Know the way to Bunhill Fields?"

"Bone Hill, I calls it," the man replies. He's a red-faced yokel with a twist of chewing tobacco between his teeth and a filthy cap slung low over his forehead. "It'll cost ye a shilling, matey."

White fumbles in his vest pocket. Only a few coins left, and he has to consider the return trip to his rented house on the Embankment. He pulls out his pocket watch. A pint or the appointment?

"It'd cost ye lots more in one of them fine hearses that goes up there regular." The man laughs. "But I guess ye wouldn't mind if ye was in the coffin, like."

"Just get me there, please." *And shut up while you're at it.* He hops up beside the yokel. A touch of the reins and the cart horse plods into the road, lifting its tail and discharging a clump of dung as it moves forward.

White tries to keep a lid on his anger. He's always smouldering these days, as he thinks of his failed legal career in Jamaica and the wife and children dependent on him. But who knows, the pastor may solve his problems. His brother-in-law Sam Shepherd got him the appointment. "I hear they need an assistant at Horsleydown Church," he told White. "Why not apply? I'll set you up with John Rippon. He's usually at Bunhill in the afternoons." Sam has been White's staunch friend and patron since they studied law together at the Inner Temple in the seventeen eighties. And for some years, since Sam has become his brother-in-law, they've grown even closer together.

Horse and cart plod on for some time. The driver chews away at his plug of tobacco and spits on the horse's tail. There's no need for conversation. Dead tired from his long trek, White closes his eyes.

His head snaps forward as they come to a halt. "Here we be," the driver says. "Where to now, matey?"

White looks around. They seem to be at the top of the hill, and they've just come through a spiked gate. Two long rows of huge plane trees line the road forward. Beyond the trees on both sides of the road stretch hundreds of gravestones. How on earth is he to find Rippon in such a vast space? Perhaps there is an office somewhere?

He alights, pays the yokel, and sets off down the road between the avenue of plane trees. He has not gone far when he hears a strong bass voice singing a familiar hymn, "O God, our help in ages past." Without further thought, he joins in the final lines: "Be thou our guard while troubles last,/ And our eternal home!"

"Over here," the deep voice calls. White is lost for a moment as he looks about for the man who beckons. No one is visible. Strange. Then he sees what's up.

A black-clad figure is sprawled on his side between two graves. As White approaches, he notices the man has a pen and a book, and an inkhorn in his button-hole, and he appears to be copying the epitaph on one of the stones. When he sees White, he struggles to his feet.

"Mr. White, I presume? I'm Pastor Rippon. Excuse my informal posture. The inscriptions on these gravestones fade so quickly, and before I am gathered to my fathers, I want to copy all the words on the stones and publish them in several volumes that will in future years pay tribute to the worthies buried here."

He's a much younger man than White expected, having heard his friend Sam speak eloquently of his many accomplishments in the promotion of Calvinism. Indeed he's probably not much more than forty, a decade older than White himself. He is tall and has a shock of black hair and a ruddy complexion.

"Let's find a bench," he says and points towards a wooden seat a stone's throw away. "Oops, forgot my wig," he adds, pulling a scalp of white curls from the top of a nearby headstone.

"You have a pleasant voice," he says to White. "Always an asset to good preaching."

"It's one of my favourite hymns." He's happy his meeting with Rippon is off to a good start.

The pastor tucks his hair under the wig and points back at the headstone that was its temporary home. "Sir Isaac Watts's memorial. What wonderful music he wrote. Too bad anyone who's non-conformist has to be buried out here in the back-country. People like Watts and John Bunyan should be in Westminster Abbey."

"And Daniel Defoe, too?" White noticed Defoe's memorial as he walked down the lane.

"Defoe should be put in a charnel pit, in my view. Free up more space here for the worthies of this world, I say." Rippon scowls.

"You don't like *Moll Flanders* then?" White knows he shouldn't say this, but he can't stop himself. He enjoyed the book. He loves Moll's courage in the face of hardship.

"Incest and whoredom? No God-fearing man could like such a book." Rippon's words spill from his mouth, flakes of spittle speckling the air between them.

*Well, that's that. I should have kept my mouth shut.* He's spoiled his chances. He'll have to go through the motions, though. So he takes a seat beside Rippon and waits for the next question.

"I shall say no more about Daniel Defoe whom you evidently admire. Your brother-in-law assures me that you have a strong personal faith. But I must ask you: what inspired you to move from the legal world to a desire for the Calvinist ministry?"

"My time in Jamaica, sir." And saying this, White gathers strength to make his case. "I went there as a lawyer two years ago. But I was not able to work with the clients who came to me for legal advice. Every one of the devils was the owner of a sugar-cane plantation, and they wanted me to help them with land disputes and contracts with British and African entrepreneurs for buying and selling slaves. And I could not. I could not . . ."

Long pause. Rippon says, "Ah yes, the slave trade. Deplorable in many ways."

"In *all* ways, surely."

"We must not judge. It is for God to judge. He saves some; he allows others to go their own way along the path of sin to eternal damnation. It is possible that some of these slave owners will achieve salvation if they are predestined to do so. It is the same with the slaves. Some will be saved; some damned."

"If you could have seen what I saw in Jamaica, you would not talk about salvation for slave owners. Every one of them should face eternal damnation. While I was there, the slaves revolted against their tyranny. All they wanted was a small wage for their labour. They burned a few warehouses filled with sugar-cane. They did not kill anyone. But for their transgressions, hundreds of them were

8

hanged in the public square. Others had their limbs mutilated. Some were broken on a wheel, their bodies pulled apart and their bones broken. There were cages in which they were . . ." Remembering the skeletal face of a young boy in one of those cages, White wipes his eyes with his fist.

Rippon reaches over and puts an arm round White's shoulder. "My dear man, you are upsetting yourself. All is God's will. He has a purpose. It is not for us to question it." With his free arm he pats White's knee. "But you have not yet explained why you have embraced Calvinism."

"It was a Baptist minister who made me see the light, sir. A brave black man who, from the pulpit of a chapel that welcomed slave congregations, exhorted them to rebel. And when they did, those 'God-fearing' plantation owners killed him and burned the chapel." White stands up suddenly, breaking free of Rippon's embrace. "I would choose hell rather than give legal advice to such people. Or . . . now that I think of it, preach to such scoundrels. I fear that you and I have differing views on slavery, Pastor. I have wasted your time. Good day, sir."

He strides down the pathway towards the spiked gate. The cart driver has long departed, but White no longer needs him. He is charged with fresh energy. He must get free of this place, this sanctimonious pastor, his wretched smug certainties.

He breaks into a run down the long hill, past the pub which no longer tempts him. Farther along the road back into London, he collapses with the fatigue of his hike. Seated on a rock by the wayside, he counts the money in his pocket; there is some left. He'll go to his club in the heart of London. There he'll seek oblivion. Tomorrow will be soon enough to reconsider his future.

# Chapter Two

John White's head bumps against something hard and he jolts awake. Where the hell is he? It takes him a moment to realize he's slumped on the top step of his rented house on the Embankment and his head has hit the iron balustrade by the front door.

He wipes the drool from his chin and crawls to his feet. In the moonlight he squints at his pocket watch. Midnight. Earlier than usual. He has no memory of how he got home. But his aching skull and the shouting from the revellers on the river force him to remember the bowl of rum punch he drank. And the money he lost at the gaming-tables and the notes of promise he signed.

If he can sneak into his house without his wife hearing him, all will be well. With trembling fingers, he takes the latch-key from his pocket-book. The door opens with the squeak his wife never gets around to oiling. All is quiet inside. The dining-room door on his left is ajar, and he sees the maidservant asleep, her head on the table. He tiptoes past her. Let her sleep. She is not a slave, but she works hard for her pittance.

He fumbles up the staircase, pitching forward on the top step. The door of the first bedchamber on his right is slightly ajar. He peeks in, expecting to see Marianne's head on the pillow, her mouth open in a soft snore. But the bed is empty, the coverlet still in place, and the bolsters undisturbed. He stumbles into the room and takes the lid off the pisspot. Nothing in it. So she hasn't been in her room all evening?

Maybe one of the children is ill . . . ? He goes down the hall into the nursery, the carpet cushioning the sound of his footsteps. All is quiet there, too. Ellen asleep in the big bed, Charles dreaming peacefully in the trundle bed beside it, and baby William in a pullout drawer in the walnut chest, so quiet that he puts his hand on the tiny back just to feel the gentle exhalation of breath.

But no Marianne. Where on earth . . . ? He suddenly feels completely sober. He lights a candle and stands at the top of the staircase listening to the clocks sounding the half hour. Then he hears a soft tap on the front door, the servant's footsteps, and the familiar squeak of the hinges. A whispered greeting, then the click of his wife's dress pumps on the staircase. He moves forward, candle in hand.

"Marianne, what the devil—"

"John, my God, I thought . . ."

"Thought I wouldn't be home so soon? Is that it? Where have you been?"

In the shadows, her face seems ashen beneath the white powder that covers it, her lips, a scarlet gash. Her hand trembles as she pulls at the heart-shaped patch that covers the smallpox scar on her forehead.

"Look at you!" He gestures at her breasts bulging from the tight corset which encircles the tiny waist he once encompassed with lustful fingers. "Where have you been?"

"Brother and I, we went to the theatre. But we didn't spend money there. Only tuppence to the orange girl. It was *Macbeth* and I wanted to see the murder. But Haymarket doesn't charge if you only stay for the first act, so we walked out and—"

"If you walked out after the first act, woman, where have you been?" He grabs her wrist and twists it. She whimpers.

He can hear the servant girl at the bottom of the staircase. "Ma'am? Ma'am?"

He pushes his wife into her bedchamber and slams the door. "Where? Where?"

"We went to supper in Drury Lane. Oh, it was lovely. And it didn't cost you a penny. Brother paid. Sucking-pig and gooseberry pasty." A smile creases the white mask of her face. And now, as he leans over her, he can smell the

11

opium and brandy on her breath, the stench of that vile laudanum she buys at the greengrocer's on the next block. For her toothache, she has told him, though it's a lie. Her perfect teeth shine through the rouged lips that grimace up at him.

He pushes her onto the bed and raises his fist. She starts to cry, and he moves away, appalled by the hot rush of blood that has pounded into his cheeks and forehead. Leaving her snuffling against the bolster, he runs into his own bedchamber and douses his face with cold water from the washbasin opposite his bed.

To hit a woman was the most contemptible of acts. And he came so close to it. If he has now sunk so low, what will come next? Marianne is intolerable: he cannot be sure anything she says is true. Knowing her brother's stinginess, he can scarcely believe the man paid for supper. But what of his own actions, the boozing and gaming that consume him nightly? He has not a penny in his pocket at the moment to pay the rent. *I am as bad as she is, truth be told.*

Throwing his wig onto the chiffonier, he climbs into bed where he stares at the canopy long into the night.

By next morning, when the servant girl pulls back the bed curtains and lays his tea on the table beside him, he knows what he must do. He'll have to throw himself on his brother-in-law's goodwill once more.

# Chapter Three

Samuel Shepherd practises law at Lincoln's Inn in the tree-lined inner sanctum of the Inns of Court. As John White climbs the wide walnut staircase to the second floor where Shepherd has his offices, he is forced to contrast his brother-in-law's success as a barrister with his own abysmal failure. *Damnit, my marks at law school were as good as Sam's.* He remembers being lauded for his "elegant and precise" writing.

But Sam has been blessed with good fortune. For one thing, he made a sensible marriage. He didn't allow himself to be smitten by a beautiful face and a bounteous bosom. And then, too, he has been fortunate in having captured the praise of Lord Mansfield, former Lord Speaker of the House of Commons. Sometimes it's who you know that makes the difference between success and failure in this world.

Sam's secretary, a pompous old gent named Wilkins who rules the roost in the outer office, makes White sit and wait. It's a comfortable chair, yes, but it faces six engraved copperplate prints of Hogarth's "Marriage-à-la-mode" on the walnut-panelled wall opposite. While the pictures do not exactly reflect the specific messes of his and Marianne's marriage, they sum up its unhappiness all too well. White feels his head begin to pound.

A door opens, and his brother-in-law appears. "John," he says, coming forward and grasping White's hand. "Got your note this morning, and I'm sorry to hear our scheme with Rippon fizzled." He glances at the secretary who appears to be hanging on each word. "Come in, come in, where we can talk privately."

In the inner office, the door shut firmly against Wilkins, Sam puts his arm around White and pulls him close. "Don't worry about Rippon, old man," he says. "It was a stupid idea. You're not meant to be a clergyman. You're a barrister, and a damn good one, too. I've got a perfect idea for you."

White feels the tears start behind his eyes. Why does he deserve a friend like this? He takes the armchair opposite Sam's big mahogany desk.

Sam moves to the chair behind the desk and pulls out a folder from a top drawer. "It's all here," he says, "just what you want. My friend William Osgoode told me about it yesterday. John Graves Simcoe has just been made Lieutenant-Governor of Upper Canada. Simcoe has appointed Osgoode as Chief Justice, but he still needs an Attorney-General." Sam pauses. His prominent eyebrows arch over his eyes, and he stares, it seems, directly into White's soul. "You are it."

"It?"

"Yes, old man, you will be the Attorney-General of the newly established Province of Upper Canada." He takes a letter from the folder and pushes it across to Sam. "Read this. I wrote it this morning as soon as I got your note about Rippon."

*Lincoln's Inn, September 8*
*My dear Osgoode:*
*This letter has two purposes. First, to offer my heartfelt congratulation on your appointment as Chief Justice to Upper Canada. Second, to entreat your intercession with Colonel John Graves Simcoe on behalf of my brother-in-law, John White, Esquire.*

*Mr. White is a person of liberal education and correct understanding. His character is without reproach. He is well established in his profession, having studied at the Inner Temple. He was admitted to the bar in 1785 and worked as an attorney in Jamaica before re-establishing himself in this city.*

*I know that Colonel Simcoe needs an Attorney-General to support his new government of the Province of Upper Canada. Let me heartily recommend Mr. White.*

*Yours faithfully,*

*Sam Shepherd*

"It's a fine letter," White says, "offering me everything I could want." He takes out a handkerchief and wipes his face and eyes. He looks down at the letter again. "But I can't do it."

"You're turning this down? I don't believe it. It's your big opportunity to start over."

"It's Marianne and the children. I can't . . . take them with me to a new world. Why, Marianne can scarcely cope in this world. You know the woman. You know what she is—"

"I've thought about her, old man. My wife and I will keep an eye on her and the little ones. You will go to this new world alone. You will get yourself established. Your salary will be three hundred pounds a year, a substantial income in those dark forests beyond the sea. When you are ready, you will send for Marianne and your family." Sam pauses. He stands up, reaches across the expanse of his desk and retrieves the letter. "Wilkins will make a copy of this. You will show it to Marianne and make clear to her what you intend."

"Dammit, Sam, it's crazy and wonderful what you do for me. But you don't know everything about my wife. She has an opium habit. She goes out at night unsupervised. She—"

"I know what she is. But there is a solution. My old governess needs work. I've been paying her a pension in recognition of what she did for me when I was a youngster, but she feels guilt in accepting it. Now I'll put it to her. Ask her to go to your quarters here in London, live in with your family, and keep an eye on everything." Sam laughs, the white cravat at his neck bobbing up and down over his Adam's apple. "Believe me, nothing untoward will go on while Nanny is in charge."

White feels hope wash over him, wiping out his worries and drowning him in waves of happiness. He moves around the desk and embraces his friend.

\* \* \*

Next morning, at breakfast, he hands Marianne a copy of the letter he read in Sam's office. The mantel clock ticks, ticks, ticks while Marianne reads the letter, her mouth framing the words. At last, with a trembling hand, she sets it down beside her plate.

"You will take this position if it is offered, husband?"

"Yes."

"But what are we to do, me and the little ones?" Marianne's voice is shrill.

"You will stay here in England. There will be a stipend to live on, but not enough for suppers of sucking-pig and gooseberry pasty, or bottles of laudanum. My sister and Sam will keep an eye on you. And there will be a live-in governess for the children. If you can manage to behave yourself, I shall ask you and the children to join me in Upper Canada in a few years hence. Perhaps there we can make a new start."

He throws down his napkin, stands up, and moves towards the door of the breakfast room. A plate crashes on the wall beside the oak-panelled portal, spattering egg on his coat and narrowly missing his head. He exits, holding his hands to his ears to shut out Marianne's screeches.

# Chapter Four

*Gananoque, Upper Canada, June 1792*

The batteau going up river from Ganonoque is not ready, so John White leaves his baggage on the wharf to be loaded later and sets out on foot for Kingston, accompanied by Chief Justice William Osgoode. In the long weeks they have spent together sailing from England, they have become good friends. White is glad to have Osgoode's company on this overland trek, and if they "stick to their guns" (an expression he learned from a military man on board their vessel), they will arrive at Kingston in time for Colonel Simcoe's swearing-in as Lieutenant-Governor of Upper Canada.

They have no compass, nor do they need one. "Walk westward, keeping the river on your left hand," a logger told them. White has never seen such a blue sky or woodlands so green and thick. The air he breathes is scented with pine and a wildflower the natives call bunchberry. The broad river is dotted with at least a thousand islands, some of them no more than small lumps of granite with a pine tree or two sticking up among the rocks.

He's a bachelor again—at least for awhile—and in a few years, when he is established at Niagara, the new capital of the province of Upper Canada, he will have his wife and children come out. Perhaps by then he will have a spacious stone residence—there is so much stone in this new country—and servants will be plentiful and cheap.

"I've never been happier," he says to Osgoode. "In fact, I feel like one of Dionysius's satyrs."

"S..s..satyrs?"

"When I was in Jamaica, some fishermen brought up from the bottom of the sea a statue of a satyr. When they got the barnacles scraped off it, there it was, the loveliest thing I've ever seen: a nude male dancer in bronze with his hair thrown back, his arms flung wide, one leg kicking behind him, and his eyes, oh those eyes, they had such a crazy look of ecstasy." He laughs at the memory, and then he makes an impromptu leap into the air.

Osgoode laughs with him. "Very good, White. And I know you're cold s..s..sober too—unlike the s..s..satyr. But maybe it's these insects that are making you dance?" He swats at one of the critters that have landed on his forehead.

"Mosquitoes they're called, so an Indian told me." These tiny, pestilent "buzzers" are, in fact, the only thing bothering White at the moment. Except for the heat. The noonday sun now tops the sky. He'd been a fool to buy all those new coats and breeches before he left England. The garment he has on now—a coat of superfine with a velvet collar and buttons—might be fine for tea with the Colonel and Mrs. Simcoe, but it is ridiculous in this weather. More important, he's starting his new life with a tailor's debt of sixty-seven pounds.

He looks over at Osgoode. His friend is wearing a jacket of fringed buckskin he got from an Indian woman on the wharf at Quebec in exchange for a linen handkerchief. While at times Osgoode seems not to know where to set his feet next, on other occasions he puts them firmly on the right path.

They stop for a pipe opposite a tiny island of granite a few yards off shore. It is hot on the rock where they sit, and the water beckons, reminding him of youthful summer days on the River Wye near Hereford. He stands up, strips off his fine jacket and breeches, his shirt and stockings. The wig he left in his baggage. In this new country, he intends to wear it for formal occasions only.

"Come on, Osgoode," he yells, leaping into the water. It's deliciously cold, and he strikes out at once for the island. He plunges his head and shoulders beneath the surface and swims with a school of trout, trying to keep

18

pace with the stragglers. At Hereford, he was sixteen, alive with the exhilaration of youth, the certainty that everything was possible. And now at twice that age, the promise of success stirs him again. In a new life, in a new land, a man of intelligence and drive cannot but succeed.

He holds his breath to bursting, and when he surfaces, like a cormorant, he finds himself close to a square-cut rock that forms the first step of a granite staircase leading to the top of the tiny islet. Up, up he goes, reaching the pinnacle where he looks down on Osgoode standing in the water clinging to the rock on which they had smoked their pipes. "I can't s..s..swim," he calls, "I'll hold on here."

*A man who can't swim in a country of lakes and rivers? Surely that must be a metaphor for failure. I'm set to dive into whatever comes.*

With a hoot of derision, he plunges downward into the crystalline depths.

# Chapter Five

*Kingston, July 1792*

Eliza Russell settles herself for a nap on the sofa in the rented quarters her brother Peter has procured for them at Kingston. It's a spacious stone house, owned by a rich merchant who is currently absent in Quebec, and staffed with eight servants who have placed themselves at her disposal. Kingston is a town of about fifty houses, a garrison, and a barracks, with only one mansion of stone. She feels mighty pleased to be in this mansion, the largest house in town, especially considering that Colonel Simcoe and his lady inhabit a small log dwelling near the barracks.

She, Peter, and Mary will be here for only a few days, of course, since they must move on to Niagara with the Colonel and Mrs. Simcoe, but solid ground is what she needs at the moment. Near eight weeks of rough weather and contrary winds on the Atlantic, followed by much to-ing and fro-ing in a batteau from Quebec to Kingston, have undone her.

Mary sits at the window, stroking the cat they brought with them from England and from which Mary declared she would never be separated. She's a frail child, ten years old, bones not yet firmed up, and Eliza feels she would be the better for agoing out into the summer sunshine. Already Eliza worries about the Canadian winter ahead. One of the servants in this house has told her about the deaths of children in the cruel weather of December and January.

"Look at those violets," she says to the girl, pointing to the open field behind the house. "I've never seen anything so grand and beautifully romantic in my life. And over that slope, just before you get into the woods, there are those wild strawberries. Please put that animal down now and go out and pick some for your Uncle Peter's tea."

"If there are any left. You must have noticed I've been gobbling them whenever you send me outside." She sets the cat on the Pembroke table near the window, grabs a birch bark bucket—made by some Indians, so Eliza has heard—and runs out without another word. Eliza gets up from the sofa and snatches the cat away from the dish of bonbons it has already put its nose into.

She must get to her nap and then prepare for the to-dos of this afternoon and evening. She's mighty glad to have a few minutes to herself. Mary has lately begun to pester her with questions about her parentage. Perhaps she feels adrift in this strange new world and needs to seek a secure place. Eliza has made up a convenient fiction about how her mother and father drowned at sea in a sailing vessel that broke into bits upon rocks, and how a sailor who survived the disaster delivered Mary, who was then a small babe, to her and Peter for raising.

"Really, Aunt Eliza?" Mary said this morning as she smacked the shell on her boiled egg. "How did the sailor know your address? And why would you take me in, since you say my parents were only 'friends' of yours? Weren't there some other relatives who might have raised me?" And on and on she went, tearing at every detail Eliza fed her. Eliza knows she's not a good liar, and it's tiring having to spin out this silly tale, but she's determined Mary must not learn the truth.

Now, looking again at the mantel clock, Eliza realizes she has no time for her nap. She must ready herself for the swearing-in ceremony. Her brother is to be Receiver-General in the new capital. It's an illustrious position, and for him to be given it at the advanced age of almost sixty illustrates for her the kindness of Colonel Simcoe, who recommended him to the bigwigs in London. And the Colonel's lady appears to be an agreeable woman, too, without the least pride or formality.

For certain, it seems to be a pleasant group of people surrounding the Colonel in this new land. On the long voyage from England, she enjoyed the company of the Attorney-General, Mr. White, a handsome man with a pleasing countenance, always cheerful and good tempered. She is grateful he did not put her to the blush by asking questions about Mary, saying merely that she reminded him so much of his own daughter, Ellen. She also likes the Chief Justice, Mr. Osgoode, who is friendly and unassuming. He's not handsome like Mr. White, but he has an excellent fair complexion, and very blue eyes. His stammer endears him to her, putting her in mind of her friend Lizzie who lives in Harwich and whom she already misses so much.

She has still to meet the Jarvises, who are not yet arrived. They chose to sail from England in a separate vessel. From what she's heard, they are Yankees who lived in London a short time only. Though they may indeed be loyal to His Majesty King George, they will undoubtedly have some low habits and unfortunate turns of speech.

The back door slams shut, and Mary appears suddenly in the withdrawing room. She thumps the bucket of strawberries down on the Pembroke table, so lately occupied by the cat. "There," she says, "I hope that will be enough to fill Uncle Peter's gut." She laughs and adds, "Though I doubt a bowl of strawberries will serve to fill *that* gut."

Eliza opens her mouth to protest the use of such vulgar language, but shuts it again as Mary produces from the pocket of her pinafore a bunch of violets. Thrusting them at her, Mary says, "And these are for you, Aunt Eliza. They *are* beautiful, and maybe you want to have a romance? So I thought you might like to have them."

"Thank you, my dear. I shall wear them in the bodice of my costume for the swearing-in ceremony."

How can she not adore this difficult but lovable child? She pulls Mary to her and plants a kiss on her pale, hot cheek.

* * *

Colonel Simcoe takes the oath of office at four o'clock in a small frame church called St. George's. He is resplendent in the traditional scarlet and gold uniform of a British army colonel. Eliza is mighty pleased to be seated in the front pew of honour beside Mrs. Simcoe where she has an excellent view of her brother who stands on one side of the Colonel with Mr. Osgoode on the other side. Peter looks very well in his new double-breasted frock coat and stock, his breeches buckled below the knee to show his still well-shaped legs. She is glad she took his wig for cleaning, dear though the cost was, for it was alive with fleas.

The Chief Justice, his face very flushed, speaks many words, most of which she does not understand, but the gist of it seems to be that the Colonel, by laying his hand on the Bible and reciting some long-winded phrases, is now the Lieutenant-Governor of the Province of Upper Canada. She makes a mental note to remember to call him "Governor" from this moment.

Mr. Stuart, the minister, has just started his sermon when there is a clatter at the back of the church. Eliza tries not to look around, but when she sees the Governor's lady turn sharply, she does the same.

It's a man and a woman, and they appear to take their seats without the least embarrassment. The Jarvises undoubtedly. They've been expected for more than a week. William Jarvis is to be the Secretary and Registrar of the province. Peter met him once in London and calls him "an indolent fool." Since both husband and wife are Yankees born and bred, they undoubtedly feel free to flout the King's protocols. As if to outdo the Governor, Mr. Jarvis is wearing a gaudy chain, some sort of office. What could it be? He has thrust his left leg out into the aisle. And now she notices also that around his left calf, he has tied a strange buckled dark-blue garter.

It may all become clear when the assembly meets in the Kingston Barracks for the supper which the Governor and his lady are giving this evening to honour the administrators of the new capital at Niagara. Meantime she must try to focus on the Reverend's sermon.

23

# Chapter Six

*Kingston Barracks, July 1792*

John White finds the Officers' Mess stuffy, but perhaps it's William Jarvis's conversation that's bringing on one of his headaches. There must be twenty-five people crammed into this tiny space, and it's impossible to escape from the man and his drivel.

"You are not aware, sir, that Lord Dorchester himself appointed me the Grand Master of Ancient Masons? He came to our London house as we were in the throes of packing, and sat down among us, quite as if he were a comrade and not His Majesty's illustrious ruler of Upper and Lower Canada. In deference to the Governor, I have not tonight worn my chain of office, but I thought this adornment was appropriate for the occasion." Jarvis pats a huge gold pin on his left breast, its circle containing two triangles, one of them upside down. There's a gold ball in the centre of it all. "These triangles, as you may know, symbolize—"

"I don't think it would be a good idea to mention Lord Dorchester to the Gov," White says. "According to the rumour mill, they don't see eye to eye on anything."

Just then there's a burst of cannon fire from the wharf. The Governor and his lady have arrived, thank God. He turns away from Jarvis and heads with the crowd to the dining hall to welcome their hosts.

"Good evening, Mr. White. I'm happy to see you again."

White turns. Just behind him in the line-up is Eliza Russell. She's dressed in the same drab black garment she

24

generally wears, but she has put a rather wilted bouquet of violets on her bodice and daubed some paint on her sallow cheeks. "Miss Russell," he says, "I wanted so much to talk to you this evening. I have a gift for Mary." He hands over the small package he's been holding during his interminable conversation with Jarvis. "I had only a newspaper to wrap it in, my apologies."

She opens it quickly as the line to the dining hall moves forward, pulling out the little buckskin moccasins with a beaded daisy on each toe. "Lovely," she says. "Mary needs new shoes so bad. Her feet have grown a size since we left home, and I had no idea where to procure some. They are so pretty with the beading. Moccasins, are they called?"

"That's the word. I bought them from an Indian woman on the wharf today. I noticed Mary limping, and I thought at first she had some sort of paralysis. But then I thought of my own daughter Ellen, how she limps when her shoes pinch."

"I'm mighty pleased with them, Mr. White. And with you, too." She smiles broadly at him, and folds the moccasins into her reticule.

The dining hall is a large room dominated by a long pine table pitted with marks from a thousand nights of spilled beer and ringed by at least two dozen wooden chairs, plain in structure, with stretchers holding the legs together. The sole picture on the walls is a portrait of Simcoe in the full dress regalia of the Queen's Rangers. White is reminded that the Governor is a military man who will know little of legal parlance and governance. Perhaps this is a good thing. Perhaps he and Osgoode will have more freedom to set up the judiciary and establish policy. From what he hears, anyone who barks can be a lawyer.

He is happy to find himself seated midway down the long table, in a position to observe and hear both the Governor and his lady. The great man is tall with plump, flushed cheeks, and he controls the conversation in a deep, loud voice. He directs one of his first comments to White himself.

"So you are now a member of the Legislative Assembly for these counties, Mr. Attorney-General?"

"Thanks to your good offices, sir. You put my name forward and supported me throughout." He does not bother to say he spent a week on horseback canvassing the back concessions about Kingston and has only this day got his walking legs back. The settlers are an ignorant bunch, concerned chiefly with the establishment of non-conformist churches and the problem of the Indians encroaching on their clearings. He wanted to tell them that the case was probably the reverse. Were they not building their miserable huts on Indian territory? But he remembered to keep his mouth shut. His stabbing back pains this evening serve to remind him of the day of his victory, when the settlers dragged him about on a chair to the diversion of the crowd and his own inconvenience. The physical pain also brought to his mind the pain of the expense he incurred to get elected: two barrels of porter and quantities of bread and cheese. *But to be an elected member of Upper Canada's First Parliament, surely that is an accomplishment to be proud of.*

A serving-wench has just dumped two carcasses onto his plate. He cannot identify them. Too small to be rabbits. He pokes at them with his fork. *My God, can they be rats?*

"Black squirrels," Mrs. Simcoe says from the bottom of the table, no doubt observing the horror on his face. "As good to eat as a young hare, especially with lots of mint sauce." White reaches into the centre of the table and dumps half the pitcher of sauce onto the corpses. He begins to understand Marianne's longing for a meal of sucking-pig. When he gets back to the small room at the inn which he shares with Osgoode, he must remember to take a strong emetic.

Mrs. Simcoe is tiny with a sharp nose and thin lips, not at all his idea of feminine beauty. She appears to be a woman of great—though strange—enthusiasms. During the serving of a blueberry tart, which proves an excellent antidote to the squirrels, she rises and goes to a corner of the room. There, in a slatted wooden box he had not at first

26

noticed, is a large grey snake with white markings. She picks up a stick beside the box and pokes at the reptile which shows a pair of long fangs and issues forth a sinister rattle.

"Is it not amusing?" She laughs, turning to her guests. "A Mississauga Indian came this morning to our lodgings and presented me with it." She takes one of the squirrel corpses from a platter on the sideboard and throws it into the box.

The Governor smiles indulgently. "Give it a little mint sauce as well, my dear." Then he turns to Osgoode who is seated next to him. "We go in three days' time to Newark," he says.

Osgoode looks bewildered. "Newark, Governor?"

"Yes, I have renamed Niagara after a town I love in England. You undoubtedly know it, Mr. Chief Justice, Newark-on-Trent. I intend to give English names to replace all these strange Indian appellations. Indeed, my entire mission here is to establish a bit of old England in this young land."

White looks down at the last crumbs of his tart. *Did this young land and its native inhabitants not provide the blueberries for the tasty dessert? Even the squirrels for the main course? And the reptile that provides such fun for the lady? Well, those are paltry things. But what of the judiciary? Does the Gov envisage planting the entire legal system of England in this land without pruning? Does he not realize that Indians, if they are to act as jurors, may not wish to swear on the Christian Bible?*

His thoughts are diverted by the shrill voice of Mrs. Simcoe, deep into one of her strange enthusiasms. "Last evening, I walked in a wood set alight by some bonfires left unextinguished in an encampment. You may have no idea of the pleasure of walking in a burning bush. The smoke keeps the mosquitoes at a distance and when the fire catches in the hollow of a tall tree, the flame makes a fine leap into the sky." She throws up her hands to illustrate. "And where there are only small sparks, they look like the

27

stars in the heavens. It is all so beautiful. Tomorrow I think I shall have some woods set on fire for my evening walk."

While most of the invited guests make their sycophantic murmurs of approval, White watches the dismay on the face of the serving-wench who, across the table, is just removing a plate from in front of Eliza Russell. Perhaps the girl lives in one of the pitiful log cabins close to that wood Mrs. Simcoe intends to set afire.

\* \* \*

Back at the inn, he hopes to engage his friend Osgoode in a discussion of the evening. But by the time he has a tankard of beer with the friendly innkeeper and climbs up to the small rented room, Osgoode has settled himself to read in the only comfortable chair. A candle flickers on the rough-carved table beside him, and he is deep into an ancient tome, *Coke's Reports*, and looks up only when White moves to the washstand.

"You at last, White. Pack your baggage. The Governor told me that we are to s..s..sail with them on the *Onandaga* to Niagara tomorrow morning."

"Newark, man, Newark."

Osgoode snorts. "The bloodiest boring place I've ever been. King John died of dysentery there. Doesn't that s..s..say it all?"

"Why now? I thought he said in three days' time."

"I think we must accustom ourselves to the man's whims."

Well, no time for the emetic. He'll just have to hope he hasn't contracted a terminal disease from those damned squirrels.

28

# Chapter Seven

*Niagara (renamed Newark by Governor John Graves Simcoe)*
White stands on the deck of the *Onandaga* as it leaves Kingston and heads into the open water of Lake Ontario. It's a fine square-rigged, two-masted schooner. It sails briskly in the light breeze, and he loves the feel of the wind pushing his hair back. He looks around him. No one in sight. He does a leap into the air.

"Ah, Mr. S..S..Satyr," says Osgoode, appearing suddenly from the stern of the ship. "Enjoy yourself while you can. One of the s..s..sailors has just told me the winds are changeable on this lake."

And Osgoode is right. About seven miles from Kingston, the wind calms, and the ship stops. Osgoode pulls a book from his portmanteau and goes below deck. White stares into the bottom of the lake. It's so transparent he can see schools of fish swirling around in the depths.

He's relieved the Simcoes have left Kingston before the lady could set fire to the woods. But he's sorry the departure was too rushed for Eliza and Peter Russell who are taking a couple of extra days in Kingston. He would have enjoyed talking to Eliza. A sensible woman with a kind heart, she is so unlike Marianne. He likes the way she looks after her brother. Peter Russell seems to have settled into his new role. Osgoode has told him Russell once went to prison for his gambling debts. White is happy to know someone else has come to this country to make a new beginning. If only Russell could be a little less serious. His face with its folds and bags reminds him of a bloodhound's.

He sighs. How long will it be 'til the wind picks up again? Hours probably. He'll find some paper and write a letter to his daughter Ellen and one to his brother-in-law, Sam Shepherd. *To Sam I can brag about being on board ship with the new Lieutenant-Governor and his lady. Quite an honour and far removed from my dead-end life in London with a thwarted career and a wife like a noose around my neck. Sam has been a friend indeed.*

But how will he get his letters to them? Is there a postal service in this new world? He asks one of the sailors who has just come on deck to check the rigging.

"Give it to us, mate. When we gets to Niagara, we'll carry it back with us. There be a ship sailing down the St. Lawrence to the sea in a week's time, I wager."

* * *

Two days later, he's back on deck in the same spot, but now they are far from Kingston. Beside him are Osgoode and a smart-looking young officer called Lieutenant Talbot who is the Governor's private secretary. The Simcoes are several feet away, sitting on chairs the sailors have placed for them. The lady is sketching, probably trying to capture the view of Burlington Bay into which they have just sailed.

Lieutenant Talbot shouts. "The spray, I can see the spray!" Sure enough, when White follows the direction of Talbot's outstretched arm, he sees the mist rising from the great Falls of Niagara.

A mere hour later, as the schooner turns south into the Niagara River, they catch a glimpse of the garrison of Niagara on the east side and a few minutes later, they see a half dozen log houses on the land rising to the west of the river.

"Can this be it?" he asks Osgoode.

"Let's hope not," Osgoode says. "It's most likely just a cluster of those s..s..settlers the Governor was talking about yesterday. Butler's Rangers, I think he s..s..said."

But the schooner is now tacking towards shore. In front of them at the water's edge is a forlorn-looking wooden building. Members of the Queen's Rangers in their green uniforms stand at attention on the wharf, waiting for their commander's arrival. "My God," White says to Osgoode, "this *is* it."

"Navy Hall," Lieutenant Talbot explains. "It's the barracks where seamen used to bunk during the winter months. And now, so we're told, it's been thoroughly renewed as a home for Governor Simcoe and Mrs. Simcoe and for government offices."

But White can hear the doubt in his voice. If the outside looks this bad, what can the inside be like?

Moments after they make their landing, the Gov sweeps into Navy Hall accompanied by Talbot and the Queen's Rangers while the rest of the *Onandaga's* passengers remain on the wharf and the low land in front of the Hall. They hear muffled, barked commands, and then the Gov is outside again.

"A damn miserable place," White hears him say to his lady. "I have given instructions for an extensive renovation. But it will always be an old hovel. Even if it's properly decorated and ornamented, it will still look exactly like an ale-house in the slums of London."

The lady remains calm. "Well then, my dear, we must live in the tents you brought along."

The Governor turns to the Queen's Rangers. "Set up the three marquees on the hilltop behind this place." The soldiers rush towards the schooner. He turns to White and Osgoode. "I have bad news for you, gentlemen. I understand from the Rangers there are no rented rooms to be had in the settlement. But do not worry. You will live in one of the tents at our expense until we can find you a place. A second tent will accommodate our children and the servants. The third one will be designated for me and Mrs. Simcoe. It will all work out."

\* \* \*

And it does. White soon becomes accustomed to the wailing children—a girl of three and a boy who's little more than a baby—and the marital discourses which at times are all too audible. He loves to open the flap of his marquee in the morning while Osgoode is still snoring and look down at the light glinting from the river. On hot summer evenings, everyone sits outside their canvas tents to catch the breezes. The only routine of the day that he cannot stand is the litany of long-winded prayers that the Gov conducts every morning in the oak bower.

The oak bower is almost like another room. Huge oak trees stand in a semi-circle behind the three canvas tents, enclosing them within their circumference. Early breezes often stir the leaves, and pretty red-crested birds called, fittingly, cardinals whistle all the day from high in their branches. When the rains come, the heavy leaf canopy shields them from the worst of the storm.

White often dines here with the Simcoes at the edge of the plain which they now call the commons. He notices how the lady appears to enjoy equally the companionship of her husband and Talbot. Though he has heard much from Mrs. Jarvis about Mrs. Simcoe's wealth and position in English society, she seems happy in the relaxed informality of her new life. A huge black dog called Trojan lies panting at their feet as they dine, and he notices the lady often slips a piece of her whitefish to him.

Supper is invariably whitefish and sturgeon or sturgeon and whitefish, occasionally enlivened with turtles from the creek cut up like oysters and served in scallop shells. At least there have been no more squirrels.

He is happy to save money in this arrangement. The only expenses he has are his dinners at Fort Niagara across the river, and though he has not taken to gambling, he does drink too much when he's there, out from under the close surveillance of the Simcoes. At the garrison, in the crowd of military men and their women and the noisy music and dancing, he feels free. The garrison is on Yankee territory, but will remain in British hands until 1796, so he's heard.

After that, he'll have to find another place in which he can cut himself loose from the shackles of his narrow circle.

The Simcoes do make an appearance at Fort Niagara from time to time, but they go in their own canoe, leaving him and Osgoode to find their own transportation. Last week, Osgoode returned across the river early with the Indian paddler they hire for these occasions, and he'd been forced to share a canoe with Mrs. Simcoe and Lieutenant Talbot. The Gov himself had stayed in the marquee, laid up with gout. The lady and Talbot seemed decidedly cosy in each other's company, ignored him almost completely, and kept up a conversation he was incapable of following in his drunken state. Talbot did the paddling. He tied on a headscarf and faked a voyageur accent which greatly amused the lady.

That night, inside his canvas wall, White wrote in his diary: "Very tipsy. N.B. Resolve to dine less often at the Fort."

"Truth is," he says to Osgoode, telling him this story over breakfast. "I'm beginning to need a woman in my life."

"S..s..stay c..c..celibate. Less trouble in the long run."

"No uncomfortable passions, you understand. Just someone to indulge me in a little coquetry, the sort of thing Talbot and Mrs. Simcoe seem to enjoy."

But he's taken the measure of the women in his immediate circle. *Who is there in this place to have fun with?*

# Chapter Eight

*August 1792*

An advantage of being in close quarters with the Simcoes is that White has an opportunity to be near to the Gov and to observe his ways. As Attorney-General, one of his duties is to help the Gov draft bills for passage in the new Parliament of Upper Canada which is to be housed for this session in the squalid little Freemasons' Lodge in the centre of the settlement.

"I intend to abolish slavery," the Gov says to him one morning as they sit together in a musty room at Navy Hall, damp from a recent rainstorm. "I am deeply troubled that many settlers in this community, including at least three members of my own administration, own slaves. It is an abomination and I will put an end to it."

"You have my heart and soul in that endeavour, sir." He tells the Gov about the horrors of the Jamaican slave trade that drove him from the island.

"You are the very man I need for the drafting of this bill which will set all men and women free. Let us begin now, shall we?"

For several days they work together, from early morning until far into the night—while the candles gutter and die—and the ensuing bill gives both of them great pleasure. All slaves currently in Upper Canada are to be set free, and any further importation of slaves from anywhere is to be considered a crime that will bring dire consequences to the offender.

"I thank God for decent, far-seeing men like yourself, sir," White says to the Gov. "When I think of the wretched slaves in those damnable sugar plantations in Jamaica, I rejoice to be here, part of an enlightened new society."

The Gov smiles complacently. "We can plant new ideas here, sir, and watch them grow and flourish. Let us have a celebratory drink in the oak bower now, eh, Mr. White?"

They have finished one bottle of wine from the Gov's stores when David Smith appears on the scene. He is a man of "overweening ambition," according to Mrs. Jarvis. But White knows him to be a capable young sprout who the Jarvis woman perhaps fears may one day be given her incompetent husband's position as administrator of land grants.

At the moment Smith has one foot firmly placed in the political sphere, being the elected member for Suffolk and Essex. He has also curried favour with the Gov by taking on the role of acting deputy surveyor-general, a post which at the moment carries no salary. White feels sure he will be on the Gov's side in this war against slavery, if for no other reason than to further his own advancement.

Simcoe passes the slavery bill to him. "Look over this, Smith, while you have a glass of my best claret."

White opens a new bottle, passes a glass to Smith, and settles back to await the accolade.

Smith pulls out a quizzing glass from a pocket of his coat. He waves it about so White can catch the glint of diamonds on its rim, then holds it close to his left eye, at the same time managing to keep the wine glass steady in his right hand.

Moments pass while he squints at the document. *What on earth can be taking him so long? My penmanship is the best, and I spent two hours last evening copying the document over so that there are no cross outs to impede its reading by the Clerk of the House.*

Finally he replaces the quizzing glass in his coat and heaves a sigh.

"Well," the Gov says, "let us hear what you think."

"With abject apologies, Your Excellency, it will not work in its present form."

"Why not?" the Gov says, his face growing red.

"Think about the people who will vote on this bill, Excellency. Half of them are military men who have fought in the West Indies and America where slavery is still deemed immutable. Half are the peasants of this province who have no interest in anything beyond the needs of their bellies."

"Surely you are wrong about the people who voted for you," White says as he tries not to think of the ignorance of the folk who voted for him in Leeds and Frontenac.

Smith laughs. "I got the goodwill of my peasants by roasting three oxen whole and giving them six barrels of rum with which to wash it all down. They had not the slightest interest in anything I said to them. When they finished belching, they lurched back to their farms to see that their slaves had rooted out the turnips." He pours himself another glass of claret. "You must agree with me, White. You are familiar with the peasants in the backwaters of Kingston."

He cannot disagree. But why should such peasants influence the outcome of this important bill? He can only hope that the Gov will stand firm for what he believes in.

Simcoe leans back and folds his arms across his chest. White has come to recognize the gesture. It's what he does when he's under siege from a verbal attack.

"What would you suggest then, Smith?"

"A compromise, Excellency. Perhaps let the peasants keep the slaves they have now, but outlaw any further importation. That way you'll still have the moral high ground, and you'll get their vote. They can't think beyond the end of their noses. And they don't give a damn what happens after they're dead and gone."

"Capital idea. White and I will work on it tomorrow."

*Damn, damn, damn. I'm to work on the watering-down of a bill that has taken us days to write and that says everything that needs to be said against slavery?*

"And if I may offer another suggestion, Excellency. I should advise not introducing such controversy at the

36

opening session of our Parliament. Perhaps in the second session?"

To this, Simcoe responds by running his hands through his hair. It's an abundant thatch and this gesture has the effect of making him look like one of the scarecrows White has noticed in a settler's vegetable garden. *Don't give in on this point, Gov. Don't, don't, don't.*

White waits for Simcoe to speak the words that will tell Smith to take himself off to perdition. The minutes tick away while the Gov looks down at the bill Smith has thrust back at him, and White contemplates throwing the wine in his glass at one or both of them.

Finally the great man speaks. "I believe you are right, Smith. We can find a compromise surely, first getting the settlers on our side in this parliamentary session and then—"

"Mealy-mouthed compromise is to be better than hard and honest speech?" As he says this, White stands up, knocking over onto the grass the small table and the bottle of the Gov's fine claret.

"Calm yourself, sir. What you call 'mealy-mouthed compromise' is surely better than utter failure. Be at Navy Hall at eight tomorrow morning and we shall begin drafting a new bill." Simcoe bends down to retrieve the upset bottle and the remainder of its contents.

*I must restrain myself. It would be fatal to my prospects to antagonise the Gov this early in the game.* "Perhaps you are right, Excellency. I shall retire to my tent now and contemplate some phraseology we may use for amendment."

# Chapter Nine

*Late August 1792*

Eliza Russell has opened the front door of their log house to let out the fug of smoke that has set off a coughing fit in poor Mary. The place is intolerable. There are but two small rooms. One has a hearth with a chimney that does not draw properly, a spinning wheel she has no idea how to use, and a crude table and benches. Job, the Negro slave whom Peter bought when they were still in London, sleeps on a mat in front of the hearth. The other room they call their bedchamber. Here she and Mary must sleep crosswise in a narrow bed while Peter takes the bed built right into the wall, no more than a mere platform of wood with a scattering of straw for a mattress. There is scarce enough space left for their pitcher, washbasin, and chamberpot, and no room at all for any degree of privacy. Nor can she get much sleep with Mary's coughs and Peter's snores. What's more, they are in continual dirt, and when visitors come to tea, she is put to the blush by the wretchedness of their quarters.

Things may improve. This morning, Peter told her he has started to build a commodious house on the commons above Navy Hall. But he also complained about workmen's wages and the fact he expects to have to pay more than twenty-four hundred pounds out of his own pocket. And will this house be ready by winter? She scarce dares to hope.

From the front stoop, she can no longer hear Mary coughing. Perhaps the girl has gone down to the wharf on the river. She likes to see the catch the Indians bring in their canoes. She will herself take a break now from her constant sweeping and sit on the back stoop in the sunshine and enjoy the view of the river and Fort Niagara on the Yankee side. The Fort is still in British hands at the moment, and Lieutenant Talbot, the Governor's personal attendant, is always paddling the Governor and his lady across to parties and dances. She can, of course, take no part in these affairs. The bedchamber must be kept as Peter's place to put on his evening attire. Even if she had a fashionable gown, she would have no maid to help her ready herself and no chamber to dress in.

As she is about to close the front door, she espies Mrs. Jarvis coming down the well-worn trail that leads to their hut. No chance of escaping the woman, nor does she really want to. Her visit will be a diversion. But she will go in now and make sure the rocking chair by the hearth is well dusted and moved close to a tiny window that can be opened. Mrs. Jarvis will deliver her fourth child in a few weeks' time, and no doubt will need to keep her lungs clear.

"Yoo-hoo!" the woman calls, banging the knocker. It is a vile American greeting, and Eliza opens the door quick so she won't have to hear it twice. Mrs. Jarvis is in full regalia as if she were attending a tea party in Grosvenor Square. Her hat is puffed out with a balloon-shaped crown and a wide brim, and she clutches at it with one hand.

"Do let me out of this wind, Miss Russell. My hat has almost flown across the river." She is a sturdy woman with pink cheeks and clear brown eyes that don't miss a thing. Eliza is thankful the bricks in the kitchen floor are reasonably clean and Job has left water on the boil in the hearth.

Eliza spoons some tea into the pot and pours the water over it. There are a couple of wedges of pie left from the previous night's dinner. Job made it from what he calls "pie-plant," a tall plant with big leaves and thick sour red stalks that cook up splendid with lots of maple sugar. She plops one of the pieces onto a tin plate and passes it to Mrs. Jarvis. Then she pulls one of the rough benches over to face the rocking chair in which her guest is ensconced.

"In a mere month, dear William has managed to procure a supply of logs and a carpenter to add a decent room to *our* hut," she says. "We now have four rooms in this town that God has forsaken." She looks around at Eliza's abode, one eyebrow quirked. "Shall I ask William to give the name of this capable man to your brother?"

"I thank you, but Peter will make his own arrangements." No doubt Secretary Jarvis's focus on the wrong things is, as her brother says, the reason why very few land grants have been processed during the weeks they have been here in Newark.

"Why the Governor dragged us to a spot on the globe that appears to have been deserted in consequence of a plague, I will never understand. We might have stayed in Kingston and been a good deal more comfortable. And then he has the nerve to rebuke dear William for not having brought parchment and beeswax and a screw press from England for the affixing of seals. I expect it is that wife of his that is behind it all. Petticoat rule, that's what it is."

Eliza does not reply. Her brother is a staunch supporter of the Simcoes and she will say nothing to this woman that might become the subject of her tittle-tattle.

"And that so-called bachelor, Mr. White, is a piece of work as well. I see him prowling about the neighbourhood like a feral dog. I wonder what bits of meat he will find."

Eliza is not sure what her guest means. She knows only that she must find a way to defend her friend. But before she can speak, Mrs. Jarvis is in full flight again.

"William tells me Mr. White is helping the Governor draft a piece of legislation outlawing *slavery*. How are we to *manage* without slaves? You and the Receiver-General have a slave, I believe. What else can we do for servants in a land where the price of household help is beyond reason?"

The back door opens, letting in a gush of fresh air. "Aunt Eliza —" Mary's greeting is cut short when she notices Mrs. Jarvis in the rocking chair. She bobs a curtsey and heads for the bedchamber.

"Quite the little savage your . . . *niece* . . . has become."

*What on earth is Mrs. Jarvis referring to now? Mary curtsied, did she not? And why does she come down hard on the word 'niece'?*

"Those moccasins she's wearing. Where on earth did she get them?"

"Mr. White gave them to her. And grateful I was for the gift. She has grown so much since we left dear old England. Dear Mr. White bought these for her in Kingston. Pretty they are with their beading and so comfortable, Mary tells me."

"Ah, so he is a friend of yours. Well, I shall say no more. But now you must tell me something. I notice the child calls you 'aunt.' Forgive my ignorance, but I did not know you and the Receiver-General had another sibling."

Eliza tells the story she has told so many times before: the shipwreck and the drowning of their friends, George and Anna Fleming, the rescue of the babe, and her delivery to their house in Harwich. But while she is telling it, she feels her face grow red.

"Indeed." The one word tells Eliza that Mrs. Jarvis believes not a particle of what she has just heard.

"You must allow me to give you some advice, Miss Russell. You really must get out and about more. I understand you are somehow related to the Duke of Bedford. I know you are elderly—as is your brother—but you both have a responsibility to show people in this forsaken backwater how to behave."

This is more than Eliza can bear. "Scarce *elderly*, ma'am. I am thirty-nine years of age, no doubt much older than you or the Governor's lady, but not *elderly*."

"Forgive me. I did not intend to be rude. But your brother is then twenty years older than you, is he not? That seems a great difference . . ." Mrs. Jarvis has set her plate and cup on the long kitchen table and now plants herself again in the rocking chair as if she wants to stay rooted there for ever.

"Peter is my half-brother, ma'am."

41

"Your *half*-brother?"

This is said in a tone that indicates she and Peter must somehow be living in sin. Eliza feels she must vindicate herself and her dear brother.

"He is the only son of my father's first wife. I met him for the first time when I was almost seventeen. He had been many years serving in a regiment in North America and the West Indies. He charmed me, so kind he was and so helpful. He went back to America and came to me again when I was twenty-eight years of age. Oh, I did need his advice then." Even as she is saying this, Eliza knows that she has given too much away.

"Needed his advice? What do you mean?"

No retreat is possible now. *So out with it.* "I then had the charge of Peter's step-mother, my own mother. By the time he came back again to me from the New World, she was insane. She suffered violent rages in which she had a mighty strength. She would bite me and strike me. My body would be covered all over in welts and bruises. On the very day Peter arrived back in Harwich, as he was a-coming into our drawing room, he saw she had pushed me down on the floor and was a-strangling me. Peter managed to pull her off and then he helped me to my feet. My dear brother saved my life."

Remembering her terror and the relief she felt when Peter saved her, Eliza cannot hold back her tears. Mrs. Jarvis leans towards her, puts her arms around her. Eliza can feel her huge belly against her breasts.

"Oh, my dear Miss Russell, how dreadful. And what happened next?"

"Peter summoned the serving girl and sent her to the apothecary on the corner to buy a bottle of laudanum. He showed me how to add it to the broth my mother consumed nightly. In a day or two, the fits of rage vanished. She would fall into deep slumber, and I be once again able to rest myself and control her. Oh Lord, I will ever be grateful to dear Peter. We have since been a faithful couple for these many years."

Has she said too much? At any rate, Mrs. Jarvis asks no more questions. She stays only a few minutes longer, but on her way out she manages to open the wrong door and look into the bedchamber. "Pardon me, Miss Russell," she says. "These days—it must be my condition—I get so thoroughly confused."

# Chapter Ten

*October 1792*

White looks out the door of the rented log house which he and Osgoode now occupy. The black bear is there again in the "back forty," an expression he's just learned from an American farmer. Though he has no desire to meet the animal up close, he rather likes to watch it munch on the rotted apples that have fallen. There is a pleasant cleared space just behind the house where he hopes to plant a garden in the spring.

He and Osgoode have a woman to cook for them. Her name is Yvette LaCroix. She's what the settlers here call a "half breed," having a French father and a Chippewa mother. The Frenchman accepted no responsibility for Yvette's upbringing, so she has been raised by her mother's Indian band. It's a common occurrence in these dark Canadian forests.

Much as he enjoys Osgoode's friendship, he realizes they have few common interests. Osgoode is always content to fall to sleep at ten o'clock each night reading his favourite book, *Boote's Suit at Law,* but *he* needs more stimulation. It's a relief, though, to be in this rented hut and to escape from the gimlet eye of Mrs. Simcoe. By early fall of next year, he may have his own house. The builders are working on it now. Though it has a good view of the river, it's a far cry from the stone mansion he once envisaged. But four rooms to himself, even in a house of logs, will be heaven.

Four rooms to himself? Should he not ask Marianne and the children to come to him here in the wilderness? *No, postpone it.* There is but one doctor at the garrison, no school for the children, and not even a church for their spiritual enlightenment, only an itinerant Church of England preacher who conducts his services in a room in the Freemasons' Lodge. Eliza Russell, bless her good heart, would tolerate Marianne, but how would his wife fare with the Gov's lady? He tries to imagine Marianne engaging in a conversation with the lady about pet snakes, or the best way to cook a squirrel, or worst of all, sitting with Captain Brant, the Mohawk chief, at an official dinner. *She would undoubtedly ask him how many scalps he had taken.* He needs must put off these potential embarrassments for as long as possible.

The Parliament of Upper Canada which convened in the Freemasons' Lodge has been prorogued so that the farmers can get home to harvest their crops. White was at first worried about his role in the new assembly, but it soon proved to be the same as government anywhere: too much talk and too little action. But what can he expect from what David Smith has called a "lair of warriors and peasants"? It's true that half the assembly is made up of former military men who have no experience in the world of politics and the other half of farmers who are mostly illiterate and untutored in the ways of the world.

Though the amended slave bill has been postponed for the second parliamentary session, White is happy enough with the current passing of bills which set up the district courts and the Court of King's Bench. That at least establishes a framework of justice. But he's determined now to see regulations enacted to ensure lawyers, magistrates, and justices in this new world are properly trained for these courts.

He heard over tea with the Jarvises last week that Peter Russell intends to supplement his income by sitting on King's Bench. Mrs. Jarvis can sniff out gossip like a foxhound routing a fox.

"The old fool knows nothing about the law," she told him, her face flushed with joy at imparting bad news, "except what he learned when he was sentenced to Fleet prison."

White had protested against this slur, of course, but she'd whacked him down. "Surely, sir, you've heard of his gambling losses and the ten months he spent in the Netherlands before atoning for his debts like a proper gentleman."

Well, yes, Osgoode told him about Russell's time in debtors' prison, but this is the first inkling he has had about the man sitting on King's Bench.

*If the woman is right, I'll have to face Russell and try to talk him out of getting into the courts as a judge.* Russell is a friend, and he dreads the moment of confrontation. Even now, Russell's horse is tethered to the railing on White's stoop. "It's yours when you need it," his friend has told him many times.

His worries have made him restless, bringing on the headaches and nosebleeds that plague him. He made the mistake of mentioning his woes to David Smith, inveterate teller of tales, who passed on his information to virtually everyone in the community. Mrs. Jarvis sent along a bottle of castor oil, and Mrs. Simcoe, a package of pigeons' gizzards dried and ground to a fine powder. He'll send the ladies thank-you notes, not mentioning that he dumped both concoctions down the groundhog's hole.

It's a fine fall day, Indian summer they call it here, so he's decided to allay his worries with a change of scenery. He mounts Russell's black horse and sets out for his first visit to the Falls of Niagara.

On the road he passes Major Small and his wife in a calash pulled by two fine steeds. Small must have a private income, White surmises. Either that or he's living well beyond his means. The man is aptly named. Though he's tall and well-built, he has but a small status in the Legislative Council. He's a mere clerk, a recorder of minutes, a position well below White's own exalted one. But in this gossipy settlement, niceties must be preserved, so as he canters up behind them, he waves a greeting.

"May I present my wife?" Small calls, pulling on the reins.

Mrs. Small is a petite, attractive woman with an ample bosom which the current fashions show off to advantage. Her eyes match her hair—dark and lustrous brown, like chestnuts. He's seen her from time to time at Fort Niagara, but like the bear, never up close. She's wearing a soft fur tippet, and her cheeks are flushed with the nip of the autumn air.

"We're on our way to the Falls. And where are you going?"

"Just out to enjoy the day." He finds it presumptuous that Small should be questioning him. *Best to put him in his place and perhaps make an impression on the lady at the same time.* He adds, "After I have breakfast with the Hamiltons."

Small has nothing more to say. So White tips his round hat, lately bought at Hamilton's large emporium, and turns his horse towards the huge stone house visible from the well-travelled road on which they have stopped.

Hamilton is a wealthy merchant, the sole provisioner of the garrison. The Gov has tried to break his monopoly, but has had to recognize the realities of life in the wilderness. "A Scotch pedlar and a damn republican," the Gov calls him, though White knows Mrs. Simcoe is a great friend of Mrs. Hamilton, whom she calls "Catherine."

The Hamiltons live in a Georgian two-storey mansion with side wings, located high above the river at the Landing or Queen's Town, though since Hamilton has started to drop the "w" from his mercantile papers, people are calling the place Queenston. This new appellation is one of the grievances which the Gov holds against the man.

Hamilton's abode is exactly the sort of house that White once dreamed of owning, though he has been forced to realize his dreams are unrealistic. He's been in this country almost five months and has not yet received a penny of the salary owed him from England. He has been forced to open a private law practice in order to pay the rent. Perhaps the Gov's letter to the Colonial Office will bring results.

White and his hosts eat breakfast in a covered gallery—which the Yankee settlers call a "veranda"—overlooking the Niagara River and the dark woods on the American side. There's some excellent porridge with cream and the maple sugar he's come to love, along with good bread from a bake oven, an asset owned only by the rich.

Most of all, he enjoys the coffee, not the vile chicory that Mrs. Jarvis serves up, but the real thing. "Ordered in special, and just arrived yesterday," Hamilton tells him, pointing down to the batteaux unloading casks of rum and scotch at the wharves. The man is a self-satisfied lout who gives himself the airs of a gentleman, but his wife is pleasant enough. She's a thin woman with a lined face that suggests hard work and the burden of a large family.

It's almost noon when he gets back on Russell's horse and sets out again for the Falls. He's drunk a tankard of beer along with the coffee, so he dismounts from time to time to void by the wayside. *No need for pisspots in the forests of Upper Canada!*

When he gets to the Falls, he finds the Smalls already there. He can see their calash parked along the row of trees that fringe the top of the steep heights leading down to the cataracts. Mrs. Small waves at him, and he joins them. They stand for a few minutes taking in the view that almost matches the praise heaped upon it a hundred times by Mrs. Simcoe.

"A vast and prodigious cadence," White shouts above the roar. He does not bother to attribute this statement to its author, Father Louis Hennepin, whose seventeenth-century account of the Falls he read before leaving London. His sole motive after all is to put Small at a disadvantage and to impress the beautiful Mrs. Small.

"Vast and prodigious, indeed," she says to her husband. "I must descend. That big flat rock down there will be a perfect spot from which to get a better view."

"My dear, you must not. It is not safe. And there will be rattlesnakes."

"Nonsense," she says, throwing her muff at Small and stepping towards the edge, ready to make the descent. In a second, they can see only the top of her head.

"Oh my, oh my, whatever possesses the woman?" Small whimpers, wringing his hands. "I cannot follow her. I'm . . . I'm . . . Whatever am I to do?"

Opportunity knocks. "Don't worry, man," White says. "I'll go down with her and keep her safe." He's less confident than he sounds, but he scrambles after her.

Down, down they go, laughing and grabbing at tree branches to slow their precipitous descent. He catches her hand from time to time to keep her from plunging too quickly, and at every jump, the lady's fine ankles and slender legs are on display. As they slide from branch to branch, he forgets his fear in the exhilaration of conquest. By the time they reach Table Rock, they are breathless and exuberant.

"Oh, Mr. White, what fun," she says. "Thank you for saving me from certain death."

*Yes, she is the one I've been looking for. Next step: find out her first name.*

# Chapter Eleven

White receives a note three days later, delivered by one of the little Indian boys he often sees skipping along the narrow path that links the log houses set into the forest. He reads it while the lad waits for an answer: *Come to dinner tomorrow at noon, do, Mr. White. My husband and I will be alone and will welcome company. Betsy Small.*

*Halleluiah, just what I wanted.*

So he borrows Peter Russell's horse again, and trots two miles or so south along the river to the Smalls' house near the Landing at Queenston. He wears his blue Bath coat with gilt buttons. It seems somewhat ridiculous to get dandified for dinner in a log house, but he wants to impress the lady.

Mrs. Small's cook sets before them an excellent meal of grilled pork with apple compote.

"It's been so long since I've had a cutlet," he says.

It's served up on pretty white-and-green porcelain tableware, and he can't help but notice the walnut dining table and the gilded clock on the rough wood of the mantel. Small's salary is much less than his. How can the man afford this display of wealth?

They've just settled into plates of gingerbread with rum sauce when Small pulls out his pocket-watch. "Oh Lord, Betsy, I am late for my council meeting with the Governor." He removes the napkin tucked under his chin and sets it down by his plate. "I have the calash and can drive you to your lodgings, White. Russell's horse can be tied behind the cart."

"No, no, my dear, Mr. White must stay and take time to finish his gingerbread."

50

Small departs. White enjoys his gingerbread, and Mrs. Small pours him another glass of wine.

"Do have a cigar, sir," she says, taking one from a pretty brass jar on the sideboard.

"You have none of the usual prejudices, then, about a gentleman smoking in your presence?"

"Good heavens, no. Why, when I resided at Berkeley Castle in Gloucester, Lord Berkeley always insisted I stay with him in the dining hall while he enjoyed his port and cigar. Why should a lady be relegated to a drawing room to gossip with biddies if she can enjoy a real conversation with a gentleman?"

White takes the cue offered him. "Lord Berkeley, ma'am?"

"One of my dearest friends. Oh sir, I had such merry times during my long sojourns at the Castle. When I see this forest, this log dwelling in which I am. . . incarcerated . . . I think of those happy days and mourn."

*Clearly, I am to be impressed.* "Please, ma'am, I long to hear about those happy days."

She rattles on about the baronial hall with half-timbered ceilings, the dining hall with the magnificent family silver, the chamber with the ebony bedstead where Sir Francis Drake slept, the green where Elizabeth I bowled.

"Edward II was murdered in Berkeley Castle," she says, dabbing at her eyes with a handkerchief she pulls from her bosom, "and dear Lord Berkeley told me that on the last day of his life, the guards shaved the king's head and beard in cold water from a ditch. Then they stabbed him in a chamber at the top of the castle."

"Horrible," White says, feeling like the Chorus in a Greek play.

"Most horrible." She pauses and sighs. "Often when I stayed at the castle, I would be awakened at midnight by his ghostly shrieks." She closes her eyes for a second, giving him an opportunity to admire her long black lashes.

*I don't believe a word of it.* Her accent is common, though her grammar is good enough. She may have visited

51

the castle on a country outing. But as a friend of this Lord Berkeley? Not bloody likely. People often embroider their past when they move to a new country. He's done it himself. He told the Gov and his lady that Marianne stayed in England because her health was poor. He invented a touching tale about how much he missed her. Mrs. Simcoe's eyes had clouded, and she'd reciprocated with a story of her own longing for the three little daughters she left behind at Wolford Lodge.

No, the Small woman's tale is mere poof, but he admires the flash of her white teeth and the tears which make her dark eyes shine as she tells it. Her corsets push her breasts into prominence, and when she dives into her bosom from time to time to retrieve her handkerchief, he feels his prick stir.

The ormolu clock on the hearth mantel sounds. He counts. *Four* bongs. "Dear Mrs. Small," he says, rising, "I have taken your afternoon. My apologies. But your account of Berkeley Castle and Lord Berkeley was so riveting that I quite lost track of time."

She comes close to him and puts her hand on his arm. "You must come and sup with us again soon."

He looks down into her cleavage. "It will be my greatest pleasure, dear Mrs . . . may I call you Betsy?"

"And I shall call you John."

An afternoon well spent, for though nothing has been enacted, much has been set in motion. Quite a feat, really, in a four-room cabin with the sounds of their young son and servants in a neighbouring chamber. Betsy—oh, how the name trips off his tongue—knows how to make the most of an opportunity.

\* \* \*

The Russells' cabin is a short ride north of his own log house, and as he trots by his dwelling, he sees Osgoode hailing him from the front stoop.

"What's up, my friend?"

52

"I'm glad to have caught you before you get that nag back to Russell. Be warned: he's in a foul mood. But perhaps you know this already."

"I didn't see him when I picked up the horse. Miss Russell came to the door, and directed Job to saddle up for me. Is he angry because I'm late returning? I had a rather good time at—"

"Tell me later. Just get over there. I know it's about that Writ of Attaint you dished up at court. I thought it was pretty damned funny when you told me about it last night, but Russell obviously thinks differently. Get moving, man. I'll have Yvette make up a bowl of rum punch for us, and we'll drain it dry before s..s..sunset."

White slaps the whip on the horse's flank and the beast takes off at a trot. He can imagine what's bothering Russell. And he's sorry. The man and his sister are two people he can trust for friendship. But dammit, the justice system in this backwater must be righted.

# Chapter Twelve

Eliza Russell has just lain down for an afternoon nap in the bedchamber when she hears the front door slam. Oh, oh, that means for certain that dear Peter is in a pet about something. She looks at Mary, lying beside her. The girl is snoring softly, thank the Lord.

She tiptoes into the main room. Job is making soup in a large cauldron on the pine table. She looks at Peter. He's standing by the door, and his whole face is one mighty frown.

"Go out now, Job," she says, "and pick us some of those windfall apples. You can slice them outside on the back stoop and put them over the hearth later for drying."

Job glances at her, glances at Peter, and leaves quickly. For certain he knows there will be a to-do.

"Peter, sit down." Eliza pours a mugful of rum from the cask in the corner and hands it to her brother. She waits while he downs half of it.

He slams his mug on the table. "He made a fool of me yesterday, sister, that man to whom I have always been a friend. Is he not at this moment riding the horse I let him have?"

*Oh dear.* "What has he done, Peter?"

But before he can answer, there's a knock on the door. Eliza answers it to find the culprit himself on the front stoop. "Excuse me, Miss Russell. I must talk to your brother and make my explanations and apologies."

She stands aside. Mr. White enters and sits down opposite Peter.

"A glass of whisky, sir?" she asks.

"If rum's good enough for me, sister, it's good enough for this blackguard and hypocrite."

54

"Blackguard perhaps, Russell, but not hypocrite. Have I not maintained in the parliament and in private that those people concerned with administrating the laws of this country must be fully qualified?"

"But that damned Writ of Attaint, you bugger—"

"That is a coarse term of abuse I will not listen to. We must discuss the matter like gentlemen, or I will leave this instant." White throws the rum in his mug into the hearth and stands up.

"I cannot tolerate this language either, brother," Eliza says. She hears her voice rise in a wail. "Please, please, let us be quiet." She sits down at the head of the table.

Peter looks contrite. "You are right, sister. I apologize. But let us now hear what this . . . this . . . man has to say for himself."

Mr. White turns towards her. He sits down again. It seems that he wants to talk to her directly, and she feels flattered.

"I will summarize the matter in a few words, ma'am, and your brother must interrupt me if I represent any of the facts incorrectly. He sat upon King's Bench yesterday—"

*What in the Lord's name is this King's Bench?* "I do not understand, Mr. White."

"He was the judge at a trial yesterday. I was the legal counsel for an Indian man named Big Canoe whose brother had been murdered by a settler here in the early summer. When Big Canoe failed to attain justice in white man's court for his brother's murder, he took his own rough justice. He seized a tomahawk and cut the settler to pieces. The settler's wife found his corpse in the woods, scalped and mutilated."

Eliza is unable to hide her shock. "How terrible!"

"Yes, but you must remember the Indian never willingly seeks quarrels with the white man, but once wronged he does not forget nor forgive. 'He kill my brother, me kill him.' Those were the seven words with which Big Canoe defended himself."

Eliza ponders the words she has heard. "Rough justice, for certain. But why in tarnation was the settler not punished for the murder of this Big Canoe's brother?"

"It is shocking, yes, but these misfirings of justice are common in this country. You must remember the jurors are always white men. In any trial, they side with the white man, always. The settler was *not* punished. And Big Canoe had no chance in this trial yesterday. He would have been sentenced to hanging for the murder of the settler if—"

"If you had not brought in this bloody Writ of Attaint."

"Tainting Rights? What are those? What does my brother mean?"

"A ploy by which I succeeded in getting this jury of white men to exonerate the Indian. I told them if they did not let Big Canoe go free, I would invoke the Writ of Attaint to redress the wrongness of their verdict. I said the punishment inflicted on them would be severe: they should forfeit all their goods and chattels; their lands should be seized into the government's hands; their wives and children should be thrown out of doors; their houses and lands should be razed; their bodies should be cast into jail . . ."

Eliza is now thoroughly confused. "Surely, sir, you were right to remind the jury to bring in a verdict that was fair." She looks at her brother. "Was Mr. White not right, Peter?"

Peter laughs. It's a laugh that shows he is not mighty pleased with her question. "Sister, you must know that the jurors did bring in a verdict of not guilty for Big Canoe, and—"

"But I ask you, brother, was this not fair?"

"Perhaps. But White's manner of wresting this verdict from them was *not*. The Writ of Attaint has been *obsolete* since the end of the fifteenth century. So Governor Simcoe told me this afternoon. I did not know that. White has made an ass of me and the whole judicial system."

Mr. White speaks up. "Dear ma'am, I needed justice for my Indian, and I perhaps used a questionable means of achieving it. But in the process I surely made clear my

56

point that all who sit on King's Bench must be qualified. Your brother is *not*."

He pauses and takes a deep breath. Turning to dear Peter, he continues, "I have embarrassed you, sir. I did not think you would find out the truth about the Writ of Attaint. If no more is said about this case, however, it seems to me you will be safe. If the trial does evoke discussion, however, it is the *jurors* and *I* who will be deemed the greatest asses, not you."

Another long pause while Mr. White seems to stare into a space far beyond the confines of their small chamber. Then he says, "I was wrong to invoke an obsolete law in order to get justice for my client. I will not do it again. But I will now pledge one more thing. Until the day comes when Indians are allowed to sit on juries with white men, I will avoid all cases that deal with Indians. I cannot stay in this land otherwise."

"Get White another mug of rum, will you, sister?"

Eliza does as she is bid, feeling that in a few short moments, the friendship between her brother and Mr. White has somehow been firmed up. Two fine men have settled things. She goes to the cupboard to get a dollop or two of the Indian corn flour pudding Job made earlier in the day. It will be tasty with the cream she and Mary whopped up earlier in the afternoon.

# Chapter Thirteen

*March 1793*

At first, Eliza Russell was mighty pleased with the Canadian snowfall. Snow in England, if it came at all, was slush and muck. She and Mary made snowflakes from bits of paper dear Peter procured for them, and they'd hung them all over the cabin for Christmas time. But now she just wants this wretched season to be gone. It's so cold, her fingers are almost numb, and the smoke from the chimney is intolerable.

"I do wish you would stop your moaning and groaning, Aunt," Mary says, between the coughs that rack her small body.

*I must have been talking out loud and not realized.* "Sorry, child. Why don't you get your book and read it?"

"Ha. Don't you remember, Uncle Peter snatched it from me at breakfast. Said he would not give it back until I finished eating. As if I could stomach one more mouthful of that cornmeal porridge."

"Now *I* am a-wondering who is moaning and groaning?"

Job gets up from his chair in the corner of the room and stirs the soup on the hearth. It creates a diversion, and Eliza knows that's what he intended. He's a good man and a good cook, and Eliza knows not what she would do without him. Even with his help, she and Mary are housekeepers, seamstresses, and chambermaids. Thank the Lord that the slave bill, according to Peter, has been put aside until the second session of the legislature opens in May. Not that it will much change Job's life as a slave, but it may give him ideas above his station.

There's a thump on the door. "It's that horrible Jarvis woman," Mary says, peeking through their tiny front window. "I'm not staying around to hear her call me a savage. I'll take myself and my moccasins into the bedchamber."

Job retreats again to his corner. Eliza has not time to ready herself except to remove her apron, stained red from a jacket she had been dyeing in madder.

Mrs. Jarvis holds a babe in one arm, a healthy-looking infant she calls Samuel Peters, named after their little son who died of diphtheria in the fall. She sweeps into the room, wriggles out of her mantle, throws it onto a hook in the wall, and before Eliza can say "please sit down," moves the rocking chair so that its back is to Job. She then pulls out the linen strip that fills in her low-necked bodice, and bares her breast.

"What a blessed relief," she says, as the babe sucks. "He screamed the whole way here. No wonder William says he has not the same affection for him as he had for our dear departed son."

She looks around the room. "How do you manage, Miss Russell? William tells me your new house is in the making and you will soon be out of this hovel."

"It is scarce ready, ma'am, and I will not be a-going from this place for many a month."

"A pity indeed. William and I now have the most comfortable cottage in the province. Why, our very cellar is larger than this room. You should see it. William has stocked it with wine, apples, butter, maple sugar—one hundred and fifty pounds of it—flour, cheese, coffee, and loaf sugar."

"That must be dear, ma'am."

"William thinks only of the comforts of his family, Miss Russell. He spares no expense." She frowns. "And you do not get out and about much, do you? I have not seen you at our subscription balls over at the Fort."

*I'm not a-going to tell her I have no money for clothes for dining out. My brother has spent more than a thousand*

59

*pounds on the new house, all out of his own pocket.* "I have been ill with the ague, ma'am."

"Let me send you some castor oil. It is a panacea for all ailments, I have found."

She pops out her other breast and transfers the babe to it. "Have you heard that the Lady Simcoe is searching for a wet nurse for her new infant?" She makes a noise that's more a snort than a laugh. "I'm thinking of seeking the job myself. The woman has too much money to throw around. That's why her husband married her. She's got him right under her thumb. Petticoat rule, that's what it is."

*She does like that expression, I've heard it a hundred times.* "Tea, ma'am? Mr. Hamilton procured some for us from Montreal before the lake froze."

Mrs. Jarvis watches while Job puts some tea leaves into a pot and pours boiling water from the copper cauldron over it. "You have only one servant, Miss Russell. He seems efficient. My kitchen maid Fanny was a perfect Devil incarnate. She ran off with a sergeant at the Fort, and yesterday William told me the man shot himself through the head one month into their marriage. Now I have a Scotch girl, a nasty, sulky, ill-tempered creature. Richard, our manservant, has turned out to be a perfect sot. Rum, dear rum, is his idol . . ."

While her guest rambles on, Eliza catches Job's eye. He stands behind the visitor's chair and makes a gesture that reminds her of a fiddler playing a reel. His gesture is amusing, but it puts her to the blush.

"How red you are, Miss Russell. Perhaps I should not discuss the servants in front of your man. I must now find some slaves, though they may all run away on me this summer when our Bachelor-at-Large and the Governor pass that piece of chicanery that frees all negroes."

"The slave bill, my brother says, forbids the import of more slaves, but for certain does not force us to give up the ones we have now. So you would be the better for getting your slaves now, ma'am." *I'm mighty pleased to set the . . . bitch . . . straight on that one . . .*

60

"Well only God knows what the Simcoes are up to. Or our Bachelor-at-Large either, for that matter." She puts the babe against her shoulder and administers a slap to its back. It gives a loud burp.

*Time to pretend ignorance.* "Bachelor-at-Large, Mrs Jarvis?

"Your dear friend, Attorney-General John White, and lately thief of large chunks of my husband's salary."

Eliza is now genuinely at a loss. "What do you mean, ma'am?"

"The Governor has done nothing but complain about William's supposed slowness in administering land grants. He has now allowed that man, who is nothing but a sycophant and a liar, the right to collect *half* of the fees on land patents. And William must still pay all the expenses of his office. You can have no idea of the cost of parchment which must be imported." She slaps the babe's back again.

"Parchment, ma'am? Why does Mr. Jarvis have the expense of parchment? My brother told me Mr. Jarvis issues his land grants on *paper,* so he should not have to charge for parchment." *Now I have undone things. Not that I care. The sooner she is a-going from my kitchen, the better.*

"I have no more to say, Miss Russell. I can see that you know little about the affairs of this godforsaken world. Though I might pity you for your ignorance, perhaps it is best to be ignorant. Then you have none of the cares and worries that beset me."

Mrs. Jarvis hands the babe to Eliza while she tucks the linen strip back into her bosom. Eliza has not held a babe for many years, and as she looks down at the toothless smile the child bestows on her, she remembers . . . *"No," Mary's first word, the bunch of dandelions the wee lass picked for me and arranged in a pickle jar, the . . .*

"What you have to smile about in this place, Miss Russell, eludes me. I shall go home now. I cannot think that all this smoke can be good for my son." Mrs. Jarvis has donned her coat and now takes back the babe. "I shall send over the castor oil for your ague with a servant this afternoon. Thank you for the tea. Good morning."

The door has scarce closed when Mary comes out of the bedchamber. "Oh Aunt," she says, "let me pour you a large glass of rum. You'll need it to wash down that castor oil."

For a moment, their shared laughter warms Eliza's hands and conquers Mary's ever present cough.

# Chapter Fourteen

*July 1793*

Following the second session of Parliament and the passage of the amended slave bill, White has invited Osgoode for a meal in his cabin. The Chief Justice now has his own residence, but the two friends often share meals together. They have just finished a supper of whitefish and drunk two bottles of dandelion wine. Yvette, who has stayed on as White's cook, brings a third bottle from the kitchen.

"Not as vile as I imagined," White says, filling his friend's glass, "though I was upset, I can tell you, when those rogues from the ship dropped a case of my French claret onto the wharf and smashed every bottle. Especially as I'll be lucky to get more before freeze-up. Fortunately, Yvette had an alternative. It was that or Hamilton's filthy rum for which he gets a pretty sum."

"Here's to the dandelion," Osgoode says, emitting a loud belch. "And here's to you! Let us drink to your victory in the legislature today." He stands up, steadies himself with one hand on the table, and shouts, "Down with s..s..slavery. Long live free men!"

"Thank you, friend. But sit down and face the facts with me. The bill was a sad compromise which will do nothing to free those already enslaved in this country. I regret that."

"But no new s..s..slaves can be imported. And children born to s..s..slaves here can go free at twenty-five years of age. That is a victory. Upper Canada is now the first place in the British Empire to abolish the abomination. And you drafted the bill. Rejoice, man!" Osgoode drains his glass and refills it to the accompaniment of a second belch.

"I try to be happy, but . . . moping melancholy, that's what I feel."

"Moping melancholy? That's a good one." Osgoode laughs. "Just a few short months ago, it seems, you were Mr. S..S..Satyr. And now you're Mr. Moping Melancholy." He pushes the dandelion wine towards White. "Drink up and tell me what's bothering you."

"Money, for one thing. This new house I'm building has drained me dry. Fancy being out of pocket for a four-room log house in a forest. I still have not received a shilling from the Colonial Office, though both the Governor and Russell have written letters. I've had to draw on my brother-in-law Sam Shepherd, and that hurts because he was the one who got me this position in the first place. It makes me seem ungrateful."

"You are getting s..s..some tin from Jarvis, are you not?"

"That's helps, yes. But the strain of dealing with the man wears me out. He dawdles and dithers, and I find myself making out most of the deeds. That labour entitles me to at least half of his fees, but the man disputes every penny. Lord, how my head aches each time I enter his office. But part of that may be due to the smell of bowels that pervades his whole house, thanks to Mrs. Jarvis's belief in the powers of castor oil." He manages a strangled laugh.

Osgoode moves his chair closer and pats his arm. "My apologies. I have made light of your troubles. But we had a good time together on the c..c..circuit this winter, did we not?"

*Shall I tell him the truth?* "On the whole, yes. It was good to get out of this place and travel. And I was grateful to you, as you know, for handling those Indian cases I wanted no part of. But — "

"The duel in Kingston, I know, was a flea in your wig. I have chewed over our fight about that one. But out with it, man, you are not s..s..still angry?"

64

"It festers in my brain. It brings on my headaches. I can't forget the injustice of that trial. I acted as the prosecutor of the man who shot another man dead and I expected you, as the Chief Justice of Upper Canada, to support me. But instead of setting the black cap upon your head and sentencing this murderer to death, you *fined* him thirteen shillings and fourpence and set him *free*. A man's life, Osgoode, *a man's life* is to be valued at thirteen shillings and fourpence?"

"I did what I considered right, damn you. The victim was determined to duel, even though the man you call "murderer" was willing to negotiate. Did the victim not s..s..seal his own death warrant? And the jury decided, did they not? They gave their—"

"You, sir, acted virtually as defence counsel from King's Bench, and the jury gave in to your devilish persuasion, even though they deliberated for hours . . . "

Osgoode rises from his place at table. "Perhaps I should leave now. You are ups..s..set. We have been through it all before, and no good can come from raking up muck again. I am Chief Justice of this province, and I endeavour to do what I think right." Osgoode says this in a tone White has never heard from him before. Though angry, it is also sorrowful, as if he regrets this quarrel.

*My God, I can't break with the man. He's my chief support in the administration of law in this place.* "Sit down, friend. This vile wine has addled my wits. I have one good bottle of port left in the house. Let us drink it. I proffer my apologies and ask you to forget what I have said."

Osgoode stands quiet for a moment, hand on the back of his chair. Then he sits down. "We have had an argument that grieves me. But s..s..since you are willing to s..s..sacrifice that last bottle of port to atone, I know you must deeply regret your words."

Yvette brings the bottle of port to the table along with two clean glasses and leaves them to it. In a few minutes, she comes back, holding another glass, her face rather flushed. "Mr. White, sir," she says, "His Excellency is here." And sure enough, coming through the door behind her is the Gov himself, wearing sturdy boots and carrying his walking stick. The dog called Trojan is with him. The animal leaps up on White first, leaving dirty paw marks on his white breeches, and then treats Osgoode to the same warm welcome. The Gov, seemingly oblivious to the animal's depredations, pulls out a chair at the table and pours himself a glass of port as he sits down.

"We are c..c..celebrating the passing of the bill, Governor," Osgoode says.

"Good work, sir," White chimes. *Too late to do anything about that damnable lukewarm mess now.*

"Yes, I am happy," the Gov says. "But I have not come here seeking praise. I was out for a walk with Trojan. I saw the two of you through the window and decided to come in to tell you my plans."

They wait obediently while he downs his port.

"Another glass, sir?" White asks. *Just enough left for one glass more, but what am I to do if he wants a third glass?*

"I thank you, no. I have at present a gouty pain in my hand. I fear it is moving to my foot. I have had to limit my wine to a mere bottle a day."

White hears himself and Osgoode making sympathetic noises. The Gov's gout is a favourite topic of conversation.

"Mrs. Simcoe and I shall embark at the end of this month for Toronto."

"Toronto?" Osgoode and White say in unison.

"It's an unfortunate name. I intend to rename it York. With me will be one hundred men from the Queen's Rangers."

"One hundred Queen's Rangers?" *Sophocles could have surely have used us as Chorus in one of his plays.*

"That is what I said. They will begin work on a new naval base. I fear the Yankees. Here we are across the river from them with no protection. When Fort Niagara is handed over to them in 1796, anything may happen. A naval base at York will provide a means of attack if they get out of hand. I was there in May, as you know, and I have only praise for its fine harbour. It is an excellent site for a town."

"A wise decision, Excellency," Osgoode says.

"Mrs. Simcoe and I shall take a canvas house with us to provide accommodation. I shall supervise the building of the garrison. We expect to be absent from this place many months, but I shall make short visits here from time to time. I leave Newark in good hands." He nods at them and rises. "Russell will administer affairs here during our absence. You gentlemen will, I know, lend him your support."

He gathers his walking stick, makes a clucking noise at Trojan, and departs.

White waits for the door to thump shut, then says, "Oh, oh."

"Oh, oh? Are you implying s..s..something, man?"

"'An excellent site for a town.' What do you think of that phrase?"

"I hope it was just a phrase in those short and s..s..simple s..s..sentences the great man utters. Do you read more into it?"

"For a moment I thought he was planning to establish more than a naval base."

Osgoode shrugs. "Not likely. But I do have a question about the way he talks. Do you think that an exalted position in the Queen's Rangers precludes the use of s..s..subordinate clauses?"

"Undoubtedly. Surely a colonel who has spent a lifetime barking out commands to subordinates must avoid unnecessary subordination. But a word or two barked at that damn four-legged subordinate of his might have saved my breeches."

They laugh together and drain the last dregs from the bottle of port.

# Chapter Fifteen

*November 1793*

White strolls through his new log house. It seems palatial when he compares it with his stuffy little corner in the Gov's tent and the subsequent rented rooms in the cabin he shared for several months with Osgoode. This dwelling is a squared-log structure, so his builder has told him, and though he at first had no idea what the man was talking about when he jawed on about adzes and hewing hatchets, he can see now that it's a vast improvement over the round-log cabin he lately occupied. For one thing, the walls have plaster, so he'll be able to put up pictures.

There's also a big kitchen with a bake oven and open hearth, flanked by a small separate dining room, an alcove for his books and desk, and a loft for his bed and washstand.

One of the best features is the well at the back door. His cynicism nearly lost him that asset. He remembers a wizened little Indian man sitting on his back stoop, holding a forked branch in his hand. He'd ignored the man for several hours—Indians often rest on settlers' stoops during their treks back and forth on their forest trails—and then he'd asked him if he needed some food.

"Not need food," the man said. "You need water. I get water. You pay me."

Much palaver had followed, the gist of it being that the Indian was a "witcher" who could find him water with his forked hazel wood branch. Trickster, not witcher, had been White's thought.

The man had said, "Watch me." Back and forth across White's "back forty" the Indian had walked, holding the two ends of the fork in his hands with the butt of the branch pointing forward.

*Mumbo-jumbo.* Then, while he was muttering to himself, the forked branch twisted in the Indian's hand and the butt of the branch moved downwards as if an invisible force was yanking it from his hands.

"Water right here," the Indian said.

"Dig me a well then," White had replied. "I will pay you English coins if you find water." *Not bloody likely that you will . . .*

But two days later, the well was dug, a pump installed, and four English pounds put into the witcher's outstretched hand. And sure enough, there was fresh water for every need. *If Marianne had told me this story, I'd have accused her of an opium dream.*

He has purchased most of his furniture from local carpenters to save money, but several dozen hock glasses which he'd ordered from a Montreal merchant were stolen on the wharf here when the packet boat landed. These building and furnishing costs have left him deep in debt to his long-suffering friend and brother-in-law, Sam Shepherd.

He knows, too, that Sam has borne most of the expenses of his family in London. Not one word has he heard from Marianne in the months since he left London, but Ellen, dear Ellen, has sent him a note giving him news of herself and her small brothers. She misses him, that is certain, but there is nothing in the content of her letter to show that William and Charles even remember him. Her writing style has improved, though. Sam's governess has obviously been of benefit, but he is upset to learn Ellen has been in an altercation with his sister, Sam's wife, over the purchase of ribbons. Marianne should surely keep the child from incurring extra expenses!

*Time is running out. I must soon resume my role as husband and father. But for now . . . carpe diem!*

He looks at his pocket watch. *Yes, carpe diem.* He is due for dinner at the Smalls' house. There have been many dinings and suppings, embracings, and snugglings in the last few weeks. In his own house now, away from Osgoode and with the Simcoes far off in Toronto, it's easy to arrange trysts. Even the deep woods, red and golden now in their autumn foliage, offer opportunities. What's more, he can walk over to the Smalls from his new house. That's a relief since his constant borrowing of Russell's horse might have raised some suspicions.

Yvette has come with him to his new abode, so he has not had to find another cook. She enters the kitchen now from the back door with a huge squash from the root cellar, enough for many meals, he fears. Roasted squash and whitefish are her major culinary accomplishments. Though the kitchen has a fine bake oven, she has not the faintest notion of how to make bread. White brought her a bottle of the milky white liquid which Miss Russell calls yeast, but the girl, not knowing what it was, threw it into the hearth. Dessert is inevitably Indian corn flour pudding, but flavoured with maple sugar, it is tasty enough.

He looks again at his pocket-watch. *Best to get going.* "Goodbye, Yvette," he says. Her back is to him. She's cutting up the squash, and her reply is muffled. She's a quiet, unobtrusive young woman, a pleasant change from the chatterers in his circle. She has seemed even more withdrawn lately, and he wonders fleetingly if there is some problem.

\* \* \*

The Smalls' dinner is capital: vichyssoise, lamb cutlet with mint sauce, and bread pudding. Good food is part of Betsy's allure. As always, she and White bide their time, addressing each other formally, and waiting for the departure of the unwanted husband. Usually Small leaves for his work at Navy Hall soon after their dinners, but today he lingers, much to White's annoyance. Perhaps he's taking advantage of the knowledge that the Gov will not be around to record his absence.

"Smith is newly arrived from York," he says to White.

70

"York? I was unaware he'd gone to England." Then he remembers. The settlement at Toronto was renamed in August after the Duke of York's military victory somewhere or other. A yawn escapes him, as he moves his foot under the table until it just touches Betsy's. She takes her cue.

"Is it time, husband, that you went to Navy Hall? You said you had some letters to copy."

"In a moment, my dear. I wanted to tell White the latest gossip. Smith has been making maps for the Governor of the harbour and the settlement there, and he thinks there's something brewing. He suspects the Governor may be considering it as the new capital of Upper Canada."

"Bloody not!"

"Language, language, dear Mr. White," Betsy says.

"No details, mind you. Just a rumour. York does seem to be a wiser choice for our capital than here where we are at the mercy of the barbarians at the gate. Dear Betsy and I will of course comply with whatever His Excellency decides."

*Sanctimonious upstart.* "But I've just laid out six hundred pounds for my house. And what about Russell? He's just moved into his magnificent new house on the commons. And Smith himself is about to move. Why, this backwater is just starting to metamorphose into a decent settlement. Dammit, the Gov cannot be so insensitive to our needs."

"Drink up, dear sir," Betsy says, pouring more claret into his glass. "Just a rumour, as my husband says. You know how Mr. Smith loves to tell tales."

*That much is certainly true. Perhaps the Gov just made one of his random remarks and Smith happened to overhear it.*

"And that's not all. Here's something you'll be specially interested in, White." Small takes another pull on his cigar and exhales a fug of mint and tobacco. "Smith tells me that as he was coming in early this morning, he saw Richard Tickell and your half-breed cook in a carnal embrace a few yards from where the boat docked."

White opens his mouth to protest the phrase "half-breed" when Betsy shrieks, "Mr. Tickell with a squaw? I don't believe it!"

*Why is she so concerned about Tickell's amours? A mere clerk, subordinate even to Small, with unseemly ambitions to become a lawyer?*

"I wish Smith would shut up," White says. "Yvette LaCroix is surely of more value to this world than Richard Tickell. Her affairs are her own business, and I hate to see them bruited in common gossip."

Betsy seems to have got over her outburst, but her face is red and she's fanning herself.

"Well, I am sorry to have caused upset," Small says. "I am off to Navy Hall now, but I hope you'll stay, White, and have another helping of pudding. My man will drive you home in the calash. I'm riding my horse."

White and Betsy look out the window, waiting until Small is out of sight, then they turn to each other. Betsy seems calmer now. She rings for the cook, orders more pudding for him, then disappears to another part of the house.

*I wonder what she has in store for me today. It had better be good enough to take my mind off Smith's disturbing gossip.*

He finishes his pudding and pours another glass of claret. He sips it slowly, hoping it won't botch his "performance," as he calls these interludes. Suddenly she's there behind him. She puts her hands over his eyes and giggles.

"Picture a hot day by the sea, a fishing-boat tethered by the wharf, a villa with Corinthian columns, a beautiful woman in a chiton dancing on the piazza, and you, dear John, drinking your wine and singing a madrigal."

*What now? Wish she'd take her hands down and let us get on with whatever she's planned . . .*

"Now, open your eyes and turn around. It's my costume for the subscription ball next week at Wilson's Tavern."

When he turns, he sees a face and figure that might reasonably have belonged to Helen of Troy. Her costume is one of those two-tiered things he's seen in books of classical mythology—*a chiton, is that what she said?*—which clings to her beautiful breasts and shows off her narrow ankles and delicate feet. She carries a bow and arrow. *Why?*

Evidently seeing his bewilderment, she says, "I'm an Amazon, of course."

"With two breasts?" he asks, trying to keep things light.

"Silly John. So you really believe the Amazons could not fire off their arrows without two bosoms? Have a look, do." She steps into the space beyond the dining table, strikes a pose, then pulls the bowstring taut. The top tier of her costume drops dramatically revealing that, yes, there are definitely two of them.

That prelude leads quickly to the next act. He jumps from his chair, grabs her, and locks her into a hot embrace. Her "chiton" falls to her waist. He pulls off his wig, undoes the flap on his breeches, and then . . .

There's an urgent tapping at the door to the dining room.

"Ma'am, ma'am," says the voice of the maid, "Mrs. Jarvis is here."

In a swift movement, Betsy sets her dress aright. "For God's sake," she hisses at him, "fix your flap." He does so, and has just retrieved his wig from the chair when Mrs. Jarvis sweeps in.

He's aware of his heavy breathing and red face and the ridiculous spectacle he presents. But Betsy is as cool as an early breeze off the Aegean.

"Do be seated, Mrs. Jarvis. You're just in time to admire my costume for the ball. Mr. Small likes it excessively, and I have tried it on for Mr. White who has kindly offered to drive us to the tavern tomorrow night."

*Silly woman. Surely she should remember that Mrs. Jarvis knows I have no horse and carriage!*

With utter *sangfroid,* Betsy pulls the bell for the servant and orders tea.

Mrs. Jarvis, of all people to detect them in this manner. Perhaps she suspects nothing, but if she does, she will certainly use the information against him. She's no fan of his, especially since he's had to take over the making of the land deeds for her incompetent husband.

One thing he knows for certain. He'll have to break off the affair. *For no woman will I jeopardize my career.*

# Chapter Sixteen

January 1794

White dons the snowshoes given him by the Indian called Big Canoe whose murder charge he allayed with the Writ of Attaint that scared the breeches off the white jurors. The man appeared on his doorstep one morning just after the first big snowfall of the winter. He had a load on his back, the weight distributed by what the Indians call a burden strap, a sort of tumpline secured along his forehead with a strip of knotted wool from which hung the strips of elm bark fabric that contained the load. He took from the burden strap a pair of snowshoes that he thrust at White, then gave a salute as if he were one of the Queen's Rangers, and disappeared into the woods without a word.

He'd never seen snowshoes until his first winter in Upper Canada. Then he'd looked with envy through the window at the Indians floating by on top of the snow. He himself had felt trapped by the drifts. Every time he put a foot into those piles of snow, he'd sunk to his knees. Winter that first year in Canada had been a trap that he could not get free of until the spring sunshine led him out of doors to walk and ride.

Yvette has shown him how to tie the snowshoes to his moccasins with leather straps. At first the bent wood frames interlaced with all those rawhide strips seemed heavy and awkward, but after a day or two, he'd mastered the manoeuvres. Soon they seemed like a huge pair of shoes that flattened the snow around him, enabling him to pass along the embankment like a master of the universe.

This morning's sunlight is bright on the snow as he tramps towards Queenston. The Hamiltons will give him a good breakfast, and then he will ask Mrs. Hamilton if she has a remedy for Yvette who seems ill today. From his loft above the kitchen, he heard her crying during the night. He knows she went out somewhere into the snow at midnight, and he did not fall to sleep again until he heard the door shut quietly hours later.

As he climbed down from his loft for breakfast, she slammed the lid on the chamberpot in the kitchen, but not before he saw the blood in it. He questioned her about it, but she did not answer. *Women's problems, some form of uterine bleeding.* He has heard Mrs. Jarvis speak to Eliza Russell of the maidenhair fern as an efficacious remedy. Mrs. Hamilton can give him advice and possibly sell him the dried fern as well.

He clumps briskly over the thick snow, the frozen river far below him on his left, and the Hamiltons' stone residence a mere half-mile ahead. Someone has already made a trail through the woods. Possibly an Indian trapper, because there are trickles of blood on the white surface. The powder snow swallows noise, and he's within a few feet of a timber wolf before the animal senses his presence and skulks into the forest. It leaves behind some fresh kill, a rabbit perhaps, though as he gets closer, he sees it's not a rabbit. It's a bloody bundle of something. He moves closer and looks down at it. *No, no, surely not. . .*

But yes. It is . . . a tiny infant, probably newborn, wrapped in a knitted scarf. Which he recognizes. *Yvette's, the knitting project she's been working on at the kitchen table for the past couple of months.* The wolf has torn away part of the scarf and chewed at the infant's belly. What is this all about?

Suddenly the shadowy images at the back of his mind become clear: the gossip about Yvette and Tickell, the crying, the disappearance into the night; the blood in the chamber pot this morning. He stands looking down at the dead babe, trying to sort out what to do. One thing for certain, he's got to get this bundle out of here. Before the wolves eat it. Before someone discovers it and traces it back to Yvette. Any woman who tries to conceal a birth in these parts is guilty of infanticide and sentenced to death by hanging.

White looks around. The woods are very still. The wolf has disappeared. He has an empty leather satchel slung over his back. He takes off his snowshoes. Leans in close to look at the corpse. Besides the eaten-away belly, its head is badly mutilated, no discernible features, just the bloody mess the wolf left behind.

Trying to ignore the pain that has risen from his chest into his throat, he picks up the bundle and stuffs it into his satchel. Gets the snowshoes on and turns back to his house.

*Why did I not notice that Yvette was with child? Too damn wrapped up in my own worries. And what now? What are we to do?*

When he comes through the back door of his house, his satchel bulging with the dead body, Yvette cowers in a chair, covering her head with her hands as if she expects him to strike her. *"Non, non!"* she cries over and over.

"Listen to me," White says, kneeling in front of her. "I don't want to know what you've done. I just want to help you. Please."

"Bébé dead when born," she says, "I not kill bébé."

*Stillborn? Perhaps. It doesn't matter. We've got to figure something out.*

"Yvette, think of somewhere we can hide this baby. If it were spring, we could give it a decent burial in the garden somewhere. But for now, we must get it out of sight."

He soon realizes he will get no help from Yvette. The night's horrors have killed everything that is rational in her. She's still hiding her face and head as if she wants to block out him and that infant corpse. Never one to say much— perhaps because she speaks an Indian-French *patois*—she can now utter only *"Non, non!"*

He sees the cut-up squash on the table and an idea comes to him. *That's it. The root cellar. But I'll need a box. Yes, my book box. Up in the loft.*

Leaving the satchel beside the hearth, he climbs up the ladder. His box of books sits near the washstand. He upturns the box, the lid swings open on its hinges, and the books spill onto the floor. He descends the ladder, places the satchel inside the box, and snaps the lid down. It's all done in an instant, and he's careful not to let Yvette see the horror of her babe's half-eaten body. It's a neat little casket, and it will go into the root cellar until spring when he can dig a hole near his back stoop away from the marauding animals in the woods.

He notices that Yvette is no longer moaning. Her face is wet with tears, but she's sitting up now, watching.

He takes her hand. "Let us stand together, Yvette, and pray." He places their hands on the lid of the box. "Jesus said, 'Suffer the little children to come unto me, and forbid them not: for of such is the kingdom of God.'" For a moment he reflects on his own children, grateful that they are alive and well. They will come unto him if he can only get a comfortable haven for them in this far-flung kingdom.

He does not know whether Yvette fully understands the words of the prayer. But she says "Amen" with him. Then she sinks into the chair again.

He takes the box down the back stoop to the place where a trap door leads down into a pit. Opening the door, he descends the rough wooden steps which the carpenter has planted into the earth. It's cool here in the dark. On the shelves facing the steps are the carrots, squash, and potatoes which Yvette got from one of her Indian neighbours. There's an empty corner on the top shelf. There he places the box, its lid jammed against the earth ceiling. No one will ever see it there.

Some more words come to him now in the quiet darkness of this earth tomb. In a loud voice he addresses the devils that lurk outside this hole, the Tickells of the world especially: "Take heed that ye despise not one of these little ones; for I say unto you, That in heaven their angels do always behold the face of my Father which is in heaven."

He stumbles up the steps to the open air and closes the trap door. Back in the kitchen, he says to Yvette who is weeping in her chair, "This must be a quiet day for the both of us. Do not cook any meals for me. Rest here on your pallet by the hearth fire, keep it stocked with wood, and keep warm. I will stay upstairs in the loft."

In his bedchamber he pulls his morning gown over his clothes, slides his feet out of his boots and into his slippers, and takes up a book from the pile he so recently emptied upon the floor. But the pain in his head defeats him. He seeks oblivion in the bottle of whisky which he has stashed in the drawer of the wash-stand.

# Chapter Seventeen

*April 1794*

Spring has finally come to Niagara, and as John White looks out his back door one morning, he sees violets in bloom in his yard. Interspersed among them in patches are the three-petalled white flowers with yellow centres that the settlers call trilliums and the Indians call wakerobins. White prefers the Indian name. There's a fat robin among them now yanking a worm from the earth.

"Come," he calls to Yvette who is stirring something on the hearth, "it's time for the burial."

No more words are necessary. She goes down into the root cellar while he takes the shovel that is propped up against the back wall of the house. He selects a spot in the midst of the violets and starts his digging. Yvette emerges from the root cellar and sits on the ground near him holding the small casket. The smell he feared is scarcely discernible. The lid of the box has kept that terror inside.

For a few minutes, the only sounds are birdsong, Yvette's soft crying, and the thump of the earth he tosses on the ground. Soon he's achieved a small, deep hole. He takes the box from her, sets it carefully into the pit, and throws the pile of earth back on top.

"Is there something you would like to say, Yvette?" he asks, pointing to the new grave.

She shakes her head. They stand in silence looking down at the piled-up earth. Then, without a word, she starts to sing. It's one of Isaac Watts's most famous hymns, "Joy to the World," and for a minute White wonders where she

80

learned it. Perhaps from one of the itinerant Methodist preachers who travel about the countryside?

Yvette's voice quavers and breaks, but White knows all the words and starts to sing with her. They are just starting the third verse—"No more let sin and sorrow grow"—when out of the woods just beyond a patch of wakerobins, Eliza Russell appears. Her scrawny form is covered in a faded brown dress, and she's carrying a bucket that is filled with spring flowers.

She spends only an instant observing the burial scene, then she sets the pail down and moves to Yvette's side, so that Yvette is now between her and White. She takes Yvette's hand and joins in their singing.

*He rules the world with truth and grace,*
*And makes the nations prove*
*The glories of his righteousness*
*And wonders of his love*
*And wonders of his love*
*And wonders and wonders of his love.*

"I am mighty happy to be part of your ceremony," Eliza says in her gentle voice when they have finished the last verse. "I was in the woods collecting some flowers that I intend to press, and I heard your singing. I shall go now and leave you to your sorrow." She picks up her pail and starts down the garden path. Then she turns and says, "'The wonders of God's love,' I need sometimes to be reminded of those wonders. Thank you."

White and Yvette watch Eliza disappear behind the trees. "Madame?" Yvette says, pointing towards the woods and looking worried.

"Miss Russell is a good woman," White replies, "you do not need to fear her. She knows how to keep a secret."

He's still humming Watts's words as he sets off for Navy Hall to finish up some work that the Gov has sent to him by the first packet boat from York. He remembers singing another hymn with Pastor Rippon in another life, another world. Would he have been happier staying in England? All things considered, perhaps not.

He passes Gilbert Field's tavern on the old Indian trail which is now a substantial path called River Road. There are several taverns in the settlement. He's heard Field often takes advantage of his inebriated customers by seizing their land grants in payment of their bar bills. Now the man is building a large brick house. *A country bumpkin who runs an ale house is a rich man while I, Attorney-General of Upper Canada, must subsist on the loans my brother-in-law doles out. Is this one of the wonders of God's love?*

There are some of the local farmers and military men sitting outside the tavern. "Good day," he says, nodding to them. Their response is baffling: a combination of laughter, loud applause, and scratching of their crotches. What's going on? Four spruce beers too many is his conclusion. He tramps onwards.

In the centre of the village, he sees some of the local bumpkins gathered around a large white sheet affixed to a fencepost. When they see his approach, they disband, sniggering as they scatter down the road.

Something's up. He moves closer so that he can read the sheet:

*Alas, Mr. Small has a very small prick*
*And Mr. White's, though large, is a dirty wick.*
*Mr. Tickell, 'tis true, likes to tickle his pickle,*
*While the bold Mrs. Small just loves being fickle.*

These vile words are written in a fine hand, one he recognizes immediately. William Jarvis's. So Jarvis is behind this? Unlikely. The man, incompetent and frustrated though he is, is not by nature vindictive. He's been put up to this by someone. *His wife no doubt.* He remembers how she found him and Mrs. Small *in flagrante delicto* that day after lunch when the woman (he no longer thinks of her as Betsy) popped out of her dress for the costume ball.

What to do? Should he go to Jarvis's house and confront the two of them? Would that make things worse?

He's trying to make up his mind when he sees Richard Tickell approaching. The man is swinging his stick as if he's a schoolmaster about to beat up a miscreant, and his face is red, right to the top of his bald head. He's obviously read the screed.

"You bastard," he yells at White. "You connived with Jarvis over this, didn't you? Just because I fucked that Indian squaw who cooks for you?"

White feels his own face redden. He thinks of Yvette's despair on the day he discovered her dead baby, of her sorrow today as they stood over that tiny grave in his back garden. But he must not show his anger. Who knows what vengeance Tickell might enact on the girl. Or on him, for that matter. *Denial, let's see if that works.*

"I do not care for the way you talk of my cook, Tickell. Her name is Yvette LaCroix. I know nothing about her private life. And even if I did, I would do nothing to hurt her. Or you either, for that matter." He points to the sheet of paper. "I have no idea what this slander is all about. All I recognize is the handwriting."

"That bugger Jarvis's. So what in hell are we going to do about it?"

"That's the conundrum. Perhaps just leave it alone and hope it fizzles out. You know what things are like in this place. Everyone's focus is gossip. Gossip is the succubus that stirs the dead air and sets emotions on fire. If we don't let ourselves get upset, there'll be some new distraction in the next few days."

"It damn well better fizzle out, but meantime I'm going to see that bugger Jarvis and have it out with him. He's not going to get away with this rot." He turns and heads in the direction of Jarvis's house.

White's head aches and his nose begins to bleed. Best to get back home and lie down. He'll have to take another route back, though. No way he can endure the ribald comments from the drunks at Field's Tavern.

He clamps his handkerchief over the top of his nose, presses it hard, and starts home. Well, the news is out, thanks to Jarvis's termagant wife. But why was Tickell's name on that sheet? Something besides pain gnaws at his head. A random thought that's lodged there . . .

*That's it . . . Betsy Small's distress when she heard about Tickell and Yvette. I wondered at the time why she cared. Why would I think that I was the only lover in her life? What a fool I've been.*

# Chapter Eighteen

*April 1794*

Eliza Russell places her pail of spring flowers on the broad oak table in the kitchen of their commodious new house on the commons. She's mighty proud of this dwelling and tries not to let herself be undone by Peter's constant complaints about how dear its construction has been. It has two storeys in the Georgian style and surrounding it are fifty acres of land, several out-buildings, and a spot near the back door where she intends to plant an extensive garden.

*Right at this minute I'm a-going to plant a flower garden between the pages of that family Bible we never look at.* She takes it from the bookcase in the withdrawing room and brings it to the kitchen table. From her bucket she takes the flowers. She has good specimens of each of the ones an Indian woman pointed out to her: red wakerobins, white wakerobins, marsh marigolds, purple crocuses, and one called Indian turnip which has an odd flap-like flower at the top of its stem.

She places a few of the flowers between two sheets of paper and inserts the papers into the centre section of the Bible, hoping the papers will keep the pages of the Bible from being stained. She has so many flowers she has to keep skipping pages so she can get them all crammed in. In five weeks, she'll take the flowers out and put them into frames or decorate her letters to her dear English friend Lizzie with them. She may even present some to Mrs. Simcoe who shares her interest in wildflowers. *And for certain, I'll take some to Mr. White to give to that Indian who cooks for him. She will be the better for something pretty to cheer herself up with.*

She has just got all of them tucked into the Bible when Mary comes in the back door. "Aunt, what is a prick?"

"You must remember, child, to introduce topics of conversation with a preliminary phrase or two. Surely you know what a prick is. You pricked yourself with a needle last week and the blood ran. That was a prick. Don't you remember?"

"No, no, Aunt, this is a different prick. It was written on a sheet of paper nailed up in the square today. Everyone tried to keep me from seeing it. It said Mr. White's prick was a dirty wick, or something like that. They wouldn't let me get close enough to read it all."

*There's something here I don't understand. It sounds almost . . . carnal.*

"Oh, Aunt Eliza, you're going to be in trouble if Uncle Peter finds out what you've done to the family Bible." Mary points and giggles.

"I think you'd be the better for not being so nosy, my dear," Eliza says, happy that the child has been distracted from her interest in pricks. "Now, help me out. Have we got something we can pile on top of the Good Book to put extra pressure on these flowers?"

Mary considers. "Why not just cram it back into the bookcase and let the books on each side of it do the pressing?"

"Excellent." Eliza pushes the Bible back into the row of books. *Good, it's a mighty tight squeeze.*

"But what will we do if Uncle Peter decides to read something from it?"

"He has some new books to read. A pile came today on the packet boat from dear Lizzie in Harwich. They're on the dining-room table."

Mary runs to look at them. "*Goody Two-Shoes,*" she says as she picks up a book from the top of the pile and leafs through it, making gagging noises. After a minute or two, though, she says, "Give me this one, will you, Aunt Eliza? It doesn't seem to be as bad as its stupid title." She takes the book and runs into her bedchamber. In this commodious new house, they all have separate rooms, thank the Lord.

* * *

Eliza awakens, the sound of the door slamming bringing her to consciousness. She has a crick in her neck, having fallen asleep in a dining-room chair, her head on the table. She looks at the clock on the sideboard. *Dear Lord, eight p.m., and Peter will be wanting some supper.*

Her brother enters the dining room before she has time to ready herself. "Sleeping, sister? Surely you would be more comfortable lying in your bedchamber?"

The crick in her neck is mighty painful, but she sits up and tries to smile. On the table in front of her is the open book she was reading when she nodded off.

Peter picks it up. "*A Vindication of the Rights of Woman.* Are you unhappy, sister, with the life you have here with me in this new world?"

"No, dear Peter. Happy I am to be here with you. I can think of no other occupation than to be your companion and support. I am reading the book because Lizzie sent it to me. It has received much praise in England. But it put me to sleep, as you can see."

Peter laughs, but there is little mirth in the sound. "You got to page five. That is a start."

Job comes in and stirs the fire in the hearth. "I have some biscuits, cheese, and apple preserves, ma'am," he says, laying the table with the silverware that has newly come from Mr. Hamilton's warehouse in Queenston.

Peter eats in silence and drinks the wine Job has poured for him. Eliza watches him, knowing from his heavy breathing and the manner in which he slaps the butter on his biscuits that he has something of import to tell her.

At last, as he downs the last dregs from the bottle, he speaks. "Where is the girl, sister?"

"She took her supper on a plate in her bedchamber. She is deep into a book from the package Lizzie sent."

"Good. For what I am to tell you is not for innocent ears." In a low voice he tells her about the notice posted this day in the public square. Though she still does not fully understand the coarse language, she understands its import.

"And who is responsible for these words, brother?"

"It's Idiot Jarvis and that wife of his. Of that I am certain. I went to his house today. It was not a pleasant visit, I tell you. The man screamed at me and denied everything. I had to stand in their kitchen and listen to his diatribe while I breathed in the stink of shit. Excuse me, Eliza, but there is no other way to describe the stench of the place—"

"Do not apologize. The woman dispenses castor oil for all afflictions. You remember she once left some of her remedy for us, and we fed it to the groundhog?"

"You understand, my dear sister." He smiles at her, then continues, "But worse than the stink were the words that Jarvis uttered when I confronted him. He told me the man Tickell had already visited him, and he is now going to challenge Tickell and White to a duel. 'My honour is at stake, and I intend to see that they pay for their slur on my reputation.' That is what he said to me. My God, the whole town is in upheaval. Since the Governor is still away and Osgoode has not yet returned from the circuit, I must deal with the matter myself. White will give me no trouble, but Tickell is a different matter."

"And what about Mr. Small? Is he not part of this, too?"

"I went to his house after I left Jarvis. Small is an amiable man. He made a pleasant little defence of his wife. He seems as certain as I am that Jarvis and his wife are behind it all, 'stirring the pot,' as he put it. But he shrugs it off. So he will not be a problem."

"Surely you are right that Mr. White will accept no challenge. He hates duels. But what about Mr. Tickell?"

"I must sort it out tomorrow. Tickell and Jarvis intend to meet behind the Freemasons' Lodge at dawn, and I must be there to stop them. As for the bastard's threat to White, I can bring in a court order for him to keep the peace."

"There was some line about Mrs. Small, was there not? I can't quite remember."

"'The bold Mrs. Small just loves being fickle.'"

"You haven't talked about her, Peter. Is she somehow the cause of this muddle?"

"Oh, sister, you might as well hear it all now. While Jarvis was denying having anything to do with that wretched verse, his woman stood by his side and spewed out filth about Mrs. Small so foul it almost drowned the stench of shit. Perhaps she just wanted to deflect my attention from her husband. Perhaps what she said was just a nasty rumour. Yet . . . I can't help feeling there's no smoke without fire."

Eliza listens as Peter tells her a story that puts her to the blush. *Oh good Lord, I must find some way to warn Mr. White.*

# Chapter Nineteen

*May 1794*

John White pulls on the tight breeches that are currently fashionable, adjusts his waistcoat, and reaches for the black frock coat decorated with gold braid. Looking at himself in the pier glass he bought in Hamilton's emporium, he is satisfied. The gold braid will distinguish him from the bumpkins whom he will undoubtedly meet on his way to Navy Hall. Since that scurrilous ditty appeared, he is anxious to seem dignified and above common scandal.

Yvette is visiting her Chippewa family today. As he descended the ladder from his bedchamber in the loft earlier in the day, he noticed that she had left him a stew of whitefish, Indian corn, carrots, and potatoes in a pot on the hearth. It's still warm now, and he spoons some onto a plate.

There's a knock at the door. He answers it to find Miss Russell on his front stoop. "Come in, ma'am," he says, "though perhaps I should warn you that Yvette is not here now, and we may find ourselves the topic of Mrs. Jarvis's gossip if she gets wind of this meeting. There may even be another ditty in the town square."

Miss Russell blushes and stammers. "Perhaps . . . perhaps . . . I should come at another time? I see you are dressed to go out."

"Perhaps you should forget my last stupid remark and come inside now. We can talk at the table here, and you might like to sample some of Yvette's stew."

"Am I holding you back from business with the Governor?"

"He can wait. After all, he has kept *us* all waiting for his return for several months. But I do not wish to seem hard. He and Mrs. Simcoe have had a sad loss this winter with the death of their baby. There are many days when I think of my own little William and my separation from him . . . I grieve . . . though our separation is but temporary."

"Mrs. White and your children will join you soon then, sir?"

"Perhaps. I can say no more at the moment." He looks around the room. "This house, though adequate for my needs, is scarcely large enough for my wife and three children."

There is a long silence. White notices Miss Russell's blush. Her breathing seems laboured, and her hands are trembling.

"You are upset about something, ma'am. Can we talk?"

"I believe you know Mrs. Small, sir?"

"Yes, of course. One cannot help but know everyone who is in any way connected, however remotely, with the governance of this province."

He watches as Miss Russell takes a deep breath. "There are rumours about her, rumours about her, Mr. White, that perhaps . . . perhaps . . . you have not heard."

*My God, is she about to confront me with my affair with the woman? Best to brazen it out.* "I know little about her, though as you know, I have had several dinners with her and Small for which your brother was kind enough to lend me his horse. *And without that damned nag I might never have met her.*

Miss Russell's words come out in a rush. "People be telling me that she was once the mistress of Lord Berkeley of Berkeley Castle in Gloucestershire. He tired of her, and to get rid of her, he paid Mr. Small a mighty sum of money to take her off his hands."

"Ah." *So that explains her connection with Berkeley and Small's grandiose life-style.* "Why do you repeat this gossip to *me*, Miss Russell?"

"Because . . . because . . . I wanted you to be wary of your to-ings and fro-ings with the woman. You have been a friend to me and—"

91

"Unnecessary advice, ma'am. But undoubtedly well intentioned. I thank you."

He says no more, sure that anything he might say at this point would make everything worse. The silence deepens. At last, Miss Russell stands up. "I have bothered you with common gossip, sir. I apologize." Her face grows alarmingly red. "But I am told the woman has procured black snakeroot from the Indians." She pauses for a minute, then adds in a strangled voice. "You must know what that indicates."

"You might better have told this story to Richard Tickell. His liaisons with the lady were . . . well, I shall say no more. It's only common gossip, as you call it."

Miss Russell departs, muttering more apologies.

*I think I pulled that one off well enough. But I am glad Miss Russell told me the rumours and that I got myself rid of the woman without contracting the clap. Black snakeroot, my God. I might have been accused of fathering a child if she had not aborted the foetus. A narrow escape all round. Time for celebration.*

He pours himself a glass of Yvette's dandelion wine. *Amazing how much I'm getting to like the swill.* He finishes off a second glass, looks at his pocket watch, and decides it's time to take off for Navy Hall. Just as he's put the cork back in the bottle, there comes another knock at his front door.

*Dammit. Now I will be late for the Gov, and he doesn't take excuses well.*

This time it's his friend Osgoode standing there smiling at him. He looks as if he has rushed from somewhere. His face is flushed and the wig he always wears is askew, so that a tuft of his fair hair slips out over his ear.

"Good day," White says. "This is a pleasant surprise. Come in and join me in a glass of our favourite tipple. I was headed for Navy Hall, but the Gov will just have to wait. My conference with the Chief Justice will be sufficient excuse." He holds the door wide open and motions his friend inside. "How was the circuit this time?"

92

"S..s..same as ever, endless hours with my derrière on King's Bench, listening to hapless victims defended by hopeless lawyers. Glad I am that you were not with me to hear the palaver those idiots s..s..spewed forth."

"By God, Osgoode, I swear I'll get rid of the incompetents in the judiciary even if I have to kill them off one by one. But there's surely a brighter day ahead. David Smith and two other men are studying law with me now, and perhaps by the time we do the circuit together again, things will be better."

Osgoode's blue eyes cloud up. "Oh, my friend, there will be no more travels together. That's why I rushed over here now, though I'm just off the batteau from Kingston. To tell you that I've been appointed Chief Justice of the Province of Lower Canada. I leave in thirty days for Montreal and Quebec."

For a moment White is speechless. Then he puts his arms around his friend's shoulders. "Congratulations. I suppose that's what I must say now. But it's not what I feel. To tell the truth, I feel such a total loss. How am I to survive the dismal days ahead without your company?"

"Let us s..s..sit down for a moment and think back to that s..s..sunny day—not all that many months ago—when you and I walked from Gananoque to Kingston. Then you told me you had never been happier—"

"I remember. I felt like that bronze statue of the satyr—"

"Free, ready for new adventures . . .  What has happened, friend?"

"So much. Penury because of my stipend that never arrives from the Colonial Office in spite of the Gov's admonitions to the bastards . . . the broken judicial system in this place . . . the spiteful revenge that Jarvis and his wife took upon me . . . " *I can't say a word to anyone about that wretched liaison with Mrs. Small.*

"All difficult to bear. But let us think now of happy things. I sent a note to the Governor recommending that you take my place as Chief Justice of Upper Canada. My pay comes through regularly, you know that, and in

93

addition to increased wages, you will have the prestige of being the Great Poobah on King's Bench. Think of it, man. Does it not s..s..seem grand?"

*More than I could ever have dreamed of.* He clasps his friend's hand. "How can I thank you?"

"By turning yourself into Mr. S..S..Satyr again. That will be my recompense." Osgoode stands up. "Come, let us walk together to Navy Hall."

# Chapter Twenty

*June 1794*

Eliza Russell adds a diamond brooch pin to the front of her gown, looks at herself in the mirror over her bureau, and removes it. It calls attention to her skimpy bosom of which too much (too little, really) is visible in the new styles Mr. Hamilton peddles in his emporium. "Grecian" is the word he uses.

She has not yet been able to find a lady's maid to assist her in dressing, so she is thankful when Mary comes in to help her. "Your hair, Aunt," the child says, "what are we to do about your hair?"

Eliza sighs. "That bad, is it?"

"No, Aunt. I have an idea. I'll just pull it back from your forehead, and we'll pin these plumes into it. Voilà!" She produces two enormous pink-dyed ostrich feathers which she has been hiding behind her.

"Good heavens, child! Where did these come from?"

"Mr. White. He left them with Job early this morning while you and I were in the shed churning butter."

"Why would he give us this gift?"

"I think they're for *you*, Aunt. He told Job he wanted to thank you for the advice you gave him. What was that all about?"

"Oh, I gave him a bottle of Job's yeast so that cook of his could bake him some decent bread." *So I wasn't wrong about him and Mrs. Small. I'm mighty pleased I went over to warn him.*

Mary succeeds in a-fixing the plumes onto her head with pins. Then the child takes the diamond brooch pin from the dresser and clamps it at the front of her head at the bottom of the plumes. "Now, look at yourself in the mirror. You're a swell. Mrs. Simcoe will be gobsmacked."

Eliza does as she is bid. The feathers and the pin do draw the eye upwards, away from her skimpy bosom. "You don't think I resemble one of those herons in the swamp?"

Mary considers, her small index finger on her chin. "Not really, they're blue and you're pink." Her laugh transmutes into a cough. "I'll go and sit on the stoop in the fresh air until the guests arrive."

The air is a bit smoky from the open hearth on which Job has been cooking since early morning. Fortunately the air is warm, so they will not have to light the fires in the withdrawing room or the dining room. The clock on the dining-room mantel strikes four. Almost time for her guests to arrive. She has planned a farewell meal for Mr. Osgoode who has been a pleasant friend to her and her brother since she first met him on the voyage from England with the Simcoes and Mr. White.

Eliza surveys the table with pleasure. She has put a fine linen cloth upon it, and set six places with the Worcester floral china she ordered in from Mr. Hamilton. In the middle of the table is a sterling silver epergne, the crystal dishes filled with the wild strawberries she picked in the woods behind their grand new home. Though dear Peter has grumbled about the expense of today's meal, she knows he will be mighty pleased when he sees the elegant effect.

The guest of honour, Mr. Osgoode, arrives first, followed shortly thereafter by Mr. White. Eliza is always interested to see what Mr. White is wearing. She hopes she can encourage dear Peter to move into some new styles. This afternoon, her friend is mighty smart in his fancy formal silk suit with tight breeches. He's wound his cravat twice around his neck and tied it in a neat knot under his chin. Mr. Osgoode is in his usual dining-out garb: a double-breasted frock coat, rather worn, of dark-blue wool.

She has just poured them glasses of sherry when Peter comes into the withdrawing room to greet his guests. He pours sherry for himself and has started to sip it when Job announces the arrival of Governor Simcoe and his lady.

The Governor seems to be in a pet. His hair is wild and his white waistcoat needs a tug-down. He starts to say something which Eliza can't quite understand, and she notices Mrs. Simcoe put her hand on his arm and point to the table setting.

"Look, my dear," she says. "Has not Miss Russell accomplished wonders in the short time she has been in her new house? What a lovely farewell meal for Mr. Osgoode!"

The Governor seems to recover himself. He adjusts his waistcoat and smooths back his hair. "Yes, ma'am," he says to Eliza, "I look forward to what you will serve up on those fine plates."

But in spite of his efforts to be civil, Eliza sees he's upset. She feels he would be the better for getting right to his food. She rings a small brass bell she brought with her from England, and Job appears with the beef stew and the chicken breasts with apples and sets them on the walnut sideboard where they can help themselves to what they want. There are some new green peas from her kitchen garden as well, and she surveys them complacently, knowing that they will be a tasty addition to the inevitable squash in a serving dish beside them.

"I fear your farm has been sadly depleted in the preparation of this meal," Mrs. Simcoe says, putting two large spoonfuls of peas onto her plate.

"All for a good cause, ma'am," Eliza says. "My chickens gave up their lives gladly. Mighty pleased they were to take their part in our farewell for Mr. Osgoode."

Job has poured the claret into everyone's glasses and when all are seated, Peter stands to deliver a toast. Eliza has always liked his deep bass voice, and he uses it to good effect as he wishes Mr. Osgoode Godspeed. But as he winds up, he pauses a moment. "There was a line from the Book of Matthew I meant to look up, Osgoode, but I'll have to wait until we adjourn after this fine meal my sister has prepared." He looks towards the withdrawing room.

*Oh my, there will be a to-do when he opens that Bible and sees what I have planted between those pages.*

"Oh, Uncle Peter, I'll be St. Matthew, if you will permit me," Mary says from her seat between Mr. Osgoode and Mr. White.

Peter frowns at first, perhaps upset to be thrown down by a girl of twelve. But he rallies and says, "Of course, my dear."

"Matthew 25: verse 21. 'Well done, good and faithful servant. Thou hast been faithful over a few things. I will make thee ruler over many things.'"

Everyone claps and glasses clink as they all repeat Matthew's words as served up by little Mary. "Your niece is a credit to you and your sister, Mr. Russell," Mrs. Simcoe says.

Now Peter is smiling, mighty glad to take credit for the girl's learning. *And she's freed me up from a set-to, thank the Lord.*

The meal proceeds. Everyone tucks into the chicken with apples, and Eliza realizes that her idea of beef stew was not a good one. Perhaps it's because of the fish stew that everyone eats in this place: whitefish from the river with potatoes and carrots day in, day out, all year. Why would they want *beef* with potatoes and carrots when they dine out?

Mrs. Simcoe, who's seated at Eliza's right, has taken a bite of stew, but now has shoved it to one side of her plate and is gobbling the chicken. The lady has a good appetite for a body so small. Withal she seems remarkably calm and cheerful, considering that she is still in mourning for the loss of her baby daughter. Eliza looks at the plain black dress she is wearing.

Seeing the menfolk intent on some topic of conversation, Eliza reaches out her hand and touches the lady's arm. "You are brave, ma'am. You put me to the blush."

"Why, Miss Russell?"

"These silly pink plumes in my hair. As I readied myself for this evening, I never once thought of your situation, ma'am. Please forgive my excess."

Mrs. Simcoe smiles and pats Eliza's hand. She is about to say something when there is a loud outburst from the other end of the table. "Damn, damn, damn Dorchester!"

The Governor has just barked, and everyone must stop eating and listen. "He's a fool. Ordered me to rebuild that fort on the Maumee River which we Brits abandoned at the end of our last war with the Yankees. I gave every excuse for not obeying orders. But at last I had to cave in. The nerve of the man!"

*I have not a clue what the Governor's talking about. What can I say?*

Mrs. Simcoe leans over and speaks into her ear. "My husband tells me that it's certain to stir up the Americans. Rebuilding a British fort on American territory! Imagine how we would feel if they came across the river into Upper Canada and built a fort right under our noses."

"There'll be war unless the commander of the fort can manage to keep the peace. And here we are, a stone's throw across the river from Fort Niagara. Which was supposed to be handed back to the Yankees in 1783. Yes, 1783!" The Governor throws his napkin onto the table. For a moment, Eliza wonders if he's going to leave the room and go to Navy Hall to wait for the cannonade from the Yankee side.

"War, Governor?" Mr. Osgoode says. "Then perhaps it's good fortune that has called me to Lower Canada at this time."

"I'm sending my wife and the children to Quebec to be out of the fray," Simcoe says, "and I intend to establish a new capital at York. This damned place is doomed."

Mr. White pushes his plate away, his stew untouched. "Sir, I have just spent my last penny on my new house. What's to be done?"

"Off to York with you, White. That must be obvious."

*Oh that uppity man. To-ings and fro-ings whenever and wherever he orders.*

"We are to sell this place we have just built here on the commons, Excellency?" Peter asks. "You must know that I too have expended hundreds of pounds establishing myself

and my sister and niece here in this commodious house."
His voice is loud.

Eliza knows now that she must speak up. "There will
be a to-do for certain, Governor, when your administration
hears this. Mr. Smith has a fine house now, and Mr. Jarvis,
too. Since we came to this place that God had forsaken, we
have firmed up a respectable settlement worthy to be called
the capital of this province." As Eliza makes this statement,
she feels herself put to the blush, but she cannot stop
herself from speaking. "You, sir, may find yourself able to
live in a canvas house, but we cannot."

Mary starts to cry. Her tears bring back the cough
which plagues her constantly. She puts her napkin to her
mouth and runs from the table.

"My dear," Mrs. Simcoe says, addressing her husband.
"This news has upset everyone. Is it not possible to talk of
something else?" In the silence that follows, broken only by
the coughs from the bedchamber, she asks, "Perhaps, Mr.
Russell, you did not hear the sad news about Mr. Tickell?"

"Just today, ma'am, my sister and I heard from Job
that Mr. Tickell had drowned. He got the news from those
bumpkins that hover at Field's Tavern."

"Drowned?" Mr. White says. "It's only days ago that
he avoided duelling with Jarvis, thanks to your
intervention, Russell. Can this be true?"

"Yes. He was on a batteau in Lake Erie. A gale carried
the boat over the bounds of the lake into a swamp. He tried
to wade through the swamp, as I understand it, but his
strength gave out. A soldier from the batteau tried to help
him, but he could only watch as Tickell disappeared into
the slough."

"You will excuse my saying so, Russell, but I do not
mourn his loss," Mr. White replies, pulling his plate of stew
towards him and taking a mouthful.

"Regrettable, but insignificant indeed," the Governor
says. "We must focus on important issues. My duty now is
to establish the new capital at York and keep my
administration safe from the damned Yankees." He picks
up his glass, then drops it, spilling its contents down his

waistcoat and onto the tablecloth. He utters a loud yelp, like one of those coyotes Eliza hears in the bush behind their dwelling.

"You are in pain, sir," she says. "What can I do to help you?"

"Nothing, alas, ma'am. My gout has got the better of me these days. But I must persevere." He takes his napkin and mops at the front of his white waistcoat.

*What am I to do about this yelping at the table and coughing in the bedchamber. Oh Lord, may this meal soon end.*

She hears her brother speak up. *Thank the Lord.*

"Now that Osgoode is leaving us, Excellency, perhaps you can give us a hint about who may succeed him as Chief Justice? We are all hoping, of course, for our friend here." Dear Peter smiles at Mr. White.

"I have, of course, recommended our Attorney-General for the post," Simcoe says, "But it is a matter for the Colonial Office." He has stopped rubbing his waistcoat and now drains the wine from the glass Job has refilled.

Eliza notices Mr. White's hand is trembling. He has set down his knife and fork with a clatter. "Do you anticipate a problem with your kind reference, sir?" he asks.

"No. You have done an admirable job as Attorney-General. You and I accomplished the passing of the anti-slavery bill which the Colonial Office recognizes as a sterling achievement. Why would they not give you the post?"

*Well, that be one good tidbit to liven this wretched afternoon.* She signals to Job who serves up slices of his pie, made from the pumpkins they stored in the cold cellar over the winter. It's a delicious concoction underpinned with a pie shell of ginger biscuit crumbs and topped with the cream she whopped. But only Mr. White and Mrs. Simcoe have appetite to eat it. Mrs. Simcoe is determined to be a good guest and Eliza is thankful to her. And she is also mighty pleased that her friend seems hopeful of a fine promotion.

* * *

Early in the evening, after the guests have left, she
goes into Mary's bedchamber. The girl is at last asleep, her
face still streaked with tears. There's a bloody handkerchief
on the pillow.

She tiptoes towards the door, but Mary stirs, sees her,
and sits up. She sweeps the square of bloody linen under
her pillow. "Oh Aunt, I am sorry. Did I ruin your party?"

"No, child. It was a disaster from the start. But you
provided one good moment."

"I, Aunt?"

"You, dear Mary. You came out with those words from
Matthew just when your uncle was at a loss for a quotation.
For a moment I thought he was going to pull out the Bible
and empty my pressed wildflowers all over the carpet. You
saved me from a good tongue-lashing."

Mary smiles. Eliza leans over to the small figure on the
bed and hugs her. It's not the moment to talk to the girl
about that bloody handkerchief.

# Chapter Twenty-One

*August 1795*

John White sits with the Gov at Navy Hall. After three years of occupancy it still smells of mould and ten minutes ago, when they opened the door of the room they use as an office, there was the sound of tiny scurrying feet. Rats, maybe, or mice. White's head throbs from the stink, and he holds his left hand to his face and hopes that the Gov will not notice his surreptitious pinching of his nostril.

"Nosebleeds again, White? Did not my wife give you some dried pigeon gizzards? She recommends them for these problems."

"Not too efficacious, sir. But I'm grateful for her concern." *I hope the groundhog in my backyard has benefited from the vile concoction.*

"Well, let us get to business. Our fourth session of Parliament will be a good one, now that the invasion of Mad Dog Wayne and his barking spaniels has been averted. No thanks to that bloody idiot of a Governor-General who put us all into peril by forcing me to rebuild that damned garrison on the Yankee side. Major Campbell saved the day. Bloody Wayne and his men came right to the gates of the fort and shouted insults at him. Wanted to get the Brits to open fire. But Campbell stayed cool. Bloody bless him."

White has a feeling that all these swear words indicate a resurgence of the Gov's gout. So he's not surprised when the Gov reaches down, tugs off his right riding boot, and throws it into a corner of the room. Then he yanks off his stocking and places his foot carefully on the seat of an empty chair. White sees the red swollen toe and hears the Gov's repeated "damn, bloody damn."

*The sooner we get through this, the better.* "What do you think, sir, of an encomium to Major Campbell in the Assembly?"

"Absolutely. What do you suggest?"

"Let us word it this way. 'Resolved that the thanks of this House be given to Major Campbell of His Majesty's 24th Regiment of Foot for his temperate forbearance and otherwise exemplary and meritorious conduct at Fort Miamis during his command in the past year.'"

"Good."

"I shall write it down now, sir."

"And I shall have a drink of bitters." The Gov rings for a servant, one of the lads from his Queen's Rangers, who puts before him a bottle of distilled alcohol (it looks like brandy) with bits of watercress floating in it. No doubt the greenery was Mrs. Simcoe's inspiration. While the Gov downs a copious glass of the potion, White takes his quill and inscribes the resolution on paper.

The Gov seems calmer now, perhaps because of the alcohol he has imbibed. He looks over the resolution and seems satisfied with it.

"Good work, White."

*Now I can ask my question.* "Have you heard yet, sir, who is to take Osgoode's place as second Chief Justice of Upper Canada?"

"No word, alas." He puts the stocking back on his foot and stands up, bracing himself against the table. "Go home, White, and look after that nosebleed. We have finished our work for this morning."

* * *

Two nights later, White dons his best dress coat for supper at the Freemasons' Lodge with the Simcoes, the civil servants and administrators of the province, members of the Assembly, the Queen's Rangers, and the women of the town. The Freemasons' Lodge serves many purposes in this forsaken world besides being the favourite place of William Jarvis and his Masonic followers. It was the site of the First Parliament. It's now the place for the Church of England worshippers, and lately, since the Yankee scare, its upstairs space has provided room for the Simcoes' parties.

He finds himself looking forward to the supper. Perhaps the Gov will have news about his appointment as Chief Justice. He feels hopeful. Simcoe and he have got on well, and he knows the Gov has backed him solidly for the position. *And one thousand pounds a year in wages! I'll be able to pay off my debts and make a new start.*

He has arranged to walk along the River Road with Peter Russell and his sister. He has become closer to Russell since Osgoode's departure for Montreal, but he still misses his friend's laughter. Russell can never see the funny side of anything.

The knock on the door alerts him to the Russells' arrival. He picks up a package Yvette has left on the table by the hearth, and soon the three of them are swinging along the road towards town. They walk into the setting sun, but the air is pleasant. There's a soft breeze from the river, and a gentle scent of roasting venison wafts from the woods to their left where the Indians have made a bonfire.

They have to pass Field's Tavern, and White imagines the spectacle they must present to the hangers-on around the front stoop: Miss Russell in a high-waisted white gown with a rather dirty hem (*no plumes today, thank God*), her brother in his unfashionable frock coat, roll-up stockings, and a pigtail wig at least forty years out of date, and himself, overdressed from top to bottom. *Why on earth did I choose a waistcoat with gold buttons?*

There's a good deal of rough laughter among the men about some joke or other, and for a moment, he hopes they may slip by without comment. Then a lout in a filthy smock spots them and starts in, "Uppity Brits! Uppity Brits!" Soon they're all in chorus, "Uppity Brits! Uppity Brits!"

"Bastards," Russell yells, waving his walking stick at them. "Didn't 'uppity Brits' give you land grants?"

"Please, brother," Miss Russell whimpers, "let us just pass on."

White offers his arm and he and Miss Russell move on, leaving Russell to berate the hecklers. The lady is trembling, and White distracts her by giving her the package he brought along. "For Mary," he says, "but you may look at it. Yvette's mother made it."

It's a small round birch bark container with a lid decorated with a pretty wakerobin made from porcupine quills.

"Mary can put her hairpins in it," Miss Russell says. "It's so pretty." Then she starts to cry.

"Don't let those damnable fools upset you, ma'am," White says. "Look behind, your brother is coming along now. He's out of harm's way."

"It's not Peter I worry about at this moment," she says. "It is Mary. For certain, she is mighty sick. I saw the bloody handkerchiefs she hides from me. Job told me this morning that for near eight weeks she has washed them out herself every day. She takes them to a tree in a clearing in the bush where she lets them dry. I had no idea. I think she is soon a-going to die."

Her news is no surprise. White doesn't know what to say. He has suspected for weeks that little Mary has consumption. He pats Miss Russell's hand, and they move forward along the road.

"Do you think I should get Dr. Kerr to come and bleed her?"

He thinks of the child, her pale face growing even paler as the blood drips from her into a basin. "No, ma'am, no. Do not torture her with that abominable procedure. Keep her as much in the sunshine as possible." *She will go down soon enough into darkness.*

\* \* \*

The Gov meets them at the front door of the Lodge. His face is flushed and he's twisting his hands together. "Take Miss Russell inside and go upstairs," he says to Russell. "I must speak to White alone."

106

"Bad news," the Gov says. "I'll get right to it. I heard it this morning. John Elmsley is to be our new Chief Justice." He puts his hand on White's shoulder. "I'm sorry. You would have been the perfect choice."

For a moment, White feels that he may drop to the floor in a faint. Then he steadies himself by putting one hand against the door frame. But he cannot steady his indignation. "Elmsley! I know him. He was called to the bar at the Inner Temple years after I was. The man is totally inexperienced. How could this happen?"

"He has connections with the Home Secretary, the Duke of Portland. Wisdom and strategy may win on the battlefield, but patronage conquers in these wars for promotion."

The Gov turns away and starts to climb the stairs. Over his shoulder, he says, "It's damnable, White. Damnable."

*Well I'm not going to get any help from him, that's obvious. But after all, what can I do? Got to keep from crying. Get through the evening somehow.* He stumbles after the Gov.

One of the Queen's Rangers is passing shrub in the second-storey meeting place. White grabs a glass from the tray. Vile stuff, but under the sickly sweetness of sugar and lemon, he tastes the brandy that will take the edge off his anguish. He drains the glass at a gulp and stumbles forward to get another one. Nonetheless, he knows his feelings must be evident when he is accosted by David Smith, who moves in so close to him that he cannot escape.

"Your eyes are bloodshot, White. Something bothering you?"

*Never give the man any information he can chew over, that's the rule in this backwater.* White attempts to move to one side. But Smith blocks his path. Along with his position as acting deputy surveyor-general, the man is now studying law with him. He appears to assume that their association entitles him to ask impertinent questions.

"Out with it, man. What's the matter?"

"Nothing, nothing. Just . . . just . . ." But now White feels the tears spilling down his cheeks, and he's forced to rub his face with the sleeve of his jacket.

"It's something His Excellency told you. That's obvious. I saw the two of you speaking together a minute ago."

"John Elmsley . . . he's . . ."

"The new Chief Justice. I know, I overheard the Governor talking to his lady about it just before you came in with the Russells. Elmsley's a fractious bastard. But he's a friend of the Duke of Portland, and that seems to be what counts. I'm not dismissing his wife's connections, of course." Smith moves even closer, evidently hoping to impart another tidbit. White can smell his tobacco breath.

"Excuse me, Smith. I need another glass."

But the man has planted himself firmly between him and the drinks, and White is forced to listen.

"Wife was the daughter of the Commissioner of Customs for the Port of Boston, time of the Boston Tea Party, you know. The old boy defended His Majesty's interests well, and those damned Yankees, two hundred of them, chased him on horseback one night, threatening to kill him. That's got to count for something with the bigwigs in London."

*A wife with connections, that's just what I need to hear. Too bad Marianne's connections are that parsimonious bastard of a brother and the local opium sellers.*

His misery is sidetracked by the call to supper. There's a stampede toward the dining table. He's relieved to find a place between Miss Russell and her brother, though on the other side of the table sits William Jarvis in full Masonic rig which seems to include a ridiculous little white apron with gold spangles on it. Beside him is Mrs. Jarvis who makes a point of keeping her attention focused on Smith who's seated beside her. White knows it will be only a matter of time before she will be able to rejoice in the news of his humiliation.

The first course is one of Mrs. Simcoe's specialties. He remembers it from the days he and Osgoode spent with the Gov and his missus in the canvas tents. Tough venison overlaid with a messy sauce of peppercorns, oil, and red wine. He pushes it away.

Miss Russell leans over and whispers in his ear. "Try a dollop of the potato dumplings. They be quite palatable."

Well, he tries them, but his stomach roils and he fears he may vomit. A regimental server moves in and gives him ale in a large tankard. For a moment or two he loses himself in its consumption. He sets the tankard down and signals for more.

Down at the end of the table where the Simcoes are seated, there is much merriment.

"True, I assure you," the lady is saying to all who must listen, "the animal is always well fed. My staff supplies him daily with everything his stomach could desire, but—"

"What is she talking about?" White asks Miss Russell.

"While she be in York these past months, that black hound of hers gobbled the maps of North America she drew and left on a table in Navy Hall. She has just told a mighty amusing tale about it."

And now the Governor rises and addresses the guests. "I have written a poem for the occasion," he announces in a ponderous voice, unrolling a long piece of heavy linen paper. "It is entitled 'Upon the Dog Trojan Eating My Lady's Maps'." He clears his throat.

Several long stanzas and a plethora of odd lines ensue, of which White is unable to remember a single word. He downs another tankard of ale, then another, and another. There is much laughter, but the ale has dulled his senses and he wants merely to give himself over to sleep. His head slumps forward.

Miss Russell rouses him with a poke in the ribs. "Dear sir, the Governor is a-going to say something," she whispers. "Please stay awake. I fear it be important."

He rouses himself, wipes the drool from his mouth, and listens.

"I have just received today confirmation . . . Jay's Treaty. . . Fort Niagara to be handed over . . . next summer . . . Americans . . ."

*Can't make sense of what the man is saying. Got to get out of here before I puke my guts out and spatter bloody Jarvis's little white apron.*

He pushes back his chair and stumbles towards the door leading downstairs. The cool air of the summer night will surely clear the cloud from his head. But in a moment, just before he closes the door behind him, he hears the Gov say, "And therefore the British garrison must move from Fort Niagara, and all civil servants are to remove to the new capital—York—without delay."

*The deadly salvo has come. Cannon fodder, that's what I am.*

# Chapter Twenty-Two

*August 1795*

A loud voice awakens White the next morning. Not Yvette's gentle greetings. It's the bellow of an angry man. He looks around, tries to assess his surroundings. Where is he? There's nothing familiar about this room. He's in a comfortable bed: surely the mattress under him is stuffed with feathers not straw. And the sun streams in through a large window. Not his house. Whose?

His head aches . . . aches . . . the bile in his throat . . . He sees a chamberpot, scrambles out of bed, and pukes into it. But in the process of tumbling down, he wrenches his back.

He crawls back into bed and pulls the linen coverlet over his head. He notices then that it's monogrammed: an $\mathcal{R}$ is set squarely in the middle of a delicately stitched border. That's the clue. The Russells' house on the commons, that's where he is. But he has no memory of how he got here. But he does remember, yes, he remembers the horrors of that supper.

The voice he hears now, coming from a downstairs room, echoes that horror. "I'm not moving, bloody not moving," the speaker is shouting, "I've spent my wife's fortune on building that house."

Ah, yes. It's David Smith. White forces himself to sit upright, plants his feet on the stool by the bedside, and steps down carefully onto the wide-planked pine floor. Someone has dressed him in a comfortable nightshirt, but where are his clothes?

There comes a soft knock at the door of the bedchamber, and Job, the Russells' black servant, enters carrying the breeches and dress coat he'd worn to that damnable supper. He sets them on a chair and departs without saying a word, though White can see his frown plainly. He realizes now he must have been in a sad condition if the Russells had to take him here instead of depositing him on his own doorstep, and Job may have borne the brunt of it. Looking at his clothes, he sees they've been newly sponged and brushed, with one dark stain still apparent. His puke?

He dresses and finds his way to the staircase, grasps the balustrade, and descends. The voices are coming from the kitchen, and he stumbles in that direction.

"Mr. White, good morning." Miss Russell, always kind and vigilant, pulls out a chair for him and plants a cup of thick syllabub on the table in front of him. He takes a moment to savour it: the whipped egg whites and cream with the sweet underlay of wine and sugar are exactly what he needs to soothe the pain in his head and the ache in his back.

At the other end of the long pine table, Russell and Smith are deep in a loud dialogue. They stop to acknowledge his presence with a nod, then resume their discussion.

"He's written to the homeland to ask for a leave of absence. Gout's got to him, I'm thinking," Smith says.

"Who?" White interjects, wiping foam from his chin.

"Who? Who'd you think? Our Governor, that's who."

"I'm afraid it's true, White," Russell says. "He told me last night that I am to administrate the province in his absence."

"You'll do that well." *Stupid comment.* But he does not know what else to say.

"Perhaps, but it will mean removing to the new capital of York, and the Governor has given us his marching orders for the summer of next year, latest. I must from this point onwards consider what am I to do with this commodious house I've just built and furnished at great personal expense."

Now Smith starts his rant again. "*I'm* bloody *not* moving. My house is the best in town, better even than yours, Russell, if I may say so. Two storeys with a widow's walk, constructed, embellished, and painted in the best style. And in the best location in town to boot. I've spent a fortune on it."

Everything the man says is true, but his superior tone is infuriating. "Your *wife*'s fortune, did I hear you say?" White asks.

Miss Russell picks up a sheet of paper from a small table near the kitchen window. "I have just this morning wrote to my dear friend Lizzie saying that I am not a-going *anywhere* until there be a comfortable place in York to receive me. Never again do I expose myself and Mary to what we suffered when first we moved to this place. Poor child, I know that wretched cabin where we once lived for certain brought on her ill health."

There's a pause while they all listen to the coughing sounds that issue from a room upstairs.

*Now they're all staring at me. What am I to say? Time to take a stand.*

"Toronto or York—whatever its name—is a savage place from all I've heard. They say it is crushed against the lake by vast forests to the north, and entirely cut off from adjacent settlements, except in the late spring and summer. Never mind that I too have gone to the expense of building and furnishing a house here. The Gov in his arrogance does not consider such trifles."

"Hear, hear!" This from Smith, accompanied by small bleating noises from Miss Russell. Only her brother is silent.

Then Russell clears his throat and makes one of those pronouncements that White has so often heard him utter from his unwarranted position on King's Bench. "This bravado is all very well, but it has no substance. We must all go to York. We must face our future and embrace it."

"Bloody embrace what you like, Russell. Kiss the Governor's ass, too, if that makes you feel good. Excuse my language, Miss Russell." Smith rises, moves to the kitchen door, and slams it shut behind him with a bang that starts White's head throbbing like an Indian tom-tom. His nose begins to bleed. He pulls out a handkerchief.

"Dear Mr. White," Miss Russell says, "Job will drive you home in our carriage." She pours the remaining syllabub from a bowl into a pitcher. "Take this with you and get right into your bed. I shall call later this afternoon and give your cook a remedy for your nosebleed. Try not to think too hard about the move. We still have time to ready ourselves."

As the horse and cart bump their way along the forest path to his house, White holds the handkerchief to his nose and watches the blood seep into it.

*There's a metaphor somewhere here. Try to remember . . . yes, something Shakespeare said . . . Macbeth maybe . . . yes . . . 'I am in blood stepp'd in so far that should I wade no more, returning were as tedious as go o'er'. . .*

"Say something, sir?"

"Nothing, Job. Drive on."

*I do not deserve this treatment. But what can I do about it? I made a brave speech this morning, but Russell is right. It's all bravado. I must move if I am to keep my position. But where can I find money right now? Maybe Sam Shepherd will come through for me again. And I've got to make a decision about Marianne and the children. Oh Lord.*

Inside his house, he pours Miss Russell's syllabub into his large pewter mug and ascends with it to his loft.

# Chapter Twenty-Three

*September 1795*

The explorer Alexander Mackenzie has stopped at Newark for three days on his canoe journey to Montreal. He sleeps in White's bed in the loft while his host has made quite a comfortable corner for himself in the alcove off the kitchen. It's a small space, but Yvette has provided him with a bear skin rug. It smells a bit—probably like a bear, though White has never, thank God, smelled one up close—but it shields him from the rough pine floor.

It's early afternoon now, and Yvette serves up her whitefish stew and dandelion wine.

"Tasty," Mackenzie says, shovelling a substantial forkful of fish into his mouth. "I call this *cuisine.*"

"Better than what you had on the Pacific Coast, is it?" White asks, thankful that he has not had to apologize for Yvette's offerings.

"You may have noticed that my teeth are ground to a thin edge?" Mackenzie grins at White. His teeth look perfectly normal, a flash of white in his tanned face. "One of the Indian tribes there gave me their *pièce de resistance,* the bark of a hemlock tree—"

"You joke, sir!"

"Not at all. It was actually a *cake* of hemlock bark, fifteen inches long and half an inch thick, but impregnated with salmon oil that made it quite tasty—especially if you consider how hungry I was after a hard day's walk over rock and through forest."

*I am to believe this?* But the man spins his yarn with a perfectly straight face.

"I gather that Mrs. Simcoe liked the fine furs you presented her with?"

"She plans to sew a shoulder cape from the mink skins, so she says. She is a pleasant woman, but I know not what to make of His Excellency. What is your opinion of the man?"

"He has many good qualities, but his health is bad. Gout is his affliction. He has applied for sick leave and may return to England if his application is successful."

"I gave him a bottle of Turlington's Balsam. He took it, mumbling something about 'damned quackery,' but I mind not his insult. He is just another snot-nosed Englishman."

"Present company excepted, I hope?"

"Too long have I been in heathen society, sir. My apologies for a stupid remark. You have been kind to me. Had I not met you on the quay three days ago, I might have had to tether my canoe and set up my bedroll within it."

Mackenzie is now tucking into the Indian pudding, and he's switched from fork to knife for the transmission from plate to mouth. White feels glad the knives have rounded edges. Otherwise, he'd have to find one of the local remedies for a bleeding gullet. Mrs. Jarvis's castor oil, he fears, would not be efficacious in those circumstances.

White has noticed Mackenzie has no difficulty spinning conversation with whomever he meets. His manner of speaking is easy, but his sometimes awkward phraseology leads White to surmise he has been long without white man's company. "This is tasty," he says now, turning to address Yvette who's hunkered down in a chair in the corner by the hearth. "How do you make it?"

"Milk, cornmeal, *des oeufs*, . . ." she answers, then she lapses into her *patois*, blushing at her failure to know the English words.

Mackenzie answers at length in her lingo, and she gives him a large second helping.

"You are at home in her language," White says.

"Well, as you know, I was for many years a clerk for the North West Company in Montreal, and when I started

116

my exploration westward to the Pacific, I often had *voyageurs* with me on my voyage. Expert canoe-men they are, the best in the world I thought, until we embarked one day with seven natives. Then I found that the *voyageurs* are actually inferior to the Indians. So I've picked some of the lingo from both sets of paddlers. I expect you know the dialects, White?

"I know very little of anything but the King's English. Sometimes I don't even understand American." He laughs. "But I have observed those canoes you talk about. When they're loaded, their gunwales are within six inches of the water, and the fate of the passengers has always seemed to me to be inevitable. Your own canoe, I see, rides barely above the water, and yet you and your crew are very much alive."

"So much depends on the paddlers. I remember once a rapid stream where we were making six miles an hour. We came to a weir where the Indians landed me and my two friends. They then proceeded over the weir without taking a drop of water, received us on board again, and on we went. Glad was I to thank them with a few words in their dialect."

To White, Mackenzie seems a creature from another planet in spite of his Scots accent, tousled red hair, and tanned cheeks. Over the three days, he's been in Newark, he has spun tales so exotic that White has been transported into a new world.

The man is talking now about his stay with an Indian band a short distance north east of a place he calls Elcho Harbour—"not Echo, mind you, Elcho"—somewhere within sight of the Pacific Ocean. "There are four elevated houses in the village," he says, "with floors twelve feet above the surface of the ground. Their length is a hundred and twenty feet, and they are forty feet in breadth."

"How on earth do they get up into these places? Or perhaps I should stay, how *from* earth do they get up into these places?"

"Easily. At the end of each house is a narrow scaffolding, which they ascend by a piece of timber with steps cut in it. The whole length of the structure is divided

117

by cedar planks into apartments, each with room for cooking and sleeping." Mackenzie pauses, sees that Yvette is busy scraping the remains of her stew into a bowl, and continues, *sotto voce*. "They thought of everything, those so-called 'savages.' At each end of the structure is an opening for them to pee or shit through. Since they remove not the heaps of excrement that accumulate on the ground below, it appears that this effluvia does not bother them."

White pushes his plate away. *Pee, shit, and effluvia in two sentences. The man has a wide vocabulary.* "You give me a vivid picture," he says. "But if you intend to write up your travels for publication, as you've indicated to me, I suggest that you—"

"Omit these details or reword them. I have not been so long in the wilds that I have forgotten the sensibilities of English readers. Indeed, even when I come to this place you call Newark, I find it a good deal like one of your villages in England, full of gossip, teacups, and evening tête-à-têtes. A week in the wilderness of Western Canada would rid these people of their narrow concepts and customs."

"You have obviously not sat at Mrs. Simcoe's table and eaten her special Upper Canada treat of roasted black squirrels. A pity. That would rid *you* of your narrow concepts about Newark parties.

"But you may be right about your impressions of life here. We do fritter away a good deal of time in petty squabbling and picayune endeavour. I fear we are often like the fox in the Aesop fable. We want the grapes, but we tire easily and give up and excuse ourselves by saying the grapes are probably sour anyway. But you, sir, are a veritable Jason. You have discovered an overland route to the Pacific Ocean and to the great furs of that far-flung land. With your Argonauts, you have brought back the Golden Fleece. I envy your accomplishments."

Mackenzie laughs and pours himself another glass of Yvette's wine. "You are generous, White. But I am no Jason. I have made mistakes like any ordinary being. On my first voyage westward, no knowledge had I of

118

compasses or chronometers, and I ended in the Arctic Ocean rather than the Pacific." Here Mackenzie pauses and looks down at his calloused fingers. "But I went back to Britain, made myself familiar with navigational skills and tried again. Second time round, I listened to the Indians. They were the ones who knew about the overland route to the Pacific, and good use I made of their knowledge of this vast land. But true it is that when I set myself a goal, I attain it. Success comes with knowledge. And endeavour."

He pulls out his pocket watch. "I must leave you now, sir. My paddlers wait for me on the river." He leans over and pulls from under the table the huge canvas knapsack that carries his worldly goods. From inside it he produces two packages loosely wrapped in pelts. "For you, ma'am," he says to Yvette, shaking off the pelts and handing her a warm-looking pair of fur-lined skin gloves. "And for you, White, a fur hat for these winter winds that will be soon upon us."

"With ear flaps and a strap to tie under my chin," White says. "Perfect."

"Not made of the Golden Fleece, my friend, but perhaps warmer."

He embraces White, waves to Yvette, and heads out the back door. White watches him from the window of his cottage. His tall figure disappears down the slope towards the river. In a moment, there is nothing left of him, only his empty glass and the gifts that he laid upon the table. But still, yes, there's an aura that remains . . . the man's air of successful endeavour, the way he speaks freely without inhibition . . . his joy in life.

* * *

White goes into the alcove, kicks aside the bear skin rug, and extracts a letter from one of the pigeon-holes in his desk. It's the latest missive from that devil Hodgkinson who has badgered him—and Osgoode, too—for months for a licence to practise law in Upper Canada. He is a scoundrel with low education and even lower morals, and he and the Chief had been of one mind in refusing his insolent requests. Now that Osgoode has departed for Montreal, White must take on Hodgkinson and others of his ilk single handed.

And herein he sees an opportunity. *Though I am not a Jason, perhaps I can find a quest of my own. Yes, I will put right the ignorant and inefficient legal and judicial system of this colony . . . But how? A governing agency perhaps, a society that will regulate the licensing of lawyers . . . I must write out my thoughts.*

"More wine, Mr. White?" Yvette stands at the door to the alcove, a bottle in her hand.

"Thank you, no. I have work to do."

# Chapter Twenty-Four

*March 1796*

White has had a quiet winter in Niagara. He calls the settlement by its original Indian name openly now, free of the Gov's insistence on "Newark." The Simcoes are far away in York, and from all he hears, set to fly like the passenger pigeons—back to England as soon as the Gov gets his request for leave of absence granted. They'll have to come back to Niagara for their goodbyes, but undoubtedly for a few days only.

Peter Russell, ever the faithful servant of the administration, has moved to York temporarily where he has bought a house that he is now in the process of enlarging. But Miss Russell reminds everyone that she is "not a-going anywhere," as she puts it, until the house is ready. So White has had her companionship all winter. She's a sympathetic listener, always willing to hear his complaints about William Jarvis who has become even more lazy and sulky in past months.

"I don't know which of them—the man or his wife—I loathe most," he tells Miss Russell now, sitting at her broad oak kitchen table and watching her whip up a bowl of syllabub. She pours the cream and whites of eggs into the bowl with wine and sugar. Then she gets to work with a whisk that she's made out of birch twigs. It's a hard task whipping it all into a heavy foam, and it takes her at least a quarter of an hour, but they talk as she works.

"That wife of his put him up to challenging me to a duel, I know, and I'm never going to forgive her for that."

"She's an uppity soul," Miss Russell says, "but it's all been settled for many months. Perhaps it be . . ." She pauses and shakes the whipped mixture from her whisk.

"I know what you're going to say, ma'am. Let bygones be bygones. And your brother did the right thing in bringing Jarvis to court and settling the matter there. When I get the legal system righted in this country, I'll see that the courts are an avenue for redress for these stupid quarrels. My brother-in-law tells me that since 1790 in England, men have begun to use the courts instead of the pistol for settling these crazy manifestations of male 'honour.'"

More swooping motions with the whisk of twigs and finally, judging by the decisive way she whacks the whisk against the bowl, the syllabub is ready. If he were a dog, he'd be drooling. She moves towards the mantel above the hearth and takes down a large tankard.

"Perhaps you could come to my house one of these days and teach Yvette how to make it. I'm not complaining about her dandelion wine, mind, but syllabub would be a delicious addition to her repertoire."

"I'd be mighty pleased." Then, *sotto voce*, she adds. "If I can escape from Cousin Willcocks for an afternoon. He gets up late—he be still abed now at this late hour—and then he expects a full meal put in front of him."

Job, the Russells' faithful servant, has evidently heard her words. From the corner of the room, where he's stirring a pot of soup on the open hearth, he heaves a large sigh.

The words and the sigh serve to herald the appearance of the man himself: William Willcocks, dressed in a banyan and slippers, as if it were eight o'clock in the morning rather than three in the afternoon. He is a fat man, probably sixty years of age, with bushy eyebrows, a mess of uncombed white hair, and a broad red nose.

"Syllabub, eh, Eliza m'dear? I'll have it." And he proceeds to grab the bowl and empty its contents into the tankard Miss Russell has just set upon the table. "How are ye today, White?" He doesn't want an answer, he's too engrossed in quaffing back the syllabub. He rubs some whipped cream off his chin with the back of his hand and asks, "Where's little Mary? You're far too easy with the girl, Eliza. She should be here in the kitchen doing a woman's work."

White watches as Miss Russell turns away to set the empty bowl in the dry sink. He senses from the heave of her shoulders that she is crying. From a room upstairs comes the sound of coughing.

"Leave it, Willcocks," he says in a whisper, "the girl is dying."

"Balderdash and bunkum. Nothing like a good day's work to set one right."

White cannot say more without upsetting everyone. He rises, gathers up his coat, says goodbye, and heads out into the brisk March breezes.

He's half-way to his own house when he meets Peter Russell coming up the path from the quay. "Just managed to catch the packet at York, the first one of the spring season," his friend says. "I have a few days now to spend with my sister and that damned cousin who's dumped himself on us for I don't know how long."

"Why is he here, anyway?"

"Only because he hopes I'll be successful in getting him some new land grants from the Governor. I got him hundreds of acres free not so long ago, contingent on his getting settlers to come over. But he buggered everything up by trying to sell the lands, and Simcoe is so angry with him that he's taken all the grants away from him. So now we have him on our hands. All he's ever done for me was to give me head lice when we had to room together years ago at school in Cork."

"Well, I've just come from your house, and your sister appears to be bearing up." *Not going to mention the bastard's callous remarks about poor little Mary. Russell's got enough to worry about at the moment.*

"Good. The more you can keep an eye on things in my absence, the better."

White notices that Russell's usual broad girth looks considerably shrunken. "How are things in York?" he asks, having heard rumours about the winter famine.

"It's been a terrible winter. I had to persuade the Governor to get food supplies from the garrison here at Niagara. Otherwise we would have starved. And now that Dorchester son-of-a-bitch has chewed him out for not getting official sanction for this most merciful action. He's blasted Simcoe for every good thing he's done in this benighted world. But I hear Dorchester's being recalled to England, and I hope we get a decent man to replace him."

Russell's eyes are red and watery and his jowls sag. *That winter in York took its toll.*

"What are you staring at, White? Better look at your own affairs. Are you coming over soon to see about getting a house ready for yourself? You do remember the Governor's deadline of June first?"

"I do. But I'm not going to rush. Didn't you say that there is no jail in the place, no court of justice, no house for the meeting of the legislature, no roads?"

"I'll do what I can, now that I'm to be in charge of things if Simcoe goes back to England. I can see getting those Queen's Rangers of his working on building and road-making. Now that we're not having to fight with the Yanks, they might as well be doing something productive. Trouble is, there's not a skilled carpenter among them, and scarcely a decent carpenter in the whole place. Someone told me a day ago that all the good carpenters are on the British ships."

"I'll go over to York with you when you leave again. Just give me a couple of days' warning." *Time to find an excuse for not going anywhere. I'm totally with Miss Russell on that one.*

They part, and White heads home. Having lost The Battle of the Syllabub, he's anxious to knock back some of Yvette's dandelion wine. It's a poor substitute, but there'll be plenty of it.

Back at his cabin, he finds David Smith ensconced in a chair by the hearth. Yvette has already provided him with a glass of her wine, and when the man sees White, he hastily holds his quizzing glass to his left eye and picks up Immanuel Kant's *Critique of Pure Reason* which he has evidently dropped onto the floor beside him.

"Careful, man. That's one of my favourite books. Haven't you finished the assignment I gave you?" White asks, annoyed to see ashes sprinkled on the cover.

"It's a hard nut to crack. And I can't see that it has that much to do with the practice of law," Smith replies. "And since you've already certified me as an attorney, I am really disinclined to read more."

"If you want to be a good lawyer, you'll read and digest it. That's an order."

"Perhaps you should have been a general in the army instead of an attorney-general in the legal kingdom, White. To answer your question, no, I haven't finished the assignment, but I will, even though my dear wife complains that she has not found me in her bed for lo, these many nights."

"Shut up," White says, gesturing towards Yvette whose back is to them, making toast in the hearth. *Why these men feel they can make remarks in front of Indians that they would never make in front of white women is beyond me.*

"Gladly. Now can't we forget Kant"—he laughs at his own joke—"while I bring you tidings of our new capital?"

"I was surprised to hear you'd been over to York, given your antipathy to the place."

"I won't move an inch until necessary, man, but meantime I like to know how the world marches. But I can tell you one thing: there isn't a place in York that matches anything here. In the last couple of years, we've built a decent town, and I've got the best place in it. And the best location—right by the Freemasons' Lodge—where I can keep an eye on all the comings-and-goings in this place. Far better, need I say it, than this hut of yours in the woods. It grieves me to have to leave the best of Georgian architecture for a hovel in a godforsaken bush." He gets out of his chair and moves to the table where a half-filled bottle of wine rests. He refills his glass and sits down again.

*By God, even in my own house I can't get a glass of wine.* White yanks off his coat and throws it on the woodpile by the hearth. "Well, what's up these days in York?" he asks Smith, finding himself able to stifle his anger when he sees Yvette move to the table with a fresh bottle and a glass which she fills and hands to him.

"Small has bought a little log house for fifty Yankee dollars," Smith tells him, "and he has stipulated that the present owner must repair the roof for the price. A cruder place you never saw—it was a fishing hut in its infancy— but fancy, he is calling it Berkeley House in honour of his friend Colonel Berkeley of Berkeley Castle in Gloucestershire!"

The image of Betsy Small swanning about in a fishing hut called Berkeley House is so amusing that White finds himself laughing out loud.

Smith has now launched into an anecdote about Peter Russell. "He's adding two windows and dormers to *his* little dwelling," he reports, "and he's chewed over the expenses so thoroughly his builder calls him 'an old miser.' Fancy, Russell himself repeated this phrase to me. He seems proud of it."

"Are expenses great in the new capital?"

"Appalling. And what will you, sir, the pre-eminent lawyer in Upper Canada, do without a court house, or a jail for that matter?"

White feels his head begin to pound. "I'm tired, Smith. Let's forget the lesson today. No charge, of course. We can resume tomorrow." He stands up and takes Smith's coat from the row of hooks on the wall.

Smith laughs. "Here's your coat. What's your hurry? Very well, I'm on my way. I know you don't like to hear bad news. But I've got one good piece of news to impart. There isn't a legislative building in the place, either, as you know. But it's not going to matter. You're not going to get re-elected for the Kingston riding anyway. I hear the merchants are too angry with you about your support of the

126

anti-slave bill. But then, what do you do anyway to get their vote? I'm out in my district every few months talking myself up and buying beef and spruce beer for the peasants. That's what it's all about: booze and beef."

Yvette, as always, has picked up unspoken messages. She goes to the kitchen door and holds it open for Smith to pass through. When he's left, she removes the toast from the hearth, spreads a good layer of butter on it and puts it in front of White. "And here's a pot of honey for you, sir," she adds, setting a large spoon into its contents.

It's all good, though he would have been happy with some of Miss Russell's syllabub to top it off. *What a pig that Willcocks is.* But remembering the syllabub reminds him of something else.

"Yvette," he says, "I wonder if your brother could carve something for me?"

She doesn't know what a whisk is, but when he draws one for her and makes whipping motions, she understands. "Brother do a good one," she says, "maybe not like this"—pointing to the drawing—"but a good one."

White is pleased. Anything will be an improvement on that wretched bundle of twigs poor Miss Russell contends with.

# Chapter Twenty-Five

*August 1796*

White has finished a hasty letter to his brother-in-law and is just putting his seal upon it when the doorknocker bangs. It's Captain Shank from the Queen's Rangers. He's leaving for England in the morning and has agreed to take White's letter with him.

"I'll deliver it myself to the Inns of Court," he tells White, putting the letter into his satchel.

"Thanks for that, Captain. And good luck with your new posting in London."

"Glad to be rid of this place, sir, to tell the truth, though it's turned into quite a smart little town since I first came here. But I want to be off on the express before I have to watch those wretched Yankees take over the fort. Better to be with Colonel Simcoe in the land that . . ." Shank salutes and heads down the path to the wharf.

White watches him until the woods hide him from sight. *What had the man intended to say? The land that God made? Does this new land not qualify as the work of the Almighty? Or does every Englishman think of it as the place to which God banished Cain after he murdered his brother?*

He sighs and climbs the ladder to his bedchamber in the loft. He is always so tired these days. It's because he knows the fragile peace he has enjoyed these past few months will soon be at an end. He'll take an hour's rest and then he'll hire someone to paddle him across the river. As Attorney-General, it's surely his duty to see the British hand-over of the fort goes smoothly and without rancour. Who else is left here with any authority?

He no longer has the Gov at his right hand here at Navy Hall, or even over the lake in York. In June, Simcoe prorogued the last parliament in Newark, ordered everyone to head for the new capital, and then took off to Kingston with Mrs. Simcoe and their two small children for the first stage of their departure for England.

White had stood on the wharf with the Russells and members of the Queen's Rangers to say goodbye. Mrs. Simcoe cried. The little boy Francis hugged the deerskin-clad legs of an Indian chief and would not let go until the man reached into his beaded pouch and withdrew a pair of tiny moccasins which he gave to the child. *Oh I remember how I too cried when I saw little Francis cling to that Indian. It was the way dear Ellen clung to me when I said goodbye to her at our house on the Embankment.*

Finally the Gov and the lady got into their canoe, the children and their attendants followed in batteaux, and to a volley of cannon from the Queen's Rangers and musket fire from the Mohawks, they disappeared from view for ever. Only Jarvis and his wife had not been in the crowd on that day.

There had followed several pleasant weeks of nothing-much, and then at the Russells' grand house on the commons last night, over some excellent pork chops and a good bread pudding, White's friend delivered the ultimatum.

"You've got to move."

"That's an order?"

"Take it as such. Now that I'm to administer the government of Upper Canada in the Governor's absence, I've got to start laying down the law."

"I don't have any money. My salary from England is late as usual."

"I'll do what I can for you in a letter. Meantime, write to that brother-in-law of yours and see what he can do. You told me in March you'd come over to York, and you haven't done one thing to follow up on that promise."

"Please, brother," Miss Russell said at this point. "Leave Mr. White to enjoy his bread pudding." She placed a silver bowl of syllabub in front of him. "And this be for you, sir, whopped up special with that wooden whooper you gave me." Then she picked up the large three-pronged forklike creation Yvette's brother carved from an oak branch and gave the contents of the bowl an expert twirl or two.

"And since Mr. Willcocks is no longer with us," she continued, "drink the whole pitcher."

"Back to my main point now," Russell said. "If I may . . ."

White let him expound at length, blah, blah, blah, while the soothing sweetness of the syllabub spread through his body and caressed the pain in his head.

* * *

Today, after his rest, he hires an Indian paddler to take him across the river for what will undoubtedly be his last close-up look at Fort Niagara. Under Jay's Treaty it was to be delivered into Yankee hands in June, after a thirteen-year delay, but somehow it's all been postponed again until now.

The canoe pulls up at the dock below the fort just before sunset. For a few minutes, White simply stands on the flats, looking up at the imposing stone structure far above. It commands the mouth of the river below it and the expanse of Lake Ontario beyond.

He remembers his first time at a ball at the fort in those days when he and Osgoode lived in the canvas tents with the Simcoes. How impressed he had been with the Mess, sometimes called The Castle: its polished wood floors, spacious dimensions, and high ceilings. The Brits were able to conjure an impressive orchestra from the ranks of the Queen's Rangers. The food and drink had been plentiful, and it had been grand to have the freedom to move about without the constant supervision of the Simcoes and their retinue.

Then, one night, as he recalls, he stumbled down a dark staircase to look for a privy or a pisspot somewhere.

Without warning he found himself in a dungeon, a black hole with no aperture for light or air, with a dank stench of blood and death. In one corner there had been a pile of filthy apparatus. Coming close to it to see better, he had stretched out his hand to look at a greasy square pillow when suddenly from behind him came a friendly east-London voice. "Want to look at it, mate? Jolly good if you wants to suffocate a Frenchie. Or a damned Yankee."

Turning round, White had confronted a British private who told him he'd been assigned dungeon duty for the evening. Then the young man—he couldn't have been more than twenty—had picked up the instruments from the pile, one by one, and put names to them. "This here's an iron collar, and this one a head cage." And so he'd run through the grisly lot, piece by piece, explaining with seeming delight the heinous punishments that each could inflict. The private had ended by inviting White to "piss on the lot of 'em," an invitation which he had no difficulty in refusing even though his bladder was full. He had finally extricated himself to return to the upper world, feeling a bit like Dante making his way from the pit of the Inferno "to look once more upon the stars." He'd taken his piss in the soldiers' vegetable garden.

As he thinks now of the horrors of that dungeon, he climbs up the steep path to the fort, reflecting that perhaps the Gov had done the right thing in establishing a new capital in York. *Yankees and Brits may be buddies now, at least on the surface, but in another decade, who knows?*

The transfer this day is remarkably civil. White watches as the new Yankee commander shakes hands with the Captain of the Fifth Regiment, Roger Hale Sheaffe. A weak and ineffectual man, in White's opinion, whose pride in his musical snuffbox seems to be his sole mark of distinction. *Perhaps the Gov chose him for that very reason: he will cause no trouble.*

"We are grateful for the vegetables you've left in those gardens behind the fort," the Yankee is saying now, as he takes a pinch of snuff from Sheaffe's proffered snuffbox. "And for the sixty barrels of pork in the storehouse."

131

"Allow me to show you around the works, sir," Sheaffe says to the relieving officer, and off they go while White sits beneath a tree looking over the lake towards York. *What will it be like there? And how soon will it be before I have Marianne on my hands again?* He turns his back on the lake and looks towards his familiar home across the river. But the sun is setting and he closes his eyes against its glare.

He's jolted awake by the cheers of the Yankees as the major and Sheaffe shake hands. In another minute, the fifty men of the Fifth Regiment descend the steep path to the flats where their guns and ammunition have already been loaded into a flotilla of batteaux.

Back in the canoe with his Indian paddler, White gets a front-row view of the Brits' progress across the river to the Niagara side where the Gov has built a new blockhouse to receive them. Before he left for Kingston, he'd named it Fort George. It's built on the high ground behind Navy Hall, looking directly across to Fort Niagara. There's something definitely confrontational about the position of this new British garrison, White reflects. *But if there's ever a war with the Yankees, at least I won't be here to see it.*

What's left to do now is to face the fact that the move to York can no longer be avoided. He has only a few more weeks to procrastinate.

# Chapter Twenty-Six

*September 1796*

Eliza has just taken a bread pudding from the hearth and set it upon the table. It is a special treat for Mary's homecoming. The girl has been gone near eight weeks to stay with a captain's widow who lives on high ground above Queenston. From what Eliza has heard from the widow, Mary has been the better for the fresh air and sunshine. Now she's coming home, thank the Lord for that. Eliza has missed her so much. Peter never sees the funny side of anything, while she and Mary can always share a laugh or two.

The pudding has rose nicely, and for a minute or two, she's mighty pleased with herself, but as she watches, its top collapses into a huge crease down the middle of the bowl.

"Good Lord, what have I done?" Eliza claps her hands together in distress.

"Dear Aunt Eliza, what have you done? You've taken the Lord's name in vain, that's what you've done. Really, you've become very naughty since I've been away."

Eliza turns to see Mary standing on the threshold, her portmanteau in her hand. "I'm mighty happy to see you, girl," she says, laughing. She wraps her arms around Mary. "Do you think the Lord will forgive me?"

"Probably, since He knows you made that pudding for me. Bless you, dear Aunt." She looks at the caved-in disaster. "Why don't we just fill the centre with whopped cream? I'll brandish the twigs, and you can sit there and tell me what you've been up to since I left you unsupervised."

Mary runs over to the window seat to hug the cat which has been sleeping in the sunshine.

Eliza produces the big wooden forklike creation that dear Mr. White gave her.

Mary looks at it for a moment. "Good for Mr. White, I say. More useful to you than those pink plumes he presented for our goodbye-to-Mr.-Osgoode party."

Mary whops briskly for a few minutes while Eliza watches. *Pale and sweaty the dear girl be. Has she been the better for that long stay on high ground? Or did I waste Peter's money and make myself lonesome for nothing?*

Suddenly the light coming in the kitchen window disappears, and a sound of ocean waves filters through the heavy walls of the house. Mary looks up. "It's the passenger pigeons migrating, Aunt." She throws down the whopper, spattering cream over the table top. "I'm off to look at them."

"Please, dear Mary, do not be a-going out. The pigeons will be—"

But Mary seems to have no idea of doing as she is bid. She's out the door in a flash, leaving Eliza to stumble after her. The girl runs across the back forty into the garden where Job is busy digging potatoes.

Overhead is a mighty vision, indeed. The whole blue of the heavens has gone, wiped out by a moving storm of wings and wailings and droppings from the sky like pellets of snow. Eliza stops to brush the dung from her dress and apron. The birds are dipping lower and lower towards the garden, their cries becoming more and more menacing, and she becomes a-feared they will strike her and Mary.

*Why, O Lord, are they a-coming so close? Mercy, mercy.* Then she sees what's up. Job has tethered a dove, for certain from their dovecot, to a stool in the middle of the garden where it's gobbling at some seeds he's put upon the ground. Those birds from above have seen it and are a-coming down. They think it's a place of peaceful plenty.

She screams, and just in time the flock sweeps upwards again. It's not her scream that's done it. It's Job and Mary. They are pelting tubers at the birds. They've hit at least a dozen of them and their bodies are flapping about in the middle of the garden. Right pretty they be, with wine-red bosoms and white patches on their dark-blue wings and tails. Eliza hates to see their distress.

"Dear Aunt, look at what we've done!" Mary laughs, but there's a nasty gargle from her throat that accompanies that laugh. "It was all Job's idea. Now we have enough pigeons for that game-bird pie I like so much. Why don't we ask Mr. White over for supper since Uncle Peter is away in York? Oh please, Aunt!"

Job is now smashing his spade down on the struggling birds on the ground. Mary counts them. "Sixteen, Aunt! We hit sixteen!"

Eliza tries to sort out what's troubling her most: the bird dung in her hair and down the bodice of her dress, the dying birds lying among the tubers, or the girl's troubling cough that was supposed to be cleared up in her sojourn on the hilltop.

"Job, get busy. Go first to Mr. White's and invite him to supper. Then dress those poor birds for our supper. Mary, get back into the house and lie down. You have undone yourself with all this running about and killing. Now I'm hearing you cough again. I'm put to distraction by it all."

"Oh Aunt, I'm sorry. But why are you in a pet about Job and me killing pigeons? You yourself have taken the head off many a chicken on the chopping block. How many times have I held the bird in place while you swung your axe? And how many times have you missed your mark and had to try again and near killed *me* in the process?"

"That's enough, missy. Get inside and lie down. Your face be all sweaty as if you have the fever. And you're coughing again, too. It would be the better for you if you'd do what I tell you to do and not try to have it your own way."

Suddenly, the girl seems to collapse in front of her very eyes. Her face becomes white and she begins to shake, as if she's cold, though her body is slathered in sweat. She starts to cry. Eliza holds her, a-feared that she's going to

135

fall to the ground. Job moves in beside her, and between the two of them, they manage to half-drag, half-carry her up the stairs to her bedroom where they lay her on her bed and pull a quilt over her to stop the shivering.

"What is wrong with you, girl?" Eliza asks. She doesn't wait for an answer. The ague, that's what it be. *The same symptoms I myself had last year. But where in tarnation did she get the ague? Not on that hilltop above Queenston, for certain. Something's up, I wager.*

In the kitchen, she takes the powdered bark that she procured from Mr. Hamilton (from South America he told her), softens it in hot water, mixes it with rose leaves, lemon juice and wine, and takes it up the stairs to the girl.

Mary struggles to get the bark tea potion down, then gags, and vomits it onto the coverlet. "Aunt Eliza," she says, "I have been a bad girl all day, and now I've ruined this pretty quilt you made me." She starts to cry.

Eliza goes downstairs, cuts a large portion of bread pudding, covers it in whopped cream, and goes back upstairs. "Dear girl," she says, "try this. Hold your nose while you swallow a bit of the potion. Then have a bite or two of the pudding, and then go back to the potion. You will be the better for getting the medicine down."

Potion pudding potion pudding potion pudding . . . it all disappears. But the process is long, and by the time Eliza has got it all down Mary's throat, the girl's head sinks upon the pillow. "So tired, Aunt, so tired," she says.

"I shall leave you to sleep, child, but tell me now, how did you get the fever? There will be a to-do with that woman if I find that she did not look after you this summer."

"Oh Aunt, do not blame Mrs. Clarke. She kept me like a prisoner there on the heights. Day after day after day, I could not escape from her. She put me outside under the oak tree in the sunshine at ten o'clock each morning, and sat with me, doing her needlework. She let me read the Good Book, that's what she always called it, for half an hour, then I was to have a bowl of gruel—you can have no idea how foul that was—and then I had to walk slow slow

136

slow across the lawn for half an hour, then back to the Book for half an hour, then the walk again, then . . ." Mary starts to cough, and vile gobs of blood come up from her throat.

Eliza wipes the girl's face. "Sleep now, Mary. You must tell me the rest later."

Mary stretches her thin arms towards Eliza. "Please pump up the pillow, Aunt Eliza. I must tell you everything now. I do not want you to blame Mrs. Clarke."

So Eliza fluffs up the pillow and fixes the bedclothes and sits down again to hear the rest of Mary's tale.

"There was a preacher coming to the Freemasons' Lodge last week, one of those evangelicals, and she wanted to go. She got out the Good Book and made me put my hand on it and swear that I would sit under the oak tree in the sunshine until she got back. So I swore. But Aunt, no sooner did I hear her cart rumble down the lane than I was rumbling, too, down the long path to the swamp on the river. "

"Lord have mercy on thee, child."

"Because I swore on the Bible and then cheated?"

"No, girl. Because it be in that swamp you got the fever. Why were you a-going to that place of hell?"

"Oh Aunt, I wanted to see the Indians harvesting wild rice. When I got down to the creek, a whole Chippewa family was on the bank of the creek ready to pole out to the edge of the big river. They saw me and welcomed me, and they put me in one of their canoes and we went right out into the rushes. It was magic. There were pretty little birds everywhere. One of them, he had an orange breast, was sitting on a reed, and I watched his tiny throat puffing out with the song he was singing. And there were some other little blue birds darting here and there and a big heron that took flight when he heard us coming, and he had a fish in his beak and—"

"Your face be flushed, my dear. You must be calm now and sleep. Tell me more when you wake up."

"You are not angry with me, Aunt?"

"No. Rest in peace, dear girl." Eliza takes the dregs of potion and pudding with her as she descends the stairs. *Oh Lord, why did I say that? It's on every tombstone everywhere. Mary is not a-going to die, no no no.* But she can't stop the sobs that shake her.

\* \* \*

When Mr. White comes to supper, Mary is still asleep, so Eliza and her guest sit down to the meal without her.

Job sets the game-bird pie on the table in the dining room. "What a treat," Mr. White says, as Job spoons large portions onto his and Eliza's plates. He tucks a napkin over his cravat and digs in. Eliza takes a forkful, raises it to her mouth, and sets the fork down.

"I can't eat it." She starts to cry.

"Whatever is the matter, Miss Russell?" She feels his touch upon her sleeve and the sympathy in that touch near breaks her heart. Job comes with a heavy white napkin and she mops at her face with it.

"Leave us for a few minutes, if you please," she hears her friend say to Job.

The door to the dining room closes, and they are alone.

She tells him everything. He puts his fork down and listens as he always does, his blue eyes still and fixed upon her. "You think dear Mary is dying?"

"I am a-feared. Brother be away in York. I have no one with me."

"We must get word to your brother then. He must come and be with you." Mr. White pulls out his pocket watch. "But the packet boat has left the wharf. Do not worry. I will go now and seek out my Indian who paddles me about. If you will scribble a brief note, I will send it with him. He will find your brother and bring him back."

"But that will take hours, sir." Eliza dabs at her eyes with the napkin. "I am so a-feared for Mary."

"You have me, Miss Russell, though I may be a poor substitute for your brother. I will be back within the hour and stay for as long as you need me."

# Chapter Twenty-Seven

*September 1796, the same night*

John White sits in a chair by the hearth and tries hard to concentrate on his book, not wanting to embarrass the child by staring at her. His mind swivels back to England, to his own daughter Ellen, whose illnesses he often superintended while his wife lost herself in the fogs of opium. He remembers Ellen's fevers, the cups of cold tea he forced her to drink, her whimpers of distress that matched his own. How he misses the girl he was once so close to. If only she and her brothers could come to this new world without their mother . . .

Mary takes sips of bark tea while Miss Russell hovers behind her, hands placed on the girl's frail shoulders. Most of the tea she pukes up into a basin beside her cup.

"Oh, Aunt Eliza, I have never before felt so wretched. Perhaps Uncle Peter can help us. You have sent for Uncle Peter, have you, Mr. White?"

"Yes, Mary. He will not be here for several hours, but I shall stay here with you and your aunt until he arrives."

The back door opens and Job enters, his face sweaty and his breathing forced. He has evidently been riding hard.

"Dr. Kerr is a-coming from the new garrison soon?" Miss Russell whispers as Job stands by the hearth, mopping his cheeks with a towel. She has turned her back to Mary so the child, who is now puking again, will not hear. The servant nods.

"Job, Aunt must give you some of her bark tea. It's sure to cure you of the sweats. But you'll need this bowl to puke in." Mary pushes the bowl of vomit towards him.

139

Then she throws her head back and summons a gurgle of laughter. *My God, she reminds me of that bronze statue of the satyr that the fishermen brought up from the bottom of the sea.* But White's happy image dissolves in the red-tinged phlegm that spews from the child's mouth followed by another eruption of vomit.

"Off to bed now, Mary," Miss Russell says, helping the girl to her feet and holding her close as they stumble towards the staircase. "I should not have let you get up."

It is eight o'clock now and the sun is just dipping out of view. "Take a break now, Job," White says. "I am here to receive the doctor and to answer any calls of distress."

Job nods in gratitude and moves towards the door. "I am in my room above the stable, sir, if you need me."

The ticking clock marks the arrival of darkness, and White takes a paper spill from the mantel, dips it in the hearth fire, and lights the candles in their sconces. From the room upstairs he hears the murmur of voices and prolonged bouts of coughing.

Minutes later, there comes a knock on the door. Dr. Robert Kerr at last. He's a man well into middle age with a large nose, pursed lips, and straggly grey hair which he has tied back in a messy pigtail. Besides his medical kit, he's carrying a large birch bark container which he sets upon the table along with a small glass bottle filled with a white powder.

"Got something to dissolve this?" he says without preliminary, looking around the room. He picks up the pot of tea, puts two large scoops of the powder into it, shakes the pot in a circular motion, and sets it back on the table.

"What is it?" *But I think I know the answer.*

"Calomel."

"Mercury? You're crazy, sir. It's poison."

"Who's the doctor here? Calomel is the best purgative around."

"Surely you've heard what Samuel Thomson has to say on the subject. He was here only a few weeks ago gathering—"

"A damned quack in my opinion. Let us say no more about him. Now where's the patient? Upstairs? Let's get to her. You take the birch bark container, if you please, and I'll carry the rest."

The lid on the container is slightly askew, and as White picks it up, he sees a slug squirming through the gap. He takes the lid off and looks into a mass of writhing black slugs, each about two inches in length with mustard-coloured underbellies. *Good God, leeches.* Only an effort of will keeps him from dropping the container.

"Careful, man, careful. I need those wigglies. They're hungry, and in a moment they'll be all over the girl, sucking up their supper. Just had a brainwave this afternoon. I have a couple of them secured on threads. Maybe you noticed. I intend to insert them, one at a time, into the child's throat where they'll feast on that bloody phlegm that's choking her. I can pull them out when they're sated. Now let's get on with it."

Kerr moves towards the staircase. White follows. *What am I to do? I know one thing: I cannot put dear little Mary through this horror.*

Mary's bed faces the open door. The girl is lying, eyes closed, apparently at rest. Miss Russell is at her bedside, holding her hand.

Mary opens her eyes. She's probably heard their footsteps. "No, no, Aunt," she screams. "No, no, no!" With the screams comes the thick, bloody phlegm, spewing forth over the bedsheets.

White says: "Stay here, Kerr. Before you go one step farther, we must speak with the girl's aunt." He gestures to Miss Russell to come into the hallway where he speaks to her in an undertone. "We cannot make the child more miserable. You have called for Dr. Kerr. He has come. But now you must tell him to leave."

"Do not listen to this man," Kerr says. "I know what to do. Purging and bleeding form my credo. Purging and bleeding. Bleeding and purging. Get rid of the foul humours in your niece's body. She will be better in the morning."

White tips the birch bark container towards Miss Russell so she can see its contents. She recoils in horror.

"Think of these leeches on her arms and throat," he says. "And in the teapot that Dr. Kerr holds is a solution of calomel. You know the word, ma'am. You know that it loosens the bowels. Mary is a wraith now. What will happen when she loses more of her bodily fluids with this barbaric treatment?"

Miss Russell has stepped away from the doctor. She folds her arms across her chest and takes a deep breath, seeming to summon courage. "I thank you for a-coming, Dr. Kerr. Send your bill, however dear it be. My brother Peter will pay. But go now."

Kerr hovers for a moment. Then he grabs the leeches, turns, and clatters down the staircase. They listen to the kitchen door slam shut.

Mary has heard it, too. She has stopped crying. White and Miss Russell tiptoe into her bedchamber. The child is lying back against her pillow, eyes closed again. There is a ghastly pallor on her face, and her nightdress is damp with sweat. Her breathing is forced, coming through her mouth in squeaks like a flute. But she opens her eyes, and seeing White, says, smiling, "Oh, Uncle Peter, you have come at last. And you sent that horrible man away. Thank you."

White moves close to the girl. "Yes, I am here, Mary."

"Uncle Peter, the pigeons . . . there were so many they hid the clouds . . . so beautiful . . . I see them now . . . I'm flying away with them . . ."

Her voice trails off. Her eyes close. The phlegm seems to boil in her throat and a bloody, slimy, scabby matter dribbles down her chin. Then there is the silence of death.

\* \* \*

White has summoned Job to make some strong hyson tea, and he and Miss Russell try to drink it. But his friend's sobs wrack her body. Job hovers, not knowing what to do. His face is contorted with pain.

"Go back to bed, Job. When morning comes, Miss Russell will wash the body and dress it and I shall summon the rector. We shall need you then."

After the servant leaves, White reaches for Miss Russell's hand. She seems glad of his touch and her sobs abate.

"You must tell me something of Mary's early life, ma'am, in those days before I knew her. You must have many memories to share with me while we hold vigil here."

"So many memories, though I have tried mighty hard to forget some of them."

"It was difficult to raise the child, was it? I expect you and your brother found that an infant thrust upon you was a care and worry. Take comfort, dear ma'am, from your bounty. What would have happened to the babe if she had not found a home with you after her parents were shipwrecked?"

These comments, intended to stimulate some comfortable memories, instead produce silence. *What have I said? Why is she staring at me?*

"I have upset you. Pray forgive me. Let us be silent then."

"Oh, Mr. White. You of all the people I have known in this new world have been the best, the kindest. Though it puts me to the blush, I must tell you the truth. Mary is my child. Mine and Peter's."

He stares at her. "I do not understand, ma'am."

Her words gush out. "Peter is my half-brother, as you know. We shared the same father, but I was the child of his second wife. I did not know Peter until I was a young woman because he had been in America with the British army for many years. When I was eighteen he came to England for a short time. I was charmed with him, sir. I was so . . . innocent . . . and he was twenty years older. He seemed such a man of the world, and though it puts me to the blush to say it, I was smitten with him—"

"Perhaps you will regret telling me this, ma'am . . ."

Miss Russell takes a deep breath, and closes her eyes. "It is a blessed relief, and I am mighty pleased to let it all out after these years of pretence. We were together for near eight weeks and then he went back to his life over the ocean. I did not see him for a decade though we wrote many a letter to each other. Then our father died. And though a daughter should not say it, he was a most evil man who gambled and left me nothing but a pile of debts and a mother who was quite mad."

"You were attendant on your mother at the time of your father's death and afterwards, were you not?"

Miss Russell's eyes are still closed as if she's back in that house in Harwich with all its stresses and grief. "Yes, sir, and I be near mad myself with the care of her. She would bite me and push me against the wall and hit me with her fists. And the day Peter arrived from America to settle our father's debts, he found me on the floor with Mother astride me. She was near to strangling me. The maid was screaming. I thought I was near to dying . . ." Miss Russell bursts into sobs.

"And your brother rescued you?"

"He pulled her off me and forced her into a chair. She became quite silent then, saying nary a word. He sent the maid to the shop for a bottle of laudanum and when she come back, he gave my mother a large glass of wine with the potion in it and made her drink it. Oh, Mr. White, she slept for hours and I was able to get myself firmed up again and ready to deal with life. And that night, dear Peter and I . . . he comforted me, sir . . . and I will ever be grateful."

*Well I can fill in the blanks, can't I?* Aloud he says, "You must be grateful, too, to have had that lovely child with you over the years."

"You do not condemn us, sir?"

"I am thankful to have known you and your brother and Mary. You have been my great friends in this new world."

Miss Russell wipes her face with the napkin Job has left by her cup of tea. "You are kind, Mr. White." She takes a deep breath. "I only wish I could have stopped the girl from running after those pigeons. I might have saved her . . . I might have—"

144

"You heard her last words, my friend. They were happy words. Be thankful she had those moments." White pauses, trying to choose words that will offer some surcease for the woman's pain. "Let us imagine that she has flown with those birds to another world, a world free of pain—"

And suddenly, they are both crying. He helps Miss Russell to her feet and places her in the comfortable rocking chair by the fire. He puts a pillow behind her neck and stands behind the chair rocking it back and forth, back and forth, back and forth . . .

When she finally falls asleep, he climbs softly up the stairs, stands in the doorway of Mary's bedchamber and looks at the child. She seems at peace. *What was that song I heard the slaves sing in the cotton fields in Jamaica?* He ponders, then remembers a line: *"I want to cross over into campground."* *Is Mary there now with those birds she loved?*

Much later, he is almost asleep, his head on the kitchen table, when he hears the kitchen door open gently. Russell has arrived.

# Chapter Twenty-Eight

*November 1796*

John White stands in front of the new pier-glass he purchased from Hamilton in Queenston. It's at present in his dining room. It should be in his bedchamber, but he and Yvette have never been able to figure out how to get it up the ladder into his loft. Not that it matters: it's the effect achieved by looking in it that counts. He wants to be at his best on this day, a day he dreads. John Elmsley is to be sworn in as the new Chief Justice. No way he can avoid the day: it's his duty to see that the ceremony unfolds correctly and that events get recorded. He claps the tie wig over his head and tucks a thatch of brown hair under it.

Then he sets out on foot for the centre of town, to the building housing the courthouse and gaol that was built more than a year ago at the end of King Street, as it's now called. It's probably too close to Yankee cannons if they should ever want to go to war, but withal it's a solid one-storey clapboard structure, plain but adequate, with a court room on the main floor and a staircase leading down to the gaol cells. *A damn sight better than anything I'll get in York.*

He can now count about fifteen solid dwellings of imposing proportions in town, all a far cry from the miserable, straggling little huts that he and Osgoode first espied on their arrival with the Simcoes in 1792. Of course, the most superior one—plunked, as the Yankees say, right in the town centre—is David Smith's. Beside the Freemasons' Lodge, it occupies almost a whole block of formal gardens, orchards, and railing in the best English

146

style. White is sick of hearing the man brag about it. *But, damn it, it is elegant and distinguished.*

And then there's Lieutenant Robert Pilkington's house on a one-acre lot, a fine house which is now vacant since Pilkington has left for Quebec. He was a great favourite of Mrs. Simcoe since they both shared a love of sketching. In his time here, he'd drawn up plans for all the finest houses in town, and his own place is in the best Georgian style. *If I didn't have to make the move to York, I might see about renting it for myself. It would be worth some extra debt. I remember how I once coveted it and planned to rent it on my thousand a year stipend as Chief Justice. Oh, what fools we mortals be.*

He steps through the front door of the courthouse to find a man in a superfine frock coat with silver braid, clearly Elmsley, waiting just inside the chamber. When he first heard the bad news about Elmsley's appointment as Chief Justice, he remembered Elmsley's inexperience. The man is young, a year younger than White himself, and it's only six-and-a-half years since he was called to the bar, apparently. *A friend of the Duke of Portland with a Loyalist father-in-law. Patronage counts.*

In his mind he had pictured a man short in stature, someone he could look down upon, but Elmsley is his own height and stares him straight in the eye. Then the impostor pulls out his pocket watch, looks at it, shakes his head, and puts it back in his waistcoat.

"I'm not late," White says, trying to quell his indignation. He pulls out his own watch and brandishes it in the man's face. "Right on the mark."

*"Accedas ad curiam,"* Elmsley replies, laughing. The phrase comes at White so suddenly that he is unable to translate it immediately, but he takes a cue from the laughter and returns a smile in reply.

From the cells below, he can hear the cries of a prisoner. "Damn," he says to Elmsley. "That wretched guard can surely postpone his whippings until we get through this ceremony."

147

Another Latin phrase issues from the Chief Justice's mouth, but White pays it no attention: he strides from the courtroom and down the stairs into the dungeon.

He gets back upstairs just in time to hear Russell's gavel banging on the podium, and the swearing-in gets under way.

* * *

White, Elmsley, and Russell go out for an early supper afterwards at the tavern called Yellow House.

They sit down near the hearth where a blazing fire staves off the encroaching cold as the front door opens and closes for the "regulars," a group of rather dirty and disheveled men, obviously labourers.

Elmsley looks them over, and says in a loud voice, "Well, it isn't the Honourable Society of Gray's Inn, but one must adjust. The Duke of Portland told me there would be very little of what we Britishers call 'polite society' here on the far side of the Atlantic, but one must adjust." He sighs. "One must adjust."

White watches Russell take several deep breaths. His friend looks tired these days. He is now officially Administrator of Upper Canada, and though he has almost finished adding wings to a fine new house in York, he keeps running back and forth between Niagara and the new capital. His sister Eliza has suffered from depression since Mary's death, and Russell has hovered near her whenever he can spare time from his responsibilities.

"Do not adjust too completely, sir," his friend says. "You know that we must resume our duties in the new capital at once. As a matter of fact, Colonel Simcoe wanted us all in York by last summer, latest. And here it is, November."

Elmsley puffs out his cheeks and barks out a response that causes the labourers to turn their heads to listen. "I have no intention of going to York. Why would I? There is no court house there, no gaol either, and what would I do there as Chief Justice without jurors for my trials?"

"Jurors, sir?" Russell is clearly at a loss. White knows what Elmsley is about to say—he's turned over the same idea in his own mind many times—but he's determined not to say anything that might seem to indicate an agreement with Elmsley.

"How are we to get jurors to travel to a godforsaken hole in the forest? There are no roads from what I hear, a harbour that is closed to access from the east, and no place to accommodate them while they are on duty. I cannot proceed with bills of indictment if there are no jurors to examine them."

"I promise you a courthouse, sir, within a few months. And roads, too."

Elmsley makes a noise in his throat and ejects a gob of mucus into the spittoon that sits by the hearth. The labourers at the next table imitate him, but their spit goes onto the broad pine planks of the floor. Elmsley sees their insolence, but he can do nothing about it except to say "dirty Yankee upstarts," a phrase that makes them erupt in laughter.

The atmosphere is heating up, and White knows he must act. If it came to fisticuffs, the three of them would be lying in the spit on the floor. "Drinks for our friends," he says to the black serving man, pointing to the table of labourers. He can ill afford the gesture, but it has the effect of pacifying them. They bury their faces in the froth of their ale tankards and begin their own conversation.

He's thankful for the arrival of their meal. It's the staple entrée of the Yellow House: boiled cabbage and fried salted pork swimming in a pool of grease. Instead of being delivered by the server to their table, the entrée is set upon a large table in the middle of the room and everyone makes a rush towards it. By the time, he, Russell, and Elmsley manage to push their way to the food, a good deal of the pork has disappeared, leaving only a few pieces in the grease. Elmsley takes a look at it, lips curled. White waits for an explosion.

"*Fabas indulcet fames*," he pronounces. Then, evidently noticing his companions' lack of comprehension, he offers a translation. "Hunger sweetens the beans," he says in a condescending voice as he picks a piece of pork for his plate.

"There are no beans here, sir," Russell says in a puzzled tone. White nudges his friend's foot, hoping that he will say no more. Irony has always been lost upon him.

Back at their own small table, they eat in silence for a time. There seems to be no common topic on which they can fasten. Elmsley asks the server for a napkin "to wipe the grease from my hands." The notion of napkins seems to be a new one, and the man has to confer for a moment with the owner who is standing behind the bar.

Dessert—puddings and creams—come next. Again they must troop to the central table to load their bowls. There are large serving spoons but no individual spoons. Even White, accustomed now to the ways of the town, is nonplussed about how to proceed. He looks at the labourers nearby. They are scooping up the contents of their bowls with their knives. He remembers Alexander Mackenzie's preference for a knife with Yvette's pudding. The method works fairly well, especially since the knives have rounded edges and can hold a good portion of pudding on their blades. But Elmsley calls for a spoon, and again, there is much consultation on the part of the black servant and his master before one is produced.

Out on the street again, White and Russell bid Elmsley adieu. The Chief Justice has rented rooms in the town. "You will have a vast acreage in York, sir, when you move," Russell tells him. "Simcoe insisted on one-hundred acre lots for each of the administration as a *douceur* to compensate for their removal from this place."

"I told you before, Russell—did you not hear—that I am *not* moving from this place. I have this day paid over a thousand pounds to Pilkington's agent for the purchase of the lieutenant's house. When my bride and her father arrive from Boston, they will find a pleasant abode awaiting them, one that, I hope, will distract their attention from the general barbarity of the occupants of this town."

White puts his arm through Russell's and pulls him away. But before they can escape, Elmsley finds more to say. "I have not mentioned my friend, the Reverend Mr. Thomas Raddish."

*The rotund, little red-faced man who looks exactly like a radish?* White has noticed him in the town, always in a clerical collar and clutching a prayer book.

Russell says, "What about him?"

"I seek a Church of England appointment for him. But I have not been able to find a church in this place. What do you suggest?"

"Nothing here for him, Elmsley. You're right, there is no church. Services take place in the Freemasons' Lodge. But we already have a rector. The Reverend Mr. Addison has looked after our spiritual lives for many months. Your friend cannot displace him."

"What am I to tell him, then?"

"There may be a need for a rector in York. Tell him to join you there."

Elmsley turns quite red with rage. "Good day, sirs."

Laughing, White and his friend walk towards Russell's house on the commons. "Blast the man," Russell says when they are out of earshot. "Blast his uppity British ways and his damnable Latin phrases. Do you understand any of his lingo?"

"Some of it," White says. "Latin was a subject I could barely tolerate, though. But I expect we'll be hearing a good deal of it in the next years: There's one phrase, though, I'll write down for you to memorize. '*Nescio de quo loqueris.*' I believe it translates roughly to 'I don't know what the hell you're talking about.' Use it when he spouts. By the way, that was a brilliant send-off you gave him tonight."

"It made me happy to see the look of rage on his face. I am writing to the Governor tonight. I'm going to tell him of the man's utter piggery." He turns towards White, his face almost obliterated by the setting sun, so that only the anger in his voice registers. "Are you with me?"

151

"Yes. Though I myself have fought against the move to York, I will not ally myself with Elmsley. Court house or no court house, gaol or no gaol, you may count on me to join you soon in York and to back you in whatever you tell the Colonel."

At the edge of the long driveway which winds towards the Russells' house, the men pause to shake hands.

White trudges towards home. "Uppity British ways," that was the phrase his friend had used to describe Elmsley's manners. *And I felt the same resentment. Have we become more Canadian than British in a mere four-and-a-half years?*

Then he remembers the drunkards in front of Field's Tavern on that ill-fated night when he learned that he had been passed over for promotion to Chief Justice. Hadn't the louts called him and Russell "Uppity Brits"?

How the world changes . . . His laughter is echoed by a barking dog somewhere on one of the forest paths.

# Chapter Twenty-Nine

*York (now Toronto)*
*July 1797*

In an effort to keep his mind off the letter he received this morning, John White has walked from his new house down to the bay. This bay at York is a place he has come to love. Dense forests line its margins, and he stops on the shoreline to enjoy the images of the trees reflected in the still surface of the water. His presence stirs the calm of early evening, and wild geese and cranes take flight.

He sees, farther along the shore, the tents of the Mississauga Indian band. He remembers how Mrs. Simcoe called them a dirty, drunken, idle people, compared with the handsome, colourfully dressed Ojibway bands from Lake Huron and the tall, well-built Mohawks who occasionally attended the Simcoes' dances at Fort Niagara. But he has some sympathy for these Indians. When he first came to this place, he heard how they had given the Gov the appellation of "He Who Changes Names." He can only imagine how they must feel to find the home they once called Toronto now metamorphosed into York. As well, they must watch the incoming flux of settlers from Niagara, all of whom will occupy the land they looked upon as their own. "Park lots," the Gov called them, which extend north into the wilderness from the street now called Queen, and "town lots" which go down to the waterfront. In no time, these Mississaugas will undoubtedly have white men chasing them away with muskets.

Despite the tranquillity of the bay, the letter from Sam Shepherd ripples his peace. He pulls it from his frock coat to read again. Its message is short. Marianne, his daughter,

153

and two sons will arrive at Quebec on a sailing vessel sometime in early August. No doubt Marianne was burdensome to his brother-in-law, but surely he could have kept them in London for a few months more. Now White must travel all the way to Quebec and bring them safely to York.

And what is he to do with them when they arrive? He can imagine Marianne's reaction when she sees the house he is currently building. Eventually it will be a decent dwelling of two storeys made of squared logs and covered in clapboard. But at present he has only three rooms covered in, and they have already cost him more than three hundred pounds. House-building in this backwoods is expensive, even with the prevalent use of unseasoned wood and a total ignorance on the part of his builder of the necessity for a solid foundation of stone.

He has, moreover, not yet received pay for the past six months in His Majesty's service, though Peter Russell has written to the Treasurer at Whitehall petitioning on his behalf.

Marianne was out of control even in the centre of London society, and he cannot imagine her coping with anything here in this backwater. Everything, except for basic food staples like milk and flour and beef and pork, has to be imported from rich merchants in Montreal and New York, after being shipped to them from England. How is he to feed a family at such prohibitive expense? He does not yet have a permanent cook, merely a slattern who comes in to prepare his meals by the day. He must put up with her wretched cooking and damnable incivility. He cannot fire her. Household servants are nearly impossible to find.

He remembers his chagrin at leaving Yvette LaCroix behind in Niagara. She had not wanted to leave her Indian relatives. But she made him quantities of dandelion wine from the new spring crops in their backyard.

He tried to reciprocate with a gesture he had long thought about. He dug up the small box containing the body of her infant and together they buried it near a clump

154

of birch trees in Paradise Grove at the edge of the commons. There, he hoped, Yvette would be able to visit the gravesite unimpeded by the new owner of his house, a Yankee just arrived from across the river. Then he and Yvette had parted. She had wept as she shook his hand, and he had felt his own tears trickle down his cheeks.

The headache begins again. Time to start home and take some whisky punch. He has already finished drinking Yvette's dandelion wine. As he passes the Indian fires, he nods to the natives. But now he feels blood trickling down his face, and he fumbles in his waistcoat pocket for a handkerchief. *Damn. Nothing. Best to get home and apply Miss Russell's remedy: cotton soaked in vinegar, stuffed up each nostril.* He starts to walk faster.

"You take this, white man," a voice calls. He turns. A young Indian has risen from his evening meal and beckons to him. The man yanks a handful of lichen off a stone in front of his tepee and hands it to White. White buries his bloody nose in the grey-green wad. It's a bit scratchy, but quite soft and absorbent, and he feels grateful to the Indian. *But it's ridiculous, isn't it? Here I am, the first Attorney-General of Upper Canada, wiping my face with a moss handkerchief provided by an almost naked native, his skin covered with some malodorous grease to ward off the mosquitoes. I have come to this. I must only be thankful that Marianne is not yet here to see it all.*

He heads north away from the bay towards his "park lot" which the Gov had laid out with his surveyors before flying the coop back to England. It's a huge block of land, and its size keeps him from contact with the John and Betsy Small, owners of the dwelling on the lot beside his. "Berkeley House" is the ridiculous name of this residence.

He has not yet had to face his former paramour. From what he has heard from the never-ending gossip of David Smith, she is trying hard to erase the doubtful reputation she acquired at Niagara.

Smith himself has built an impressive house he calls Maryville. "Being land-rich is not much use if you are cash-poor," he has said to White. But in the next breath, he

155

always goes on to brag about its startling bright yellow paint and the buildings that make up what he calls his "service court": "my stable, my coach-house, my wagon shed, my root-house, my summerhouse . . . "

White passes Peter Russell's house which faces the bay. The first house Russell purchased in this new capital burned to the ground during the winter, and he had to hire a German immigrant named William Berczy to build this one. It's quite the place, a U-shaped building in what his friend boasts is "the neo-classical style." It is surrounded by fine elm trees and a picket fence set upon bricks. It has eleven large shuttered windows, as Russell has mentioned a hundred times, and has cost him a "crushing one thousand pounds."

He assumes his friend is now in Niagara with his sister, and he hurries past, promising himself to stop the next time when he's calmer and count the windows to see if there really are eleven. But he has just turned the corner onto Princess Street when he hears a voice calling him. Russell emerges from his fine panelled front door and comes down to the gate. *Dammit. I can't shed the lichen without his seeing it.* He tries to hide the bloody "handkerchief" behind his back.

"What's wrong, White? Your face is a bloody mess."

"The usual nosebleeds. Nothing to worry about."

"What's that you have in your hand, man? Throw away that moss, for God's sake. Take my handkerchief. We're all up to our eyebrows in debt in this place, but I can afford a piece of linen."

"I thought you'd be in Niagara now, getting Miss Russell packed up ready to move over."

"The inside is not finished, and she's bound and determined to stay there on the commons until all is ready here. I'm trying to find some servants, got in mind three who've come over the border to freedom, and with Job, that should be plenty." He turns back to look at the house. "She'll be pleased when she sees it, I warrant. The neo-classic style is the latest craze in Europe, so Berczy tells me, and all those windows let in so much light."

"Eight windows, are there?" *Why am I taunting him in this stupid way?*

"Eleven. Have I not told you?"

*Let it pass. Change the subject.* He spits on the handkerchief Russell has given him and mops at his face. "I trust you will be in Niagara on the seventeenth of this month, my friend?"

"Ah, yes, the date of the formation of the Law Society of Upper Canada. I must commend you, White, on the part you have played in regulating the profession of law in this new country."

"It is the one most important achievement of my life." Tears spring unbidden and mix with the bloody mess on his face. He feels Russell's arm on his shoulder. "I could not have done it, sir, without your support here at our first meeting of the Legislature. You passed the Act that has made it all possible." *Yes, the man annoys me, but he has proven to be a staunch friend.* He leans forward and clasps Russell in a close embrace.

"And I shall be with you at Wilson's Tavern to see it all unfold. What's more, I shall invite all the gentlemen licensed to practise law on that day to join Eliza and me for a celebration—perhaps the last—at our commodious house on the commons."

For a moment, as White turns again in the warm summer evening towards his unfinished home, he forgets the impending doom of Marianne and seeks solace in thinking of the greatest accomplishment of his legal career. *I have insured that all persons who practise law in this province are competent, follow proper procedures, and behave ethically. From this month forward, there will be no more asses and apes popping up from God-knows-where and calling themselves lawyers. Surely I have, like Mackenzie, achieved a quest to be proud of.*

*Bring on Marianne. I can stand her. Bring on my children to love and cherish and to walk beside me in the years to come.*

# Chapter Thirty

*July 17, 1797*

White and Russell disembark from the *Onondaga* at the wharf at Niagara. "Shall we hire an ox cart to take us to the hotel?" White says to his friend.

"With pleasure, as long as you are willing to pay for it."

They climb up onto the wagon which has been waiting at the pier and jolt off up the road into town. It's only a mile's distance, but White is happy to avoid the sweat and dirt which walking would entail.

There's also the necessity to avoid the louts who linger around the wharf and may find his outfit laughable. Before leaving York in the coolness of early morning, he was happy with his attire, but now he fears he may look slightly ridiculous in the heat of high noon. He's wearing a black superfine redingote over white vest and breeches. He has not bothered with a hat, but his head is already itchy beneath his wig.

He looks at Russell. His friend has obviously spent no time worrying about *his* rig. His boots need a shine-up, and White fears his wig may be crawling with lice. He moves as far from him as possible on the plank of the wagon. Perhaps Miss Russell will be able to spruce her brother up when she finally moves to York.

A bone-rattling ride ensues, but fortunately it's a short one, and they arrive at Wilson's Tavern to find a crowd of people crammed into the ballroom on the second floor. He has been prepared to find John Small present. As clerk of the Executive Council of Upper Canada, he has perhaps some reason to be here for the investiture. But it's a shock to see his wife with him as well. She's deep in conversation with a tall, fair woman whom he has not seen before.

"I did not realize that ladies would be present today," he says to Russell.

"Nor I, but that bastard Elmsley told me he was bringing his wife, and then Small asked me if he could bring *his* wife along, too, and what could I say?"

"I did not see the Smalls on the ship."

"Small told me they would be coming over yesterday to spend the day with the Elmsleys. Apparently Small and Elmsley knew each other in England through Home Secretary Henry Dundas, and Mrs. Elmsley seems to have struck up a friendship with his wife." Russell points to the two chattering women. "Obviously she knows nothing about that rumpus started by Mrs. Jarvis."

"Someone will tell her, surely."

"Perhaps not. Elmsley is such a big cheese in these parts now, and Mrs. Elmsley's father is a Loyalist whom everyone here reveres. No one wants to alienate the lady by casting aspersion on her friends."

White looks towards the reading stand which has been set up at the front of the ballroom, a table with two chairs beside it. There are huge portraits of Governor Simcoe and King George the Third on the wall behind, flanking the British flag. "We had better get things started now."

Russell moves to the podium, and White seats himself behind the table. The Administrator reads aloud the Act passed earlier in the summer by the Parliament of Upper Canada. It is long-winded and couched in arcane language, and the audience shuffles and sighs and the several ladies present fan themselves obtrusively.

White has time to observe the crowd in detail. He is pleased to note that Elmsley, who has placed himself at the front of the audience, presents a clownish figure in a dark-blue redingote over a jacket and breeches of red, white, and blue stripes. *Is it supposed to remind us of his illustrious British connections?* In contrast, his wife is modestly dressed in a dark-grey gown, her cleavage hidden by a white gauze fichu. Mrs. Small has emulated her friend's decorum: her gown is white muslin with a long scarf covering the bosom he remembers so well.

At last Russell stops his spiel and calls him forward. "Ladies and gentlemen, I give you the first Treasurer of the Law Society of Upper Canada."

White's role is to provide a succinct, easy-to-understand summary of the qualifications for the legal profession. It contains sentences he has thought about and honed over many weeks. He has written them down in his best penmanship on a sheet of fine linen paper that will serve as a lasting record of the day. He begins boldly: "The Act, in brief, provides that gentlemen of education and probity shall be privileged to conduct legal procedures for fellow subjects. These gentlemen are authorized as well to secure to the Province and the—"

A cough from somewhere in the audience causes him to look down from the podium. There, near the front of the crowd, he sees the woman Small staring at him, her left eyelid closed in what is clearly a wink. He feels the heat rise into his cheeks, and for a moment, he loses his place on the sheet before him. By the time he resumes, he has lost his audience's attention as well. They have started to whisper and cough, and it is only Russell's whack on a gavel from the table beside the reading stand that forces silence again.

Taking a deep breath, White manages to finish his speech, knowing that its impact has totally disappeared. Then the investiture of fifteen men begins, and in another twenty minutes, this ceremony for which he has longed for so many months is over.

Russell pulls him aside and they walk together towards the door leading downstairs to the main entrance. "Bit of stage-fright, my friend? Never mind, we all understand what's what. The legal profession is now solidly in place, and we can go to my house for a celebratory meal." He laughs and slaps White on the back. "Eliza has made some syllabub especially for you."

# Chapter Thirty-One

*November 1797*

In spite of his resolutions to be a better husband in this new world, John White finds it hard to stifle his irritation with Marianne's views and behaviour. When he first saw her on the wharf at Quebec, he had for a moment felt happy, picturing the joy of having a warm body beside him in bed. Then as he kissed her, he'd become aware of the paint on her cheeks and those damnable artificial eyebrows she always wore in London—made of mouse skin.

And then, he had noticed his children. It was clear at once that Charles and William did not remember him. They clutched each other's hands and stood by the baggage, not moving an inch towards him. But Ellen had made up for this disappointment. "Papa, Papa," she cried, throwing her arms around his waist and stretching up to receive his kiss. Ellen alone had sustained him on the long trip up the St. Lawrence and into Lake Ontario.

* * *

Tonight Marianne is harping away on one of her standard topics. He sits in his favourite withdrawing-room chair and tries not to hear her over the pages of his newspaper. But she gets up from her chair, comes over to him, peers over his raised paper and speaks down to him from above. There is no escape. At least, he reflects, she has got rid of the eyebrows and the paint on her cheeks. That much he has accomplished.

"Why can we not have more company, husband? We live next door to the Smalls, but we have yet to invite them to sup with us. Why?"

"Small is not as many rungs up the social ladder as I am, my dear, and in this place, the rungs of the ladder are all-important. And lately he has begun to put on airs which I find intolerable. Why do you not content yourself with our friends the Russells?"

"Mr. Russell is old and fat, and that sister of his, so doleful. I wish to meet people of my age. Mrs. Small is attractive, is she not, and if you worry about the rungs of the social ladder, is she not a bosom friend of Mrs. Elmsley who is right at the top?"

*What am I to say? I cannot risk the chance of having the Woman Small anywhere near me. Though she curries favour with the Chief Justice's wife and appears to be working to restore her reputation, who knows what she might get up to if we meet at an intimate gathering? She is quite capable of talking to me behind her hand or making a cryptic allusion to Niagara days.*

"If Miss Russell is 'doleful,' as you put it, perhaps you might consider the great loss she has suffered."

"Oh, she must get over it, move on. I can scarcely refrain from telling her so. But why do you seek to distract me by talking about Eliza Russell? I want to have the Smalls for supper. It's not natural to ignore close neighbours. I know our house is not as pretty as theirs, but that's not my fault. I do have a nice walnut teapoy inlaid with mother of pearl, and those flowered cups and saucers with the orange border would make the lady sit up and take notice."

"No." White shakes the pages of his paper, causing Marianne to move back out of range.

"I'm to sit around here, am I, while you go drinking at the garrison? I might just as well have stayed in England with that devil of a nanny your sister and brother-in-law set upon me. Night and day, day and night, she scrutinized my every move, treating me like a seven-year-old. Now I want some society. I will invite the Smalls myself if you do not."

"You shall do nothing of the kind. If you dare to do such a thing, I will throw you onto the first boat leaving for Lower Canada. You can fend for yourself. But before that day comes, I must ask you to empty the chamberpots. They stink."

"Why does that slattern you hired not do these loathsome tasks? What am I to do with the slut? She told me this very day she intends to leave soon to marry a German farmer in the place they call Markham. 'When I marries my man,' she said to me, I be going into my own house and farm. And damned be to service and the paltry sums I gets from the likes of youse and them other folk from over the lake.' That's the way the slut talks to me."

*Well at least I've got her off the topic of the Smalls onto another one of her favourites.*

He reaches for the decanter again. Oblivion may be what he must seek. But Marianne leaves the room in a huff, so at least he no longer has to listen to her infernal nattering. She goes up the stairs, slams the bedchamber door with a crash, and silence descends, mercifully.

Laughter from the kitchen reminds him of his children. The three of them have been in the warmth of the hearth putting a puzzle together. Charles and William now call him 'Papa' and seem to be quite at home in York. Though he has not always been a good husband, he has been more successful in his resolutions to be a good father, and he now remembers the commitment he has made to his children's education. He looks at the decanter of wine. He has drunk most of it, yet he feels coherent enough for the task of helping them with their studies.

He calls to them, and they come into the withdrawing room, laughing and flushed from the heat of the kitchen fire.

"Look, Papa," Ellen says, showing him a large wooden puzzle of Europe which they have put together. Ellen is now thirteen years of age, a slight, pretty child with her mother's fair complexion. White is happy she seems to enjoy Miss Russell who has been teaching her to crochet. William, who was a baby when he left England, is now a

163

chubby six-year-old. Charles is eight, a quiet lad who has said very little in the weeks he has been in York. But White has watched him observe things, his large brown eyes fixed on his mother and father during their quarrels. *What has our acrimony done to him?*

He seats them at the dining-room table and reads them *Goody Two Shoes,* an old book of Mary's which Miss Russell has given him. The boys never tire of the tale, but he sees Ellen fiddling with the ribbons on her dress and senses she is bored. When he finishes the story, he sets Charles, who knows his alphabet, to making words that match familiar ones from the story they have just heard. He doesn't know what to do with William, except to take him on his knee and get him to write WWWWW with a quill, spattering ink all over his new buff breeches in the process. As for Ellen, Miss Russell, bless her, has given him an idea.

"You like puzzles, my dear?"

"Oh yes, Papa, but we have already conquered that one." She points to the map of Europe.

"Try this." He shows her a square piece of paper with twelve holes drawn onto it. "Miss Russell has drawn these," he tells her. "Now see if you can cut the paper into four pieces of the same shape. The catch is that each piece of paper must have three holes in it."

With the children occupied, he has time to reflect. This slapdash approach to education, while better than nothing, has few positive merits. Perhaps he can scrape together enough money to enrol the lads in William Cooper's school in George Street. The man provides instruction in reading, writing, arithmetic, and English grammar with, as he says in an advertisement in *The Upper Canada Gazette*, "great attention paid to virtue and morals." That would be a godsend. They get no training from his wife.

His head aches from the argument with Marianne and from the burden of his children. And now Ellen is crying. "I can't get it right, Papa. You'll have to help me."

He takes up the puzzle and tries to remember what his friend showed him. But the wine has dulled his intellect. "I

164

can't get it straight myself," he says. "We'll have to ask Miss Russell. Why don't you go over to her house tomorrow morning and ask her?"

Ellen mops her eyes with the back of her hand and starts to laugh. "Oh, Papa, I feel so much better knowing you can't figure it out either."

He laughs with her, feeling a spurt of happiness to have his daughter with him again. She is so much like Mary, spirited and funny. "Why don't you read me *Goody Two Shoes*?" he asks. "Your voice will be so much better than mine for the orphan girl."

Ellen reads. That English nanny of Sam's was a godsend in spite of what Marianne claims.

# Chapter Thirty-Two

*March 1798*

With the departure of the slattern for the green pastures of Markham, the Whites' domestic life has improved. They have a new cook now, a thin woman with a lined face, her wavy blonde hair pulled back in a thick braid. She applied for a position at the Russells' house, but they, having four servants already, did not need her. Miss Russell, however, recommended her to the Whites.

White has had the German immigrant William Berczy build a small log cabin for his new servant and her family in the back of the property. It gives him and Marianne privacy. White has no wish to have an outsider know too much about the state of their marriage.

Mrs. Page, as she calls herself, has small twin daughters who tag about after her. Marianne thought they would be an impediment, but they are happy, unobtrusive children and Charles and William enjoy playing with them.

Right now, his wife is setting out the scones which Mrs. Page has left on the hearth for their breakfast. He has looked forward to enjoying them with butter and baked apples, but he can tell by the way Marianne is banging the plates about that something is sticking in her craw.

"Is it right, husband, that our sons should associate with Cook's children?"

"Why not? It is an advantage for you, is it not? She will keep an eye on them, and you will have more free time. Eventually I shall enrol them in school and they will be off your hands during the day. You might, however, give more of your attention to Ellen. She should not be running loose through the town the way she seems to be."

"Where have Cook's children come from? Where is the woman's husband? I have tried to get answers, but she says nothing."

"You wanted a good cook and household helper. Let us enjoy her. She makes good bread, does not hold her nose when she empties the chamber pots, or offend our ears with her complaints. Servants of her calibre are impossible to come by in this world. Have I not told you the story of William Jarvis's outburst to his father-in-law? He showed me the letter one day which he wrote during the hours he was supposed to be helping me with the land grants. He pushed it right under my nose, and I read what he said to the old man. 'For God's sake, try and bring out a servant or two with you; the whole country cannot produce one fit to put in Hell's Kitchen.'"

"You never answer my questions, do you? She may well be a good servant, but I want to know something about her background."

"She dropped down from Heaven into our kitchen. Let us be thankful for her and forget about everything else."

His breakfast ruined by their marital discourse, White retreats to the coat hooks in the hallway where he dons his heavy knee-length woollen coat to face the swirling snow which he saw earlier through the window of their bedchamber.

He slams the front door on Marianne's mutterings. She has become more strident in the years she was without him in England. Her laudanum habit appears to have dissipated, and he almost regrets that. It kept her quiet and more passive. At the moment, though, he regrets most mentioning William Jarvis. The very name stirs his anger. The man is still dithering about in Niagara, loath to make the move across the water. White now writes out most of the land grants himself, but receives only fifty per cent of the money raised in the process. *If I had the lazy fool here, I'd break his head open.*

He heads for the foot of Berkeley Street where Peter Russell—the direct opposite of Jarvis—has fulfilled his promise of a court house. He has succeeded in putting the idle Queen's Rangers to work in the completion of Government House. Though none of them ever constructed a building before, the results are tolerable. The south wing is now fitted up for a temporary meeting-place for the Court of King's Bench, and the north wing is to receive the next sitting of Parliament in June. Russell is still hoping to fill in the centre of the structure with a residence to house the Lieutenant-Governor.

"It will be ready for his Excellency when he returns from his leave of absence," Russell has said to him time after time. "I'm sorry that, for the present, the cost is too prohibitive to carry out the instructions he gave me before he left for England."

"Face it, man, the Gov will not be returning," White has said over and over. "When the Brits recognize the fact, what can they do but appoint *you* as our next Governor? You have been a whirlwind in the establishment of this new capital, and your reward must surely be to take the governance of the province."

But as he says this, he cannot help but remember how he, the first Attorney-General of Upper Canada, was passed over for promotion in favour of John Elmsley, whom he and Russell both hate.

Though the court house is ready, British justice in this godforsaken backwater is largely unchanged from his time in Niagara. As he passes through the front door, he sees one of the court louts heating the branding iron in the great wood stove in the corner of the room. Daily he listens to the screams of some poor wretch forced to stretch out his hand and have burned thereon the first letter of his offence.

"Good day, your Honour," the man says to him, his face red from the heat of the fire.

"And who is your victim today?"

"One Hiram Jones. Forged a signature for nine shillings, the bugger. But he's not getting off with the branding. Thirty-nine lashes he'll have on his fat back— which I am happy to administer." He points to the whipping frame in another corner of the room where transgressors are tied in place to receive floggings. "People can come to see that one. Should be a merry old time."

"Can you put it off until today's trial is over?"

"Glad to oblige, Your Honour. It will be even a better spectacle for folk later in the day, when their work is over. But right now, I'll get to the branding."

White retreats to the small room off the main courtroom. He stuffs his ears with pieces of beeswax that he cut from the candles on the sideboard, melted, and shaped into ear stoppers which he keeps in his desk here at the court house. The screams of Hiram Jones sear his brain nevertheless. *And we are to believe that Odysseus's crew shut out the Sirens' songs with wax?*

When the torture is over, he goes back into the courtroom to wind up the case he is now prosecuting. He has been forced in this new place, in spite of his resolutions, to resume cases involving people from First Nations' bands. A man called McKewen, a member of the Queen's Rangers, has brutally murdered a Mississauga chief who went to the assistance of his sister whom the scoundrel was trying to rape. White has proceeded quickly with the prosecution, and hopes for satisfaction for his Indian chief.

John Elmsley has recently moved to York after quarrelling with Russell for months over the relocation of the courts. Now he sits resplendent on his wooden throne, throwing a spate of Latin at the Grand Jury who, farmers all, understand not a word. Finally, seeing their incomprehension, Elmsley sighs and says, "I await the Grand Jury's verdict."

The foreman gives it. "No bill. The Attorney-General has produced no conclusive proof that the Mississauga chief is dead."

*Oh my god, at every turn in my struggles to find justice for the natives, I am thwarted. Why did I hope for anything better?*

\* \* \*

169

The one bright moment in White's day is the platter of salmon which Mrs. Page has roasted on the hearth and set before them for supper. Marianne seems pleased with it, too, and the bottle of good French wine supplied on account by the King Street merchant rounds out the meal. For a half-hour, all is well.

"You bartered for this excellent treat from an Indian, did you, Mrs. Page?" he asks, as the woman comes in with more mashed potatoes.

"No, sir." She looks embarrassed and retreats to the kitchen, saying nothing more.

"Where did it come from, then?" He feels a twinge of heartburn as he wonders if Marianne has been running up more bills with the merchant.

Silence. Then Ellen says. "I got it."

"You, child? Where?"

His daughter swallows, and then proceeds in a loud voice. "I went out on the bay with Jacob, an Indian boy I know. He hacked out a large hole in the ice with his axe. Then we both leaned over the side and looked down into the water." She pauses, a smile lighting her face, and says, "It was exciting, Papa. There were so many fish wriggling and darting about. I held a lighted torch while my friend plunged his spear into a big one."

"You were out alone on the ice with a native?" White tries to remain calm, but he can hear his voice swelling in anger.

"No, no, Papa. There were several Indian women and Jacob's brothers were there, too. They were all fishing. They get a dollar, Jacob said, for six big salmon. But he gave me this one free for holding the—"

"Stop, stop! I will hear no more!" He bangs his fist on the table. Ellen screams, her mother begins to whimper, and Charles and William add their cries to the cacophony.

The sobs and screams smite him. He takes deep breaths and tries to pull himself together. "Go, Ellen," he says to her, his voice softening, "go and get Cook to make you a cup of tea."

She runs off, holding a handkerchief to her eyes. He turns to Marianne. "You, wife, you are responsible for all this. It is your fault the girl runs wild about the town. Did I not caution you about her conduct this very morning?"

But as he says this, he recognizes that Ellen is not to blame. And perhaps Marianne is not at fault either. He's sorry he has upset their fine meal. He has often complained about the scarcity of food and its expense in this desolate wilderness, and now that he reflects, he realizes Ellen probably thought he would welcome the gift. Undoubtedly she saw no reason to ask her mother's permission to go on the lake. If she hadn't been completely innocent of wrong doing, she would not have been so open about her actions.

The day has been an utter ruin. How is he to survive?

# Chapter Thirty-Three

*September 1798*

Though Eliza Russell and her brother Peter now have four servants to carry out all the chores in their fine new house in York, Eliza misses the tasks she used to do with Mary: the making of butter in the "up and down" churn, whopping up cream for the syllabub Mr. White used to like so much, picking the spring wildflowers which they tucked into the family Bible. Those flowers are now framed and placed on the walls in the hallway, and she should be mighty pleased, but she cannot bear to look at them.

For certain, it's not the tasks she pines for, but the company of the girl.

This morning Peter said to her as he put salt on his poached eggs, "Sister, I am happy that you have your poultry yard here. It must please you to collect these eggs each day. And I think your health has improved. You get out and about looking after all those hens, and that is good."

Yes, for certain she gets out and about, but it's not work in the poultry yard that has put a blush back in her cheeks. It's the hours she spends to-ing and fro-ing in the sunshine along the bay, looking across the water and wishing for Mary.

Today has been wretched. She went out with Job to pick up the windfall apples and a flock of passenger pigeons flew overhead, their wings beating with such a mighty flap that she could scarce hear what her servant was saying to her. Then, when he picked up an apple and flung it at the birds, knocking one to the ground, she was quite undone, and had to go into the house where she has been for the last hour, sobbing in her bedchamber. *Mary, Mary, my girl, come back.*

Their fine iron doorknocker sounds. Eliza mops at her eyes and waits. Peggy is to answer the door, but she considers herself too uppity for the task. There's another bang of the knocker, and Eliza knows that she must move down the stairs into the hallway to answer.

A small girl in a dimity frock and apron stands there, a basket in her hands.

*Mary, Mary, you've come back, thank the Lord.* But then she sees the dirty dress and the hair that needs a good brush. "Come in, Ellen, the sun in my eyes has made me quite blind for a moment."

The girl comes into the hallway and hands the basket to her. "Mama says she and Papa will come over this night to hear the reading. Mama is quite chuffed about it. She sends these gingerbread cookies to help out." Ellen pulls back the cloth to show her mother's offering and adds, laughing, "Don't be afraid, Miss Russell. They're real tasty. Mrs. Page made them, not Mama."

"Thank you. And thank your mother. And Mrs. Page."

When Ellen leaves, Eliza takes the basket to the kitchen and unpacks it. She slides the gingerbread onto a platter. Yes, it looks good. The Whites' cook has put some raisins into it. Only the good Lord knows where she procured raisins. Must have cost a pretty penny.

"Let us ready ourselves," she says to Job, the one servant she can abide in this fine new house. "Guests are a-coming this evening to hear your master read."

Reading aloud has become a common pastime in this place they call York. Dear Peter has a beautiful, sonorous voice, and the reading of the new book which her friend Lizzie has sent from Harwich makes a good evening of entertainment without much to-do on her part. With the gingerbread and some good cheese from their farm to the north, there will be little to make a fuss over.

She has had to pull together many suppers and tea parties since Peter has become Administrator of Upper Canada. Mighty happy she is, though, about her brother's fate. He is for certain the most important person in this new world of York. No matter that the Jarvises hate him. What was he to do when those new German immigrants couldn't get their land grants? Things have firmed up now Mr. White does most of Mr. Jarvis's work. And since Mrs. Jarvis no longer wants to visit, she no longer has to listen to the woman's blather.

Sixty-three years of age her brother be, and yet in the brief time he has ruled this new capital, he has accomplished so much. God be her witness, she will do what she must do to help him.

* * *

Her dear brother arrives home at seven o'clock. He seems tired, the pouches under his eyes swollen and grey-looking. "Remind me, sister," he says, throwing his wig onto the back of a chair in the kitchen. Though they have the finest house in York, they still prefer to talk in the kitchen by the warmth of the hearth.

"Remind you, Peter?"

"Whom have we invited for this evening?"

"The Elmsleys—" She finds herself cut off by a loud groan.

She pats his arm. "Consider, most of the time you will be reading, and the Chief Justice will have little chance to say anything. And you will be the better for seeing Mr. White and his wife, and I have also asked the Powells to come—"

"Very well, I shall suffer Elmsley, if I must. But I trust you did not invite the Smalls? That I could not endure. Small's airs in this new place are more than I can stand. Why, when I was coming across Berkeley Street just now, there was the man himself in front of that house of his with the pretentious name. He was standing at the front door in knee breeches, silk stockings, and silver-buckled shoes. 'Come to supper,' he says to me. 'We have a good spread ready.' Wanted to show off that new dining-table he keeps boasting about."

174

Peter's breathing has become quite puffy, and Eliza seeks to divert him. "Your attire is spread out on your bed, brother, and your grizzle wig has just come back from the wigmaker."

"At great expense, no doubt."

Eliza pours him a tumbler of Irish whisky from Bushmills.

"And where in tarnation did this come from?"

"It arrived this very day on the schooner from Kingston. Do not ask me what it cost, brother. Just enjoy it."

He takes the tumbler and heads for his bedchamber to change his attire. As she watches him depart, she turns to Job who has observed and heard it all. "Get Jupiter to help him dress, will you? The lad must do something for the wages he receives."

Job goes out the back door to find the boy. He is as lazy as his mother Peggy, and he lurks in the stables or fishes down at the bay in order to keep from doing as he is bid.

Eliza looks around the kitchen, searching for what she dreads. But Job, bless his kind heart, has made certain that there is not one feather of that passenger pigeon to be found anywhere.

She takes a deep breath and looks at the mantel clock. Seven-thirty. This wretched day has near passed. Now she must ready herself for the bigwigs. But seeing some fresh cream in a bowl on the table, she thinks about a treat she still has time to make for Mr. White.

# Chapter Thirty-Four

*The same evening, September 1798*

White must acknowledge that Marianne is the best-looking woman in the withdrawing room. Her muslin gown criss-crossed with ribbons shows perhaps too much of her fine bosom, but she makes Mrs. Powell and Mrs. Elmsley look positively frumpy. Dear Miss Russell has tried to enhance her severe black gown with a necklace of agates, but her red-rimmed eyes bespeak some inner sorrow. With a pang, White remembers that this day marks an anniversary of Mary's death. *I must come over tomorrow with some fall flowers from my garden.*

Marianne's shrill laugh over something Mrs. Elmsley has said grates on his ears. True, he enjoyed that fine bosom for a week or two when she first arrived in York. But now her silliness drives him mad. In sober moments, he faces the fact that he used to like silly women, especially pretty ones—as paramours, that is. *Why did I make one of them a permanent part of my life?*

But tonight is a harmless way to give her the society she craves and keep her from plaguing him with her complaints. Miss Russell is a kind woman, warm-hearted and devoted to her brother. Mrs. Powell and Mrs. Elmsley are the crème de la crème of their muddy York world. Surely here in this withdrawing room Marianne can find society of irreproachable quality.

And indeed, since they have come for the past two weeks to hear Russell read from *Gulliver's Travels,* Marianne has appeared to take great delight in the adventures of Gulliver in Lilliput. She has laughed unaffectedly at the description of the Lilliputians taking Gulliver's measurements with a rule of an inch in length, and at their protracted and bitter parliamentary wars over which end of the egg should be broken. She has even appeared to understand the satire of the Big Endians and the Little Endians.

Now, at this, the third evening of reading, White relaxes in a comfortable armchair and waits for Russell to begin.

"Tonight we shall start the voyage to Brobdingnag," Russell announces. "It contains some of my favourite passages." *And mine, especially Swift's description of the nursemaid's monstrous breast and nipple.*

Then Marianne's voice breaks into his reverie. "But surely, Mr. Russell, we have not finished all of Lilliput?"

"Indeed, ma'am, we finished last Thursday."

"But you did not read one of the best parts, sir!"

Russell's face grows red. White watches the effort with which he plants a smile on his doughy face. "I assure you I did not miss a word." He lays the book down on the table next his chair and rises to throw another log on the fire.

While he is doing this, Marianne grabs up the volume and riffles through the pages. "Here it is," she announces to the gathering, "Mr. Russell has forgotten to read us the passages about the fire at the Emperor's palace."

Elmsley hooks his thumbs into his waistcoat and laughs. "*Vir in mare excidit!*"

Russell has returned to his chair. "Confound it, Elmsley, speak the King's English. *Nescio de quo loqueris!*"

*Good man, he has actually remembered the Latin phrase I gave him weeks ago when we first met Elmsley in the Niagara tavern.* But White himself knows what Elmsley has just said. It's "Man overboard!" And it exactly sums up the moment that is surely about to happen.

Russell now stretches out his hand towards Marianne, no doubt expecting her to hand over the book. But she ignores the gesture. This is her chance to impress the Elmsleys, and she intends to make the most of it. She will show everyone, by God, that she too is a scholar.

Keeping her finger in the open book, she continues. "It's so funny. We must not miss it. The Lilliputian palace is ablaze. The little people are labouring mightily to put out the fire. But their pails are the size of a thimble and the flames are growing. So Gulliver, having drunk plentifully that evening, pisses upon the blaze and extinguishes it in seconds."

There is an intake of breath around the room. Only Elmsley laughs and repeats, "Didn't I sum it up a minute ago? *Vir in mare excidit!*" Miss Russell, very red in the face, makes a hasty exit to the dining room. Powell, who seems to have picked up a fever during a trip to Boston, mops his brow. Mrs. Powell shakes her head and one of her tight little curls pops out from under the gold fillets that bind her hair. Mrs. Elmsley's jaw is agape.

"And does Gulliver receive any thanks for this act of kindness?" Marianne continues, never one to let well enough alone. "No indeed. The empress is upset because, you see"—here she erupts in giggles—"the Lilliputians have issued an edict stating that it is a capital offence to make water within the royal precincts."

In the silence that follows this sally, Elmsley asks, "Do tell us, dear madam, how came you to read the elevating incident you have just related?"

"Why, it was my husband's book," she says, turning her head now and addressing him. "Mr. White, you recall the volume you were reading when you set sail for Canada? You left it behind in the withdrawing room, and I read it. And mightily amusing it was, I assure you."

"Let us go into the dining room now," Miss Russell says, standing in the doorway. "Time for some victuals, and then my brother will begin his reading."

They follow her towards the platters of cheese and gingerbread which the maid Peggy has set out on the walnut table. "Rum punch for everyone," Miss Russell says, "but for Mr. White, I have his special treat." She gestures towards a small bowl. "Syllabub!"

In the clatter of saucers and the clinking of glasses, the awkward moments in the withdrawing room dissipate. But White knows that the tea tables of York will be abuzz on the morrow.

178

# Chapter Thirty-Five

*October 1798*

John White sits in his cramped office off the main room of the court house. He does not have a case to prosecute today, but he is here to write a letter to his brother-in-law Sam Shepherd, and he does not want Marianne to know what he is about. She might demand to read it, and there will be an item or two in it that he must keep from her.

\* \* \*

Yesterday he placed an order for shoes and boots with a new German immigrant, name of Brunshilde, who operates his business from a small room in his cabin in the bush far north of Queen Street. When the man took measurements, cut out the necessary pieces of leather, and told him the cost, White had yelled at him. "Outrageous. You are no better than a thief!"

"Fine leather must be imported from Cordova," the man said, with a shrug of his brawny shoulders. "Withdraw your order if you wish."

He had already spent an hour walking northward along a worn trail through the woods. An hour's walk back home with nothing to show for his exertion seemed stupid. He capitulated. As he handed over the money, he looked over the man's shoulders. Behind her husband, sitting at the kitchen table, the wife smirked.

As White tramped back home through the woods, he knew it was time to confront the truth. He was bankrupt.

He'd pulled out his handkerchief and mopped the tears from his eyes.

On his way south, he met Russell, riding towards him on the fine white charger he keeps in the stable on his property. "Want to climb up, White?" he asked. "Beau can easily accommodate your weight. I'm just on my way to Kurt Brunshilde. With all the walking around I do in this new town, I badly need some good solid boots."

White recounted his tale of woe to his friend. "I grow angry," he'd said, "when I think that six years of the prime of my life have been devoted to His Majesty's service at an expense I can never hope to cover."

"Join the band, White. We wretched colonials are in hell. We work day and night, and the Brits in London don't give a damn about paying us our stipends. You made the point long ago that I had no right to sit as a judge. But I have reappointed myself to the Court of King's Bench because, as you know, I need the money. I'm administrator here, it's up to me to make all the decisions, but my remuneration for all this extra work has not increased by one penny."

White made no response. He has heard Elmsley rail against Russell's "damnable presumption" in setting himself up as a judge, and in theory he agrees with the Chief Justice. But he hates the arrogance of the man. Russell is his friend, and in this benighted country friends must stand by each other.

And it was then that Russell offered him some interesting news. "Powell is bad with the ague," he said. "Mrs. Powell was over to the house this morning to get some of the bark my sister keeps at the ready."

"How bad?" White had asked, his spirits suddenly lifting.

"The man probably won't last more than a week or two. Why don't you write to that brother-in-law of yours and see what he can do for you?"

"I'd better keep walking," White had said, "and get the letter written this morning in time for the packet boat for

New York." Not one more word had they spoken, but they both understood the intent of the discussion.

He had picked up his pace then, leaping over the rocks in his path, focusing on that ray of hope offered him by Powell's possible demise.

* * *

Now White pulls a sheet of fine linen paper from the drawer of his desk. Powell, as puisne judge of the Court of King's Bench, makes twice as much as White's stipend, and he does not have to scrape pennies from private practice and allotment of land grants.

He dips his quill into the inkwell, chews at the feathered end for a moment or two and then writes.

*My dear Sam:*

*I write to you in great haste. Mr. Justice Powell is seriously ill. If there should be the misfortune of his death, I hope you will solicit his office for me as I understand the salary is seven hundred and fifty pounds per annum.*

*I am forever out of pocket doing the King's business. I cannot live in this place on four hundred pounds. Everything that makes life supportable here must be brought in from overseas. Just this morning, I paid a shoemaker seven pounds for shoes and boots.*

*There are times when I feel hopeless, disappointed, and without prospect. My life is wretched, and yet there are people in this place who think my situation enviable.*

*I received your letter a month ago, but I have not mentioned to Mrs. White your news about the death of her sister. The wilderness here has few charms for her, and I know that the sad tidings would only upset her further.*

*Ever yours,*
*John White*

He reads the letter, then rereads it. Folds it and seals it. Pulls it open and looks at it again.

*Whiny and despicable. I have come to this: that I hope a worthy man will die so that I can have his position and emolument.*

He seals up the letter again. Looks at his pocket watch. Time to get to the wharf and catch the attention of the crew of the packet boat.

As he passes the pot-bellied stove, he sees the clerk has fired it up. He opens the front door of the stove, pauses for a moment, and looks at the burning coals within. Then he throws the letter on the coals and watches the flames leap up.

# Chapter Thirty-Six

*January 1799*

Marianne comes into the withdrawing room and hands her husband a letter. "I have written to your sister," she says. "Please affix a seal, and see that it gets overland to New York in time to catch a packet boat to England."

She looks at the case clock. "I must see to my gown for tomorrow's festivities. What a lark!" She laughs as she leaves the room.

She is in a merry mood for a change. Queen Charlotte's Birth Day Ball is to be held tomorrow, and she looks forward to the excitement of an evening out. He has agreed to go. It will be held at Government House, and there will be no rent to which he must contribute for a room in a tavern. Subscription balls are à la mode here, and usually in addition to the rent, he must donate several bottles of wine and a cold dish or two to the festivities. But Peter Russell has told him that the cost of the ball tonight will be borne by the government.

He takes the letter Marianne has given him, folds it, and reaches for the wax. But he is curious to see what news she is sending to his sister. He unfolds the letter and reads it. The first two paragraphs are the usual inconsequential blatherings about her life here. Then he comes to the last paragraph.

*Dear Elizabeth, I ask you to send by earliest post a fashionable bonnet and also whatever is most worn around the waist now.*

The impertinence of the woman to think that there is money to spare for frippery! He throws the letter on the fire. He will say nothing to her. Packet boats go down regularly, especially in these winter months, and if she gets no answer, she will assume her letter is at the bottom of the sea.

He must at all costs avoid a quarrel which will bring on the headaches that plague him. Best he should go this night to the garrison and enjoy some rum punch. Perhaps he will be able to avoid David Smith, now Surveyor-General, who last night induced him to drink nearly a bottle of port and two bottles of porter. Smith's beautiful, rich wife has recently died, and the man seeks him out for company and solace. *At least that's what I tell myself: that my drinking with Smith may be excused because the man needs my company.*

Last night's fit of indulgence was in part brought on by the sight of Justice Powell, large as life, telling a lewd joke at a table in the Mess. The judge seemed thoroughly cured of the shakes and sweats of his ague. He greeted White with warmth, explaining that Miss Russell's bark remedy had been efficacious in promoting his recovery.

Soon after that piece of news, White went with Smith to the bar and drank away the rest of the evening.

*But at least that wretched letter I almost sent lies in a pile of ashes. I have risen above the worst of the ignominy that besets me.*

Ellen is in the hallway with his stock in her hand. She knit it for him for Christmas. "Pull it up over your nose, Papa, when the wind blows off the lake. See?" She puts it over her own neck and pulls it up to demonstrate.

He laughs and pinches her cheek. Miss Russell seems to like the child and has shown her how to knit. As he pulls it over his head and adjusts it around his chin, he feels the warmth of the lambs wool and the comfort of Ellen's solicitude.

Marianne accosts him as he is donning his greatcoat. "Oh, husband, pray do not wear that powdered wig. Your hair is so abundant, and no fashionable man in London has worn such a wig for several years."

She is always harping on London fashions. But he is glad to oblige her in this instance. The wig is itchy, and he will be relieved of the expense of having it cleaned weekly at the barber's. As he takes it off, she wraps herself into the front of his greatcoat and snuggles against him.

*Things should go well later if I can just keep myself sober enough to enjoy her warm body.* "Do not go to bed too early, my dear," he says, winking at her when he notices Ellen's attention straying to the location of his gloves on the shelf of the wardrobe.

In the next minute, William and Charles have also come to the front door to see him off. He notices their wind-burned cheeks. "You have been out on the bay today, boys?" The Russells often take his sons out in their cariole on the ice, and they enjoy the wild rides behind Beau and the upsets into the snowbanks lining the icy path the settlers and the Indians have made.

"Not Mr. Russell today, Papa!" says William. "We went fox-hunting with Sam Jarvis and his papa. It was so much fun, wasn't it, Charlie?"

Charles nods and smiles. Both the boys' cheeks are round and red as apples.

Since Idiot Jarvis and his bitch of a wife have finally resettled themselves in York, they have sought "to bring new diversions to the inhabitants of this wretched place," as Jarvis wrote in a letter to the editor of one of the town's newspapers, Well, so be it. It's none of his concern. He and the Jarvises scarcely speak since he now does most of Jarvis's work and collects—at Russell's insistence—half the fees that used to go to the lazy bugger.

His sons don't need to know about any of this, at least from him. No doubt the town gossips will spread the word soon enough. "I'd like to hear about your fox hunt," he says now as he fastens his wool coat.

It's William who tells the tale of the fox taken in a bag out upon the bay and then set loose with the hounds unleashed to run it down, followed by the concourse of gentlemen on horseback and families in carioles and sleighs.

"Hoicks! Hoicks!" Charles yells.

Though he is glad to hear Charles's enthusiasm, White has no idea what he's talking about. William explains, "It's what Mr. Jarvis and Sam yelled as we chased after Mr. Reynard. We yelled it, too."

"Hoicks! Hoicks! Hoicks!" Both boys are now screaming.

"Off you go, Papa," says Ellen, "before my dear little brothers blast your eardrums to bits. They're worse than the cannons."

He walks out into his front yard. It's a full moon, and the air is still. He looks back. Marianne, Ellen, and the boys stand in the lighted doorway waving.

# Chapter Thirty-Seven

*January 1799*

It is the evening of Queen Charlotte's Birth Day Ball, and the Russells pick up the Whites in their sleigh for the short ride to Government House. The big white horse called Beau is in harness with a fine grey mare, and there is a black driver in livery whom Russell addresses as "Mundy."

"Quite a stylish rig, Russell," White says.

"Governor Simcoe insisted that I have a sleigh, a cariole, *and* a wagon. They go with the position of Administrator, he told me. Too bad, though, that I have still not been reimbursed by the Colonial Office, but I am in hopes that all will be settled when His Excellency returns to his post."

*Not bloody likely you'll ever see the Gov again. Or hear from the Colonial Office either.* But he makes a non-committal noise in the back of his throat.

The large room in Government House, where the legislature meets each summer, has been set up this evening as a dining room. Sideboards and tables are splendidly covered with hundreds of candles that catch the sparkle of the starched linen, the wine glasses, and the fine Coalport china. Menservants—White recognizes several soldiers from the garrison hired for the occasion—stand about awaiting instructions from the steward.

Fashions inspired by the French Revolution seem to be the rage among the women of the town this year. Gone are the hoops and overskirts and huge hairstyles of yesteryear. Now the party gowns are sheer muslin gauze with low-cut necklines that show pretty bosoms to advantage. White

187

stands for a moment at the doorway of the room admiring the offerings on display.

He notices Betsy Small swanning about with Mrs. Elmsley. To be the bosom companion—there is surely a play on words here—of the wife of the Chief Justice is no doubt the crowning achievement of her sojourn in York. As she comes close to him, she pauses to point at something or other on the far side of the room. Then she sweeps in front of him, drawing up her skirts at the front to show off the slender ankles that are one of her main attractions and no doubt to remind him of what he has lost. For a moment, in spite of himself, he wants to take off her pink slippers and run his fingers up to the top of her elegant legs—and beyond.

"Like the new fashions, do you, White?" a voice from behind him says, cutting through his reverie. Turning around, he sees Peter Russell's cousin, William Willcocks, at his shoulder. He can feel the man's warm, fetid breath on his cheek, and his remarks have been loud enough that Mrs. Small has turned her head to laugh.

"You are looking mighty fine tonight, Mrs. White," Willcocks says to Marianne. She dips a very proper curtsy and White feels satisfied the evening will go well. He hopes the Small woman has heard the compliment to his wife. He is pleased to note that Marianne can hold her own with La Belle Small. She does not have the woman's slender feet, but her tiny waist and ample bosom are shown to advantage in the tight bodice of her new gown. He tries to put aside his concern about the expense of the silk which he allowed her to buy at auction at M'Dougal's Tavern. That blow to his pocketbook was followed by the bill of the local German dressmaker who sews a fine seam—and no doubt feeds upon strawberries, sugar, and cream.

"If only my cousin's sister could rig herself out in something decent," Willcocks continues, pointing at Miss Russell who is standing at the edge of the crowd, blessedly out of earshot. Her dress is a sombre grey with a high neck ruff, but she has added a pretty dark-red paisley shawl.

"I believe Miss Russell looks very well," White tells the man.

"Balderdash and bunkum," Willcocks replies, "she looks like a witch about to get on her broomstick." He picks at his nose. "But it's the money that counts, is it not? The woman has a small fortune in land grants her brother has given her, so I hear. I'd be interested in improving our acquaintance if it weren't for the marital burden I already carry. But a good cholera epidemic might change everything." He gives a snort of laughter and turns away to grab at a glass of shrub being passed by one of the soldiers.

*If only I could tell Russell about the filth this cousin of his spews forth. Can he not at least be polite to Miss Russell, knowing that his promotions to magistrate and postmaster and all his land grants have come to him through Russell's influence?*

"Come, husband," Marianne says, tugging at his sleeve. "I want to dance."

"Later. Right now, let's get some of that food."

Russell knows how to order a good spread. No squirrels anywhere. There is excellent whitefish, a vegetable curry, pork roast and gravy, venison, mincemeat tart, cherries in syrup, and imported Stilton cheese.

He heaps his plate again and again, trying not to hear Marianne's repeated cries of "Oh please, let us go now and dance."

At last he lays down his plate and ushers her into the adjoining room where the musicians from the garrison are striking up a country dance. There he leaves her with Miss Russell while he departs for the card-room where he intends to indulge himself in hot Madeira and several rounds of whist.

His partner is inevitably David Smith who will not dance because he is still in mourning for his wife. Although he wanted to avoid the man, he knows Smith is a canny player, and they manage to make five shillings each.

He is about to embark on another round when he hears a fiddler in the music room strike up the familiar strains of "Ae fond kiss and then we sever." For a moment he is transported back to a tavern in London where he sang the song to Marianne before leaving for Upper Canada. Though he had been glad to "sever" from her then, they had both cried. Perhaps it had been the wine they had drunk or the poignancy of the words . . .

Those words are now lilting back into his ears. He moves to the door to listen, wondering who in this room possesses such a lovely voice.

It is Marianne. She is standing in the middle of the little orchestra in her pretty gown, singing the words that made him cry all those years ago and which are having the same effect on him now. It's not the wine this time—he is still sober—it's the knowledge that perhaps they must again part if he is to survive in this world.

The song ends. Marianne smiles, evidently happy with her success, and for a moment White is proud and happy, too. He goes towards her, takes her hand, and goes onto the dance floor as the orchestra sounds the opening chords of "Sir Roger de Coverley."

"I knew that you had a pleasant voice, my dear. But your performance tonight had a professional quality that I have not until now been aware of."

"Please, husband, spare me your condescension. When you left me alone with that jailer of a nanny, I had to do something or I would have gone barmy. Your sister arranged for me to have singing lessons with an Italian tenor from Covent Garden. And you do not need to harp on the expense. Your brother-in-law paid for it all." She seems keen to start another squabble, so when the dance is over, he leaves her again with Miss Russell and returns to the whist table.

There's a supper at midnight, a tasty repast of cold tongue, roast chicken, meat pies, and bonbons. Marianne is quiet. Her eyes are red. She picks at her food and leaves most of it on her plate. *Probably tired.*

It's past two o'clock when he and Marianne and the Russells come out the front door of Government House to find Mundy waiting for them, the sleigh firmly planted at the end of the walkway so they do not have to leap into

190

snowdrifts like several other departing guests. There is a crescent moon over the lake, and the horses' breaths mist into the fresh, cold air.

As they pull the bearskins over themselves, Miss Russell says, "It was an elegant entertainment, dear Peter. I be mighty proud of you. And of you, too, Mrs. White. I did not know until this evening you had such a pretty voice. We must for certain arrange some evening entertainments at which you can give us a dollop or two more of your talent."

In his corner of the sleigh, White waits for Marianne to respond to the compliment. Instead from under the pile of bearskins comes the unmistakeable sound of sobbing.

Russell and his sister seem embarrassed, and Russell breaks the moment with a comment about the evening's breakages. "Four goblets and two Coalport plates," he says, "replacement value ten shillings."

White makes a commiserating comment, and the moment's awkwardness passes. The Russells drop them at their house before turning around to drive back to their own fine dwelling.

Marianne and he have barely closed the door behind them when she pounds on his chest, face bright red and eyes streaming. "She called me Cinderella. S-s-said I should have stayed by the hearth and not come to the ball. And the other one laughed."

"Who? Who called you names? Who laughed?"

"Mrs. S-S-Small," she sobs. "And Mrs. Elm-Elm-sley thought it a fine joke."

*Whatever is behind this little piece of cruelty from that bitch? I'll deal with it when I can. At the moment, though, I haven't the strength.*

"Go to bed, Marianne. Things look better in the morning."

He lies awake listening to her snuffles on the other side of the bed. Eventually she falls asleep, but when the morning sun finds its way through the window, he is still awake. *Breakages indeed. Forget the goblets and the china and concentrate on the destructive tittle-tattle of these women. A passel of Lilliputians mired in petty concerns, that's what they are.* And he's Gulliver, baffled and confounded by the small tyrannies, the wholly illogical issues that consume the denizens of this frozen little world.

# Chapter Thirty-Eight

*The next morning, January 1799*

Mrs. Page serves up some strong scalding tea that helps to clear his head. He is thankful his sons have gone off to school and the room is quiet. She then takes three poached eggs and several sausages from the hearth and sets them upon a plate. "Thank you," he manages to say. "This is an unusual bounty."

"One of Miss Russell's servants sent them over early this morning while you were still abed."

Mrs. Page must once have been beautiful. Her eyes are bright blue, and there is a becoming flush on her cheeks from the fire. She always wears a spotless cotton gown covered with a capacious apron. But this morning her face is lined and tired. "You arise early, Mrs. Page. We must give you one day a week in which you can get up at leisure before beginning your chores."

She curtsies. "The mistress is not well this morning, sir?"

"We did not get home from the ball until very late. She must be tired."

Ellen has just come into the kitchen. "I think it is more than that, Papa. I went in to see her just now and she is crying. She keeps sobbing about someone calling her Cinderella. Was it that nasty Mrs. Small?"

"Yes."

"Oh Papa, I think I know what it is all about. And Mrs. Page knows the story. So I might as well tell you here and now."

She pulls a copy of *The Upper Gazette* from the middle of the table, turns to page three, and points to an

193

advertisement in the bottom right-hand corner. She reads aloud: "The merchant Abner Miles, King Street East, offers a generous price for household ashes of nine pence a bushel in exchange for merchandise."

*Oh my God, now I know what's coming.*

"Remember, Papa, how Mama wanted some new stockings for the Queen Charlotte Ball and you told her to darn her old ones?"

He nods. *Let it all come out, child, so that I can feel like the blackguard I am. And I will not tell you how your Mama sulked and refused to pick up her needle even though there was but one tiny hole to fix.*

"And then she got this idea of taking the ashes from the hearth and transporting them to Mr. Miles's establishment. You were a big help with that task, Mrs. Page."

"We got three sacks full, did we not, Ellen?"

"Yes, three sacks, three very full and very dirty sacks. And Mama, you, and I dragged them all the way to Abner's store. It was a long haul, but everything turned out well. Mama got the prettiest silk stockings embroidered with leaves and pink flowers. Oh, Papa, you must have noticed how pretty they were."

*Not really. I think my attention was wholly directed to her bosom.* "I am happy that your mother got what she wanted, my dear. But I still do not understand this Cinderella business. Is it possible that Abner told the story about town?"

Mrs. Page speaks up. "Do not blame the merchant, sir. We were on our way home rather sooty-faced, I fear, from our endeavours, and we met Mrs. Small coming down her front walk. And the mistress said, 'Oh, Mrs. Small, see what I got for three sacks of ashes.' And then she unrolled the paper and showed the woman her new embroidered stockings. I was proud of the mistress. She did not try to hide what we had done. In fact, she was not a whit embarrassed."

"I was so happy for Mama, so happy about those pretty stockings. But now that nasty woman has got her in a pickle. What are you going to do, Papa?"

He covers his eyes and forehead with his right hand and tries to think. But now his head is pounding and no thought comes forth except . . . *She will pay for this humiliation of my wife. Silly and careless as Marianne is, she does not deserve this sordid attack from a woman who is no better than a common prostitute. And I brought it on by nitpicking about the expense of new stockings.*

"Go outside now, Ellen, if you please, and see what my little ones are doing. I shall get the master some more tea."

When the door closes behind Ellen, Mrs. Page comes forward and takes a seat beside him. "If it will help you, sir, I have some news about Mrs. Small."

"Well?"

"My brother has a friend in the one of the regiments at the garrison. A lieutenant he is, and there have been rumours about him and Mrs.—"

"Let it be, Mrs. Page. I do not want to hear anything more." *I already know the woman is a whore, and by God, she will suffer if I can manage anything.*

He goes upstairs to find his wife red-faced and blotchy. "Dress yourself and come to breakfast, Marianne. Why do you concern yourself with the likes of Mrs. Small? Now you will understand why I wanted to have nothing to do with the woman. Miss Russell is one of the best women in this town, and she sees nothing in your behaviour to censure. In fact she has worried about your grief of last night. She sent over eggs and sausages for your breakfast. Come now, get dressed, and eat. You will feel better when you have a tasty meal."

He takes her hand and pulls her towards him, wrapping his arms around her. Then he reaches into his waistcoat pocket and extracts the five shillings he won at whist. "Go to Abner Miles's store today and buy yourself a bonnet and something fashionable for that pretty waist of yours."

# Chapter Thirty-Nine

*April 1799*

For once, John White has an evening free of childish squabbles and marital nagging. The house is silent. Russell and his sister, bless them both, are giving the children supper and keeping them overnight. Miss Russell is showing Ellen a new embroidery stitch for a reticule they are making together. Russell and the boys are looking at insects under his new microscope. Russell, who has quite an interest in scientific experiments, is a good influence on Charles and William. Charles has started talking more of late, so enthusiastic is he about the insect specimens he and his brother have collected on these hot spring days. They have also found some tadpoles, and Russell is helping them track the creatures' metamorphosis into frogs.

As for Marianne, she has gone to play whist at Mrs. Powell's house. The judge's wife will keep her in line. No gambling or indiscreet behaviour will take place under that formidable woman's eye.

So he is free to try on his new frock coat of blue velvet. He turns round and round in front of the pier glass, admiring the fit of the shoulders and the way the back hangs. He's run up quite a tally with the tailor Otto, but the velvet collar and cannon buttons are worth it. His head looks so much better now that he has given up powdered wigs. And the lace cravat is perfect. Really, he cuts quite a figure. There's the cost of this rig, of course, but he's hopeful that his brother-in-law will be able to help him with a loan, though he hasn't heard from Sam for far too long.

Mrs. Page comes in with a cup of tea just as he is taking one last swing in front of the mirror. For a moment, he is embarrassed to have her discover him in self-admiration. But when she says, "Quite dashing, sir," her voice is sincere and entirely free of irony. On impulse he offers her his arm, and the two of them break into a waltz in front of the pier glass. They spin round and round the room, happy together in the moment. Then she breaks away, curtsies, and leaves the room, her face flushed but smiling. *A pleasant woman, and pretty, in her way. Somehow big breasts and tiny waists no longer attract me the way they once did.*

He puts on a loose silk gown and settles himself in his favourite armchair. These warm spring nights are lovely. For three weeks now, he has not had to light the fireplaces and thus he is no longer troubled by the cough that the stink of smoke brings on. He puts his feet up on the stool and plucks a book from the parcel that arrived this day. The waterways now being open, communication between York and the outer world is again possible.

He is laughing over the ballad of John Gilpin and his runaway horse when he hears a loud thumping on the front door. Opening it, he finds John Small, now a magistrate of the town, standing on the step. Behind Small is a strange little man in a mask. Small grabs this person by the shoulder and thrusts him through the doorway.

"Look to your responsibilities, White," he says in a loud and arrogant voice. "I have had a fine run-around with this little rowdy tonight. There should be a bloody rule against these damned shenanigans. If you weren't the Attorney-General, I'd have laid charges." And with that statement, Small marches down the front walk into the darkness.

White gawks, open-mouthed, at the figure crouching on the carpet before him. Then he leans over and yanks the man to his feet, staring at the filthy masked face and dirty clothing. He's wearing a broad straw hat, plain shirt, and leather breeches covered with a heavy fabric apron. Is he a

197

butcher? Why is he here? White grabs the candle from the hall table and looks again. Not a butcher. His wife.

"What is this, woman? You went out of here at seven o'clock dressed in your tea gown. You told me you were playing whist with Mrs. Powell. What has happened?"

Stripped of her whimperings and excuses, her story boils down to this: she has lied to him about everything. The evening with Mrs. Powell was a clever piece of fiction. Though she went out the front door dressed in her tea gown, she went straight to a tavern where she met Peggy, Miss Russell's maid, who was waiting with the butcher's disguise. In a room in the tavern—her presence there no doubt observed by all and sundry—she changed from the respectable wife of the Attorney-General into a common butcher.

"Why? Why?"

"I wanted to have some fun, husband. You surely cannot think that I would have fun with that bullying harridan and her deck of cards?"

He wants to slap her, but he breathes deeply and tries to keep control. "And what stupidity did your notion of fun lead you into?"

"When I was ready in my butcher costume, I waited at the front door of the tavern. Then two carriages of men from the garrison—do not look so shocked, Mr. White, yes, from the garrison where you waste so many hours—picked me up and took me to a . . ."

"A what, for God's sake?"

"A shivaree."

*Lord, a shivaree.* White knows all about shivarees: a cursed custom that came across the border with the United Empire Loyalists and the rest of those damned Yankee upstarts.

"Old Mahoney, the butcher, died just after I arrived here, remember?"

He does remember something about the man severing an artery during an encounter with his knife while he was cutting up a carcass. "But so what? Get to the point."

198

"His wife, she's sixty-two, and this day she married Mahoney's apprentice. He's twenty-five. Wanted to have a second 'go,' I suppose."

Well, he can almost picture the next part. Shivarees always involve shenanigans by local louts who show up at a married couple's house on their first night, banging pots and pans and demanding money or booze to go away and leave the honeymooners in peace.

"It was a fine old ruckus, they made," Marianne tells him, now in full flight as she recounts the details. "The men from the garrison put their uniforms on back to front and stuck feathers in their hair like the redskins. Oh it was funny what they did. They banged and banged with their drums and rang cowbells until the apprentice came to the door. 'Give us money for whisky or we'll stay here the whole night,' they said. And he had to give in and hand over some coins to spend in the tavern."

"And what was your part in all this?"

"Why . . . why . . . I was the ghost."

"The what?" *But do I really want to know the worst?* He remembers that sometimes, on these lamentable occasions, if it is a second marriage, the hoodlums bring along an open coffin in which lies a person dressed as the first spouse. *Surely the woman, for all her stupidity, would not stoop to this?*

But of course she has. "When the young man opened the door, I stood up in the coffin and said I was old Mahoney come back to take revenge on their marriage." And after a pause in which he wonders how he can face up to the shame of it all, she adds, "Oh husband, the look on his face . . . it was so funny." A hiccough bursts from her, carrying with it the stench of cheap whisky.

*There's more, I know: the hours afterwards in the tavern drinking with the garrison rowdies, the drunken carousing, the appearance on the scene of John Small, magistrate . . . But I can't hear another word.*

"Get to bed, wife. I can stand no more."

"But nothing really happened that you must worry about. The children need not know, surely."

"The whole town will know by tomorrow, idiot woman. Do you think the soldiers at the garrison will keep it quiet? Or John Small, for that matter? Can you not imagine the joy his wife will feel to hear it all?" He puts his fingers on the bridge of his nose to stop the nosebleed he feels coming on. "This is the last straw."

# Chapter Forty

*June 1799*

Eliza Russell scarce knows what to do with the unhappy children seated at her kitchen table. Job has put before them his fresh-baked apple spice cake and glasses of milk from their farm to the north of the town, but they have not touched anything.

"We don't want to go back to London," Ellen is saying, "I want to stay here. I don't know why Papa is so angry with Mama, but he says she must go, and she says she won't go without us. What are we to do?"

"I want to stay here, too," William says. "We want to look at these wigglies under Mr. Russell's microscope." He points to a pail of strange swimming creatures he and his brother have brought with them this morning and set under the kitchen table. "Polliwogs," he tells her they are called, and they gathered them from the swamp at the edge of the bay.

"I hate London, I hate it, I hate it," Charles shouts, pounding on the table and upsetting his glass of milk.

"Lordy, Lordy, children, what am I to do?" Eliza says, as she wipes up the mess. "Have you talked to your Papa?"

"Yes, and he won't listen to anything we say." Ellen puts her head down on the table and starts to cry.

"Would things be the better if I spoke to your Papa?"

"Oh, Miss Russell, would you?" The girl sits up and wipes her eyes.

"Let me see what I can do."

Of a sudden, the three of them are up and flourishing. They drink their milk and eat their cake. William stirs the water in the pail with his hand, seeming to be pleased with the feel of the creatures on his fingers. "This one is getting little legs on it. Look, Miss Russell."

She can scarce keep herself from shrieking as he thrusts the thing towards her. But she manages a smile, mighty pleased that the children have stopped crying.

"Come back tonight, and Mr. Russell will be here to look at them with you. And Ellen, you and I must get to that reticule and finish it. Sometime in the next day or two, I will ready myself and talk to your Papa."

As they troop out the back door, she wonders how she is to manage. *Never come between a husband and wife.* She learned that long ago when she complained to her father about her mother's craziness, and he slammed her against a wall and broke her nose. *Thank the Lord for dear Peter who took me away from all of it.*

* * *

It's two o'clock. Peter is late for dinner. Job has made a cream soup from the peas in their garden, and there's beef brisket and the left-over apple spice cake. She's hoping that while she and her brother are eating the cake, she will have an opportunity to hear his views on what Mr. White plans for his wife and children. Mrs. White is a hare-brain, but he chose the woman, doubtless for her breasts, not her brain. She gets herself into a pet thinking of the stupidity of men in this world, her brother being an exception. And yet she likes Mr. White. He has proved himself a good friend. She remembers his kindness to Mary, and to her, when she lost her darling child.

She watches for her brother from the dining-room window while Job fusses to keep things hot on the kitchen hearth. At last, she sees him come through their fine gate. But he is not alone. Mr. White is with him. And for certain, there is something amiss. The two of them are leaning on each other, as if to walk down the path is too much for them. *What in tarnation is wrong?*

She looks out again. Peter's face is wet as if he has been crying. Mr. White's face is pale, and he, who is always so dapper, has one button undone on his flap. That puts her to the blush. *Lordy, what am I to do?* She calls to Peggy, "See to the front door, woman." Then she runs to the kitchen where Job has just taken a soup tureen from the shelf.

"Job, Job, you must help me. Mr. White has come for dinner with your master. And he . . . he . . . has one button undone on his flap. You must find some way of telling him."

"I shall, ma'am."

Back into the hallway she goes to greet the men. "Good day, Mr. White. I am mighty pleased that you have come with my brother for dinner. Now sit you down. All is ready and waiting."

As the men go into the dining room, she sees Job do as he was bid. He whispers something in Mr. White's ear, and a moment later, he has buttoned himself, thank the Lord. Now she must find what is wrong with the two of them.

Job serves the soup from the tureen and goes to the kitchen. Eliza watches her brother lift a spoonful to his mouth, then set the spoon down with a clatter. Mr. White is staring into his bowl. He has not even picked up his spoon.

"It be too hot, brother?"

"It is undoubtedly fine soup, but I cannot eat, sister. I have had bad news this day from England."

"His Excellency has died?"

Peter's eyes fill with tears that spill down his cheeks onto his chin. He takes the napkin and mops his face.

"It be bad, brother, but he has been ill. And though we must not seek comfort from a good man's death, at least now you will be the better for it. You are now the Governor of Upper Canada, and a good thing it be for everyone."

There is utter silence. *What is this to-do all about?*

Mr. White has such a furrow in his brow she fears he will soon have one of his nosebleeds. His voice, when he speaks, is so quiet that she leans forward to hear him.

"Your brother, ma'am, is not, nor will be, Governor."

"Not Governor? What has happened, sir?"

"Colonel Simcoe has not died, but he is not returning to Upper Canada. The Colonial Office has now made some British bastard—I do not regret my language—Governor. His name is Hunter. He will be arriving in August."

"But my brother—" She turns towards Peter. "You, my dear Peter, you have done all the work in this place for years. You have established roads in all directions, you have set new boundaries for the town, you have—"

"All this and more, sister. But what do they care, those uppity Brits? We have seen Elmsley take the position my good friend here should have had. And now they send a simpleton who knows nothing about our world here—"

"Whose chief qualification for the position is that he once put down an Irish rebellion by impaling the heads of three men on spikes over the door of a court house . . . Oh, Miss Russell, when I consider the disdain of His Majesty's government for fair play, I want to rise up and say 'To hell with it all.' Life is unsupportable."

Eliza rings for Job. "Please remove the soup. Excellent it be, but we have no appetite. Bring in some rum punch."

The punch arrives, and she watches her brother and Mr. White fill their glasses. Then she rises, puts her arms around her brother's shoulders and kisses his cheek. "Good day to you, Mr. White," she adds, clasping her friend's hand in hers. "We are all undone. I leave you to drink your punch. You be the better for it, I hope."

She stands in the hallway for a few minutes listening. Eventually she hears the murmur of voices. If they can talk to each other, friend to friend, perhaps there will be some solace for Peter. She herself will find ways to comfort him. Tonight in his bedchamber, she will hold him in her arms until he falls asleep.

And she must somehow find a way to talk to Mr. White about his wife and children. This day is not the day. But soon, in spite of all that has come upon them, she must firm herself up and speak out.

*I be scarce ready for these trials and tribulations. But oh Lord, I commit myself to doing what I can.*

# Chapter Forty-One

*August 1799*

For a moment John White has no idea where he is. Then he sees Mrs. Page standing by his bed, looking down at him. She has a pot of tea in her hand. He must have been asleep though there is light streaming through the window. He tries to sort it all out while she sets the teapot on the bureau and hands him a cloth which she has just soaked in water from the pitcher on the wash stand.

"You will want to wipe the sweat from your face, sir. You were screaming, 'I hate you, I hate you' in a most fearsome manner, and I became alarmed and took the liberty of entering your bedchamber."

"What time is it?"

"Three in the afternoon. My girls are napping in our cabin, and your sons are at school. I was in the kitchen making some Scotch eggs for supper when I heard your screams."

"But why am I here in bed? Why am I not at the court house?"

"You have been tired, sir, since you took the mistress and the children to Quebec. You have been falling asleep at all hours."

And now he remembers. *What does one call a nightmare that comes in mid-afternoon?*

The quay at Quebec. Marianne and Ellen boarding the *Triton* for the trip back to England. Him standing on the wharf with William and Charles while Ellen shouts from the stern of the ship over the rustling of the wind in the rigging. "I hate you, Papa. I hate you."

He begins to cry.

Mrs. Page pulls the rocking chair from the corner of the room to the side of the bed. Then she sits down in it. "Please, Mr. White, I'm here to listen if you want to tell me anything. As I told you, there is no one in the house except us two. And I will repeat nothing of what you tell me."

"I am so bereft . . ."

She waits for him to say more, her worn but pretty face turned towards him. And suddenly, it all spills out, the whole wretched sorry mess of the departure from his life, forever, of the wife he once loved and the daughter he still loves.

"I had to get rid of my wife, or I might have done something violent. Dear Miss Russell wanted me to keep the children here in York. She offered to look after them while I took Mrs. White to Quebec to catch the sailing vessel for England. But my wife would not leave York without them, and so we all travelled to Quebec. I cannot put words to the horror of that trip, my children crying day and night, and Mrs. White cold and sullen through it all. At Quebec, I purchased four passages on the *Triton* and reminded her of the financial arrangements I had made. She was to have one hundred and fifty pounds a year, one half my designated salary as Attorney-General. I had told her this before, mind you, and she had agreed to it.

"'I cannot raise three children on that paltry amount,' she told me as she was about to board the *Triton*. And right there on the quay, she grabbed Ellen and dragged her up the ramp. 'Keep the boys,' she told me, 'and may a curse fall upon you.'"

*I will tell no one what she really said to me, the vile accusations she spat at me as she forced Ellen onto that ship. I can only pray the boys did not understand the venom of her words. They were so happy to stay with me that they may not have listened or cared. But Ellen must have understood what she said and perhaps she believed it.*

"Surely you cannot blame yourself for the mistress's anger. She knew the terms. She was the one who agreed to those terms and then insisted on leaving your sons behind with you."

"Yes, but Ellen's words are burned into my soul. 'I hate you, Papa.' Can a father ever forget that?"

"She did not understand the ins and outs of it all."

"That is perhaps true. But I shall never see my little girl again. Never can I explain to her how I love her, how I wanted her with me always, how if her mother had left her with Charles and William there on the quay, my life would be bearable with my children beside me, but now . . ." He starts to sob again.

Mrs. Page gets up from the rocking chair, pours fresh water from the pitcher into the wash bowl, then holds it under his chin while he rinses the tears from his face.

"Can I get you tea now, sir?"

"No tea, thank you."

*I don't know how to tell her what I really need.*

Seconds pass while Mrs. Page opens the window and throws the water from the wash bowl down on the garden beneath the window. She turns back, sits down again in the rocking chair and says, "Shall I stay then?"

"Please." He reaches out with both hands in a gesture of entreaty and pulls her towards him. "Please."

She smiles. "We have perhaps half an hour, sir." She goes to the bedroom door, slides the bolt into place and turns back. She takes off her shoes and, fully clothed, climbs into bed beside him.

He turns towards her, and she moves close so that her body fits snug against his. Her skin smells of the lavender sachets she has put into every room of the house. Through her dress, he feels her breasts, small and firm, and though he has no strength left in him to do more than hold her close, the warmth of her sympathy invades his being and gives him, for a few moments at least, surcease of sorrow.

# Chapter Forty-Two

*September 1799*

Eliza Russell is for once looking forward to this day's tea. Job has set a brass teakettle of boiling water beside the tea table in the withdrawing room and laid out some tiny sweet buns fresh from the bake oven. Her guests are expected at any moment. She will have only her brother and Mr. White with her today. Though perhaps Cousin Willcocks may show up, too. He surfaces from time to time like a drowning swimmer trying to take in air. He is now postmaster of York, her dear brother having procured this position for him not so many months ago. He has settled in York with his wife and daughters. She is fond of his daughters. And all would be right and proper, if only he would stop putting his hands on her when Peter is not looking.

Of late, she has had to serve too many teas and rum punches to Governor Hunter who has replaced Peter as administrator of Upper Canada. Governor Big Wig, as she privately calls him, meets her brother here in their house day after day after day while his own residence west of the garrison is being built. It puts her in a pet to see how Big Wig relies on her brother even though Peter no longer has the official honours as administrator. Often Chief Justice Elmsley joins them for tea. Eliza can scarce be polite to these guests, and the effort is wearing her down.

There is much she cannot tell her brother, not wanting to distress him. Though he must surely have noticed the stink of Big Wig, perhaps he has not linked the smell with the man's frequent trips upstairs to use the chamber pot near her bed. And for the last few days, she has had trouble with Peggy who now refuses to empty the pot.

"Look at that," the servant said to her last week, coming out of the house to push the chamber pot under her nose while she was stitching a new frock in a comfortable chair on the lawn. Well, for certain it was a mess—loose bowels in a bloody swill—but what was she to do?

"Take it away, woman," she had said. "Do not bother me with it."

But Peggy, always uppity, refused. She put the pot down on the lawn, splashing some of its contents onto the grass, and marched off. Eliza, too, had gone back into the house, leaving the stinking mess behind her. When she looked down later from her bedchamber window, she saw Job carrying the pot away. That put her into a pet. Job has more than enough to do without the added chore of emptying chamber pots. And what is she to do about Peggy? She must soon have a set-to with that bad-tempered slut.

Today, however, she will try to enjoy herself with her brother and Mr. White, and she hopes to be the better for a rest from the trials and tribulations of dealing with Big Wig and his bowels.

She looks out the front window to see dear Peter and Mr. White coming up the front walk. And yes, alas, they have Cousin Willcocks with them. Well, he won't try anything with Peter around.

As the men come into the withdrawing room, Eliza settles herself in her wing chair, mixes the tea leaves, and pours the boiling water over them. Soon they are deep into a good tongue-wag about Governor Big Wig.

"He has gone to Quebec," Peter says, "and I have no idea when he will be back. He is commander of the forces in both Upper and Lower Canada, and I fear that the real needs of York will necessarily be set aside for who knows how long."

"Are you to be left with all the responsibilities of this town without the title? Is that what the Colonial Office considers fair play?" Cousin Willcocks's indignation does

209

not seem to interfere with his appetite. He spreads a huge dollop of butter on his bun as he says this.

"I am commanded to deal only with routine business," Peter says. He unfolds a letter that he takes from his waistcoat. "Here's how the Grand Poobah describes his role. 'I must have sole authority to govern upon the principles which my own judgment suggests.'"

"Balderdash and bunkum," Willcocks says, wiping crumbs from his waistcoat.

Mr. White refuses a second cup of tea and leaves his bun half eaten. "That damned Elmsley appears to be in the Poobah's charmed circle."

"Do not fear Elmsley, my friend. Who can understand a thing the man says anyway? And if he dares to give me any advice in plain English, I will spit in his eye."

Eliza is mighty pleased to see Mr. White laughing. She knows he has been in a pet since his wife and Ellen have left, and she has not known how to offer him comfort. "I do not think Governor Big Wig will last long," she says. "He has bad health, I wager."

"You have noticed that, sister? Dysentery and biliousness, by all accounts. It may explain why he is so prone to angry outbursts at our meetings here." Peter smiles. "Followed by all those trips upstairs . . . "

*So brother does know about the chamberpot. Thank the Lord. Perhaps he will now be able to give me some advice about how to deal with Peggy.*

"No doubt you have noticed that I have my own set of problems," Cousin Willcocks says, helping himself to another bun and holding out his cup for more tea. "I have, in fact, been a social pariah in this town since I refused to celebrate the victory of Nelson at the Battle of the Nile. The wife keeps yapping at me to fall in line with the Brits, but I have no intention of pandering to them."

"The town's need for a postmaster will trump any deficiency of respect for our great British traditions, surely," Peter says, uttering a great belch as he says the phrase "great British traditions."

"You had some windows broken, did you not? Have they been fixed yet?" Mr. White asks.

"Every last one of them was broken by those roustabouts at the garrison, and every last one of them is now fixed—at an expense I can scarce afford."

"It was undoubtedly the same roustabouts, as you call them, who caused my wife to fall into such grievous straits the night of that damnable shivaree." White picks up his bun again, looks at it, then sets it back on his plate.

The minutes pass. Eliza's brother and his cousin are now deep in conversation. She sees Mr. White turn his head to speak to her directly. "I no longer blame Marianne for my woes, Miss Russell. My miseries have come from many sources and have settled like the rock on Sisyphus's shoulders. But I must thank you for your concern for Ellen. The one thing that gave her comfort on that wretched trip to Quebec was the reticule you made with her . . . and the Scotch pebble necklace she found inside it."

Eliza wipes her eyes with the little lace-edged handkerchief she pulls from her bodice. "I have been in such a pet lately about losing your little girl from my life. And about my dear brother's loss of promotion." She sighs. "I, too have had a rock on my shoulders. But I feel the better for this tongue-wag, Mr. White."

She feels Cousin Willcocks's large boot press against her foot. The moment she has shared with her friend shatters. She swings her legs away from the brute, and almost hits the tea table with her left knee.

# Chapter Forty-Three

*October 1799*

Susannah Page is a simple woman who gives John White one of the few comforts he now has in his life. They snatch their time together in White's bedchamber while William and Charles are at school and while Susannah's girls have their afternoon nap in their log cabin at the foot of the garden of White's park lot. They sometimes also meet in the octagonal summer house beyond the cabin in the woods at the rear of the lot. They have only to keep an ear for the children, but so boisterous are they, he and Susannah can always hear them coming. Then Susannah adjusts her dress and emerges from the summer house with her tray, saying in a loud voice, "Sir, I hope my sweets today are to your liking." How he laughs.

He has told her she must stop calling him "sir" or "master" during these moments, and she has agreed to "Susannah," rather than "Cook" or "Mrs. Page." But in spite of their increased intimacy, she has told him very little about her life before she came to his house. Only that her husband was a clerk, "a good man, he died of gunshot wounds during a set-to with a neighbour." Well, that is enough to know. What matters to him is the warmth she offers him, the uncomplicated kindness of their day-to-day life together.

She seems happiest when she pulls her fresh bread from the bake oven or when she heaps the boys' plates with the cutlets and gravy they like so much. He is glad he incurred the necessary expense for the bake oven though he has no idea how he will pay for it. As for the cutlets, fortunately most of them come from the Russells' farm to the north where one of their hands kills, cuts, and cures the meat. How could he cope without his friends' bounty?

He has started to spend a good deal of time at the garrison, now that Marianne is no longer here to nag him about wasted evenings and heavy drinking. There's a certain cachet in socializing at the garrison. Civilians are allowed only if, in the opinion of the officers, they are on the same class level as officers. So the garrison gives him a chance to escape from the court louts who delight in torturing prisoners or the tradesmen to whom he owes money. Over cups of rum punch and tankards of beer, he has met people like those he consorted with at Fort Niagara.

This evening, however, he hesitates to leave his house. William, now eight years old, seems ill. Two days ago, he declined second helpings of Susannah's pork cutlets and a couple of hours later, he vomited everything up. Then he complained of pain in his joints and a headache. Tonight the child seems somewhat better though he has sweats and chills in rapid succession.

The German immigrant Berczy, coming earlier in the day to make a final adjustment to the front door of Mrs. Page's cabin in the woods, diagnosed the boy's illness as the ague. "Give him alcohol," he suggested. "Spirituous liquors are always good. Drinking the raw water in this place causes trouble."

Miss Russell has also diagnosed it as ague. "It's from those accursed insects in the swamp the lad is always a-going to," she tells White. "These long hot fall days be making our lives a misery. I've told my brother to put away that microscope the lad is so fond of looking into. Keep him in bed, and I'll send over some bark tea."

But White has been reluctant to give little William either alcohol or the tea. Miss Russell's remedy sits unused in the pine cupboard in his kitchen. He remembers all too well the night that her daughter Mary died, how early in the evening the girl sat at the kitchen table puking up the bark tea his friend had made. Mary's last hours had certainly not

213

been improved by drinking Miss Russell's concoction. If only there was a doctor in York that he could trust . . .

"Go to the garrison tonight if you wish, sir," Mrs. Page says as she serves supper to him and Charles. "I shall be here to keep an eye on William. Surely he cannot become worse in a few short hours."

So he sits in the Officers' Mess with one of his new acquaintances, a German officer, Frederick Baron de Hoen. Baron de Hoen once served with a German regiment, helping British forces quell the revolt of the thirteen American colonies. He is a military man to the core, and since he finds it difficult to adjust to his new life as a farmer, he too spends a good deal of time drinking at the garrison and swapping tales with the soldiers.

Upright in stature and sharp of speech, Baron de Hoen carries about with him an ornamental sword that he lays on the table while he talks to White. The weapon disturbs White, but he decides to say nothing about it. The Baron's stories are set in a world that lies outside the courtroom and the legislature, and while listening to him, White begins to see the injustice the man has suffered and to understand the fears that afflict him.

"I met a Mennonite man, name of Reesor, on the Rouge River Trail," Baron de Hoen tells him this evening after they have downed several tankards of beer in the Officers' Mess. "He had ridden all the way from Pennsylvania. He told me he wanted to settle in the area, and I had two hundred acres I wanted to get rid of. So I say to the man, 'I'll swap my land for your horse and saddle.' It was a fine large steed, see, full of vigour, even after that long journey.

"'Done,' says Reesor, and we shake hands.

"So he brings the horse to me with a saddle upon its back, but no bridle.

"'Where's the bridle?' I ask him.

"'Not part of the deal,' Reesor tells me. 'We negotiated for horse and saddle only.' Then the lout turns around and heads back to Pennsylvania to get his family."

"And what happened to the bridle?" White asks.

214

"Carried it on his back all the way home to Yankee-land, from what I hear."

At this point, a young man on a stool nearby the bar starts to laugh. "I wager he had one huge, bleeding sore on his shoulders."

"That would be small punishment," Baron de Hoen says, joining in the laughter. "I wanted to challenge him to a duel—I have a set of fine duelling pistols—but my wife, who was with me at the time, gave a tug on my topcoat and I knew what that gesture meant. Wives do not need words to convey messages."

More laughter, and the young man leaves his stool and joins them at their table. "I'm William Warren Baldwin, newly arrived in York," he tells them. "I'm a doctor so I know all about bleeding sores, though I doubt I'd want to preside over a fatal duelling wound."

White and the Baron introduce themselves in turn, and White says, "Are you old enough to be a medical man?" Baldwin could not be more than twenty-five, a good-looking young man with a long, straight nose, abundant blond hair, and low brows set over piercing blue eyes.

"Graduated from the University of Edinburgh last year," Baldwin says. "I'm almost twenty-six, but I wager I have much more to offer people than the old quacks I've met on this side of the Atlantic. You don't need jowls and a red nose to be a medical man, do you?"

"You're settling in this town?" White asks. He keeps the question short as he tries to avoid a belch that threatens to erupt.

"Yes. At the moment I'm staying with William Willcocks—he's a distant relative—but I intend to move on to my own quarters when I have established a practice. So far, though, I need patients. Seems we might, God forbid, need an epidemic here to give me a boost."

"What are your views on purging and blood-letting?" *Too many questions, but I've drunk so much I can't manage much else.* And in spite of his muddle, White is beginning to see an opportunity opening up, but he wants to do his own research first before he takes chances.

215

"Damned quackery," Baldwin says, his cheeks turning pink with indignation. "I spent a few days in Niagara before coming here, and I met an idiot who tried to sell me the idea of purging with calomel. Calomel, can you believe that?"

"Dr. Kerr, was it?"

"None other."

Baron de Hoen rises. "Back to the farm now," he says, putting his hand into the back pocket of his redingote, undoubtedly to withdraw a coin to pay for his drinks. There's a tinkling sound.

"What on earth is that noise?" Baldwin asks, looking about the room.

De Hoen shows him the flap of his pocket which is trimmed with tiny ornamental bells. "They discourage pickpockets. Good idea, wouldn't you say?" He puts a coin on the table, retrieves his sword, shakes hands with his companions, and departs.

"A quick diagnosis here," Baldwin says, smiling. "That sword on the table, the mention of the duelling pistols, and those tinkling bells to ward off pickpockets: delusions of persecution, wouldn't you say?"

*This may be the man I need.* "Now that we're alone," White says, struggling to clear his head to form a coherent sentence, "I want to tell you about a possible first patient."

# Chapter Forty-Four

*October 1799, later the same evening*

Dr. Baldwin makes a quick stop at Willcocks's place to pick up his medical kit, then he and White head for White's house. They have just turned up the path leading to the front door when Mrs. Page comes running towards them, tugging up her skirt so that she can move faster. Charles is at her heels, crying "Papa, Papa."

"Sir," she says, wringing her hands, "I have been watching from the front window these last few minutes. Oh, please come quickly."

They run into the front hall, up the staircase, and into the boys' bedchamber. William lies on his back on top of the quilt on the narrow four-poster bed. He usually sleeps in the trundle bed which they pull out nightly, but because of his illness he has taken Charles's space.

There is no response from the boy to their arrival. His face is pale and his eyes, closed. *Sleeping. Or dead?* Suddenly completely sober, White moans and falls onto his knees beside the bed, grabbing one of William's hands.

Dr. Baldwin has whipped from his waistcoat a magnifying glass. He holds it close to the boy's nostrils.

At the same time, William opens his eyes, looks around him, his small face contorted in pain or confusion, and then seeing the familiar faces of his brother, father, and Mrs. Page, he smiles. But the smile fades as he looks at Baldwin who, fortunately, has had the good sense to put the glass back in his waistcoat. "Papa, Papa, why is that man here?"

"It's Dr. Baldwin, son. He's going to see what's wrong with you and get you better."

"No leeches, no leeches! Please, please, no leeches!" White remembers his son's sorrow over the death of one of his school friends. He, William, and Charles had gone to the child's home to offer their respects to the parents. They looked down at the little grey-white face in the rough pine box on a low table in the parlour. That moment had been bad enough, but as they looked, a leech had inched out of the child's abundant brown hair and wormed its way onto his forehead. William and Charles had immediately started to sob, their faces pale with horror, and the mother, thinking it was grief that fuelled their tears, went into the kitchen to get wine. In her absence, White was able to reach into the box and pull off the slug. He'd held it tight in one hand, and they had all refused the wine when it came, wanting only one thing—escape. Out in the open air, he'd thrown the leech onto the ground. Then he'd looked at his hand. Smears of the child's blood lay on his palm. He'd swallowed the bile that rose in his throat. A father must always be strong for his children. *But why the devil had the women who washed the child's body not found the slug?*

"No leeches, lad," Dr. Baldwin is saying now as he puts his hand on William's forehead. "I am going to have a look at what's wrong here, and then I'll have a remedy that will make you feel better. It may taste bad, but it won't be leeches. Guaranteed."

Perhaps it's the man's youthful face, his gentle voice, and smiling demeanour that reassure William. In a moment, the lad is spilling details about his sweats, chills, and headaches.

Dr. Baldwin pulls at his hair with his fingers. It seems to be a gesture that accompanies thought. In a moment or two, he turns to White, "He has all the symptoms of ague."

"Miss Russell says it's ague, doctor."

"And how did the lady come to that conclusion?"

"I think it was the sweats that alerted her first. She's had them herself over the years. And then, of course, she knows both my lads are regular visitors to the bay and the swamps."

"Ah, the swamps. That clinches it. These hot days—Indian summer, isn't it called here?—mean those bloody mosquitoes are still about." The man runs his fingers through his hair again. "So now we have to find a remedy." He looks back at William. "I'll just talk to your father in the hall for a moment while we discuss what we can do for you. But no leeches, remember that, my boy."

Once outside the door of the bedchamber, Mrs. Page moves down the hallway and Charles descends to the kitchen. Baldwin puts his hand on White's shoulder and speaks quietly. "There are the opiates—"

"Never." White raises his voice. "Never."

"Let me finish, sir. There are the opiates, but I'll have no part of them even though the quacks of this world recommend them as a cure-all. I spent a few months in the marshy fens of eastern England where every farmer in the countryside grows opium poppies and where every shop in the place sells pills and penny sticks. I saw those opium-eating children, some of them no older than your lad here, caved in and wizened, shrunken into little monkeys. No opiates for William."

"What, then? Berczy—he's a German who did some building for me—suggested liquor, but . . ."

"There's far too much liquor drunk in this backwater." Baldwin stops with that sentence, but the look he gives White speaks volumes. Again his fingers tear at his hair. "Bark tea, that should work. But where to get it in this place? I haven't been here long enough to scout out sources."

Relief floods through White. "Miss Russell, she has some. She used to get it from a merchant in Queenston who brought it in from somewhere, I've forgotten where."

"Ah, this Miss Russell of yours is quite the physician. I must talk to her." Dr. Baldwin pulls out his pocket watch. "It's midnight. Hardly the time to disturb the lady in order to get the tea. But it's urgent. Perhaps we should try—"

Susannah hovers nearby. "We still have the jar Miss Russell left, sir. It's in the pine cupboard in the kitchen, remember?"

The stress of this evening, coupled with the beer he drank at the garrison, have so befuddled him that he'd completely forgotten.

In a minute, Susannah has measured the powdered bark according to Dr. Baldwin's instructions and poured boiling water over it. Charles, thank God, is already asleep in the rocking chair by the hearth and does not have to see what comes next.

Back to the bedchamber the three of them go. White raises his son into a sitting position and puts a couple of pillows behind his head to hold him upright. "Now then, William," he says, "you must drink this tea."

Dr. Baldwin sits on the bed close to the boy and pushes the steaming cup of tea towards him. "It's vile," he says, "but it will make you better."

William tries a sip and retches.

"Try pinching your nose, lad," the doctor says. "That way you won't be able to smell it, and you can get it down."

It works. Bit by bit, it all goes down.

Dr. Baldwin stands up. "One cup every two hours all night. You should notice a marked improvement in twenty-four hours. I'll stop by to see how he is tomorrow afternoon." He moves into the hallway, down the stairs, out the front door, and disappears into the darkness.

White picks Charles up from the rocking chair in the kitchen and carries him along the hall and upstairs to his bedchamber. Best to keep him away from William. He goes back into the kitchen where Susannah has stirred up the fire in the hearth and set a kettle of water to boil.

"Go to bed now," she says. "I'll keep watch over the boy until three o'clock, then I shall call you to take my place."

* * *

Two days later, William sits up in bed, rosy-faced and ready to eat the chops which Susannah has cut up into small pieces for him. After he has devoured them, along

220

with a slice of his favourite bread pudding, White brings in Noah Webster's spelling book and sits down beside the child's bed.

"Time now to get caught up with some of the work you have been missing at school."

"Oh Papa," William says, "I feel so sweaty." He puts a small hand on his forehead. "My headache is so bad. I have pains in my—"

"Very well, my boy, we'll let you have more time. But the day after tomorrow, you must start your schoolwork again."

White takes the speller and the dirty plates down to the kitchen where Susannah, her two little girls, and Charles are just finishing their supper.

"Why are you smiling, Papa?" Charles asks.

"Because William has completely recovered."

# Chapter Forty-Five

*November 1799*

Indian summer has passed, and crisp evening air smacks John White's face and soothes the headache that has plagued him all day. He's been stuck in the court house for hours, and he sets out now to enjoy fresh air and exercise. At the end of the path to his house he turns west, away from the Don River, wishing to avoid a possible encounter with his neighbours to the east, Betsy and John Small.

The path in front of the park lot houses is now more of a roadway than a path. In the time he has been in York, the original Indian trail has packed down to a comfortable width. Though the Indians still walk along it in single file, the white settlers often walk in twos or threes.

It would be pleasant if he had someone congenial to walk beside him this evening, but the Russells are entertaining Peter Hunter again, and the local gossips would have a good "tongue-wag" (as Miss Russell would say) if he appeared arm-in-arm with Susannah. She is at his house this evening, supervising some sort of improvised cricket game with the boys and her small daughters. The shrieks from the rear yard did nothing to help his headache, though he's happy to see William running about again and enjoying life.

Of course the choice he has made to turn west will take him past William Jarvis's house, but he hopes that at this time of day, the lazy dolt and his bitch of a wife are having a late supper in the depths of their dwelling.

The Jarvis house is a two-storey structure with an attic. Its squared-log construction has been covered with white

222

clapboard, and the effect, White must concede, is attractive. He's heard from Surveyor-General Smith about the impressive flight of winding stairs that leads from the main hall. "Must have cost the bugger plenty," his former student tells him, adding, "in fact, more than a thousand pounds from the common gossip I hear."

But Jarvis can undoubtedly recoup some of that outlay through being able to feed his family without much expense. He has fruit trees that he's brought across the lake from Niagara. White notices some marauding pigs snuffling at the windfall apples and pears. He also catches a glimpse of two cows and some sheep. Incompetent though Jarvis undoubtedly is, he does know how to take care of his wife and children.

At the Jarvis residence, White turns towards the lake and his favourite walk along the bay. There are several creeks running into the bay, and he plans to walk west briskly and to get as far as the one the local folk call Russell's Creek before turning back. By then darkness will have settled, but he always enjoys the moon and the stars and the utter peace of the place, broken only by the drone of cicadas and the occasional hoot of an owl. If he's lucky, he'll be able to avoid having to speak with anyone, except perhaps the Indians with whom he's become friendly. Unlike the white settlers in this place, they don't chatter. The Mississauga band has now largely dispersed, their land having been usurped by the newcomers. Most of them have moved westward towards the garrison. But there are still a few tepees here close to the shore.

"Good evening, White man," Abel Crowfoot calls from his campfire. He's the native who gave White the moss handkerchief for his nosebleed when he first came to York. They meet in this place often, and the salutation has become a joke between them.

White sits by the fire and takes a tin cup of lemon-balm tea that Abel pours for him. In anticipation of meeting his Indian friend, White has bought a packet of Susannah's oatmeal cakes and he passes it to Abel who hesitates for a moment and then takes one. White dips his into his tea, and he observes that Abel, watching him closely, copies his action.

They sit in companionable silence enjoying the sunset and the flapping of lowering sails at a nearby dock. As dusk falls, White rises to take leave of his friend. As he is about to shake hands, he is distracted by a movement to the right of the campfire. He turns to look. On the path by the water a woman is scurrying along. She's wearing a spencer jacket with fur-trimmed collar over her gown, and she's holding a large kerchief to her face. Though her features are covered, he has no trouble recognizing the woman's figure and her walk.

It's Betsy Small.

"My God," he says.

"You know this woman, White man?"

"Yes."

"She comes here along bay often. She meets soldier from garrison. Up to—how you say it—hanky panky." Abel laughs, evidently pleased with the phrase. It's probably something he's heard from a Yankee settler. White himself has not heard it before, but he likes it, and the meaning is clear.

So the woman has not changed her ways in spite of the spotless demeanour she now exhibits in York society. *Dammit, I'm going to confront her.*

He moves away from the campfire and places himself in the middle of the path along the bay. She sees him—no way she can avoid him—and he relishes her discomfiture.

"Mr. White," she says, pulling the kerchief away from her face and trying, obviously, to brazen things out. "It's a pleasant surprise to see you here."

"And you, Mrs. Small."

"I come here often for the fresh air and exercise."

"I do remember," he says, "how you enjoyed the woods at Newark." Out of the corner of his eye, he catches sight of a man in a dark green uniform with black facings who is trying to hide himself behind the trunk of a huge oak tree near the water. White recognizes the uniform. He's met these men at the garrison, Glengarry Fencibles they're called.

Ah, hanky panky indeed. He decides to have it out with her. "Who is that man behind the tree? From the garrison, isn't he? I know I have met him before." This is not exactly true, but he wants to see what she'll come up with in the way of an answer. He wants her to know that he's aware of what she's up to.

She looks around and shrugs. "I have not the faintest idea. The soldiers often come along the bay in the evenings. It must be respite from their toil at the barracks. I frequently see them on my walks." It's almost convincing, but White notices, even in the twilight, the blush that extends from her tits to her forehead.

"I'm so happy to have a chance for a moment of private conversation," she says. "I've wanted to warn you about a couple of things that are affecting your social standing here in this new capital. But first I must ask you about your good wife. I have not had a chance to speak to you about her return to England. A permanent separation, is it? I am aware that she was not entirely happy here."

*So she's decided to slug it out, the slut. Well we'll see who wins this round.*

She waits for an answer, but he says nothing.

"Well, I can understand if you don't want to talk about your dear wife," she says. "But if you will permit me, now that I have your ear, I must impart a cautionary message as well. Pray do not consort with Mr. Willcocks. He is, I understand, a low Irishman, with none of the proper regard for His Majesty's traditions. And no doubt his relative, that young man who calls himself a doctor, is an ill-bred Irishman as well. We English must maintain standards."

White feels a blush of rage suffusing his own face. He leans in close to her so that he can taste the delight of watching her brown eyes trying to evade his gaze. He spits on the ground beside her, purposely hitting the hem of her flimsy muslin gown that reveals all too much of the figure he once yearned for. "You of all people, woman, to talk of propriety and standards. I hope that man waiting for you

225

there behind those trees is a proper Englishman." He turns on his heel and leaves her standing on the pathway. He returns to the campfire.

"You know hanky panky woman, White man?" Abel asks.

"Yes. Let us sit and watch what happens next."

The woman Small fiddles with her reticule for a moment, then turns and walks east, not deigning to glance towards Abel's campfire. There is a hiatus of perhaps five minutes while White and Abel finish off the tea and biscuits and wait. Then the soldier comes out behind the oak tree and looks eastward, no doubt at the vanishing pleasure of his evening. He shakes his fist at White, uttering a curse, and slouches off to the west in the direction of the garrison.

Abel makes some comment about hanky panky which White scarcely hears, so busy is he trying to sort out the rush of emotion that has engulfed him. He says goodnight to the Indian and heads north towards home. *What do I feel? Triumph? No. Anger? Yes. But more, much more. Disgust and shame, that's what.*

Marianne is silly and she's had her share of addiction. But not to sex, not like the Small woman who seems to love cock of any size or origin. *And, dammit, I once provided an outlet for her lust. For a while in Niagara I even convinced myself that she found me attractive and special. What a fool I was.*

*And now the slut has the nerve to ask after my "dear departed wife" whom she called "Cinderella," she, who herself, lies in the ashes of her bespoiled reputation.*

*What's more, there was the advice I had to listen to this evening. Advice from a whore, telling me to uphold English standards.*

He kicks at one of the hens that is scuttling in the bushes at the edge of Jarvis's property. Its squawk restores him to a portion of his senses. He smooths back his hair and tugs down his waistcoat before he passes the house which sits close to the path. No point giving Mrs. Jarvis anything to speculate on if she's peeking out the window.

226

By the time he turns up the path to his own house, anger and disgust have left him. There is now only the shame of confronting his own stupidity. As a younger man, he was always attracted to a pretty face, a bounteous bosom, and slender ankles. Why could he not have looked for intelligence and devotion in the women he loved?

He settles in an armchair in his withdrawing room and tries to shake out the confusion of his thoughts. Susannah has lighted the candles in their sconces and left his newspaper folded on the Pembroke table. Beside it, she has put a pitcher of syllabub and a glass. *Ah, Miss Russell's offering, no doubt. And she must have brought it over after she got rid of Peter Hunter.*

These decent, wonderful women—Mrs. Page and Miss Russell—why could he not have married someone like them?

He sits, drinking the syllabub and thinking. Six years of the prime of his life given over to this place. What has he to show for it? Heavy debt, intolerable headaches, lost wife and daughter, a whore who gives him advice on propriety, two or three friends only on whom he can depend for succour . . .

An hour passes. He stumbles off to bed, soothed somewhat by the frothy curd of whipped cream and sweet white wine. In the course of that hour in the withdrawing room, he has made a decision.

"What's wrong, Papa?" Charles asks, coming out into the hall in his nightshirt and rubbing his eyes.

"Sorry, my boy, I must have been talking out loud. Back to bed now."

*Vengeance is mine, saith the Lord. And mine, too, saith John White.*

# Chapter Forty-Six

*December 27, 1799*

John White has mixed feelings about the ball to be held at the local tavern. Subscription balls are à la mode these days, and he will have to contribute to the renting of a room as well as donating several bottles of wine and a meat dish to the festivities. But he decides to go to it nonetheless because he sees an opportunity that he intends to seize.

"Please do not worry about the food, sir," Susannah says to him as she serves dinner to him and the boys. "I can cook something up at low cost. There are plenty of black squirrels in the back forty I can snare and cut up with mushrooms, onions, and—"

The boys make retching noises.

"No squirrels, Mrs. Page."

"Plenty of rabbits too. How about a rabbit stew then?"

White sighs, thinking of the comments people like Chief Justice Elmsley would make when they found out—as they surely would—who had brought what. "Best get a fresh chicken from the market and roast it."

"Or perhaps Miss Russell would let me have one from her poultry yard," Susannah says. "I'll ask."

Russell has already told White that he and Miss Russell will not be going to the event. "It's Hunter's idea, the cheapskate, and he won't charge it to the Colonial Office. Mind you, I don't entirely blame him. I'm still waiting for them to send sixty-eight pounds, seven shillings, and nine pence for the ball I gave two winters

228

ago. So why should I be out of pocket for this event as well?"

White groans in commiseration. He's still lacking this year's stipend. He's had to make do with some income from private practice and the pittance he gets from his share in the issuing of the land grants.

* * *

The night of the ball, he dons the formal court attire he's purchased for the occasion: a red velvet claw-hammer tailcoat over a striped silk waistcoat, and tight trousers tucked into what that devil of a German boot-maker calls "Hussar boots." Perhaps the yellow kid gloves he's carrying are an unnecessary added expense, but he wants to look his best for the evening ahead. It gives him confidence to know he will be the most stylish man in the room.

In the lower hall of the tavern, he hands Susannah's fricasseed chicken and her pumpkin pie to a serving man and proceeds upstairs to the ballroom. Fiddlers from the garrison have already tuned up, and tonight there's a caller for the growing fad called "square dancing." He sees the Smalls and the Elmsleys and two other couples swinging about to a brisk beat. Not a sign anywhere of the Glengarry Fencible!

That officer, who from behind the oak tree overheard his conversation with Mrs. Small, challenged him to a duel two weeks ago. He has Elmsley to thank for coming to his aid on that one. He met White and the officer in a room at the court house, and after a spate of Latin which included his calling the lieutenant *"pavo absolutus,"* Elmsley ordered the "total turkey" to keep the peace for twelve months and post bonds totalling five hundred pounds. Though he hates feeling indebted to Elmsley, he recognizes the man's wisdom in that thwarted affair.

Now White heads straight for the bar reminding himself he must not get tipsy tonight. But a few drinks will put him in a frame of mind to carry out the scheme that he has planned carefully with malice aforethought. A cup of rum punch in hand, he searches the crowd to find the person he wants. *Ah, there he is.*

"Smith, may I join you here against the wall?"

"By all means, White. Since my wife died, I find these events difficult. It's always good to have a friend to talk to. And you yourself must feel lonely without your wife."

The man is giving him an opportunity to talk about his and Marianne's split, but White has no intention of giving out this information to the town's most notorious gossip. "Let us drink and forget our problems," he says, reaching for another glass of punch from the server who is making the rounds with a tray. He takes a glass for Smith as well.

Their position could not be more perfect. Directly in front of them is the square dance group that contains the Smalls and the Elmsleys.

As the dance ends, Mrs. Small takes Mrs. Elmsley's arm, and steers her directly in front of him and Smith. Though Mrs. Elmsley is modestly dressed in a deep blue gown with a fichu at the neck, the Small woman wears the same pale yellow muslin dress she wore for her night of thwarted hanky panky. It has a low-cut neckline and as she catches White's eye, she tugs up her gown just far enough to display those ankles of hers.

"Quite a vision," Smith says, pulling out the diamond-rimmed quizzing glass that he always keeps on a gold chain on his waistcoat. He puts it up to his eye and stares at the women who have just passed, concentrating, it seems, on the hussy's bare white shoulders. "I wonder if all the things I hear about the Small woman could be true?"

White has been waiting for this opening. "Absolutely. She is a whore," he says in a low voice. "I had her as my own mistress when we lived in Niagara. I gave her up because I feared for my health."

"Your health?" Smith says, leaning towards White, his face flushed and his eyes avid.

"Yes. The frequency of her amours with Mr. Tickell and the officers at Fort Niagara worried me. What is more, I had it on the best authority that . . ." Here White pauses strategically and takes another sip of his drink.

"You had it on the best authority that . . . ?" Smith prompts.

"That she was, while in England, the mistress of Lord Berkeley of Berkeley Castle. He was a good friend of Small, I understand, and he asked Small to . . ."

Here White makes a show of searching for his snuff box. He takes it from the pocket of his tailcoat and opens the lid.

"Come, come, man, out with it." Smith is in a fidget of excitement now.

"You must promise to keep what I tell you to yourself," White says, trying to show reluctance to say more. He inhales the snuff and sneezes.

"I swear. Not a word will pass my lips."

*Not bloody likely. Everyone in this place knows about your loose tongue. God bless you for that!*

White has thought long and hard about the next tidbit. Whether it's fact or fiction, he knows not, not does he care. "Lord Berkeley asked Small to take the woman off his hands. He was thoroughly sick of her, from what I hear. For this he paid his friend a substantial sum—enough to establish him in this new world—and he booked them an early passage to Niagara."

"No!"

"Yes! But remember your promise to me. You must repeat none of this."

Soon after this exchange, Smith excuses himself, "to find a loo," he says. But White laughs to himself when he sees the man walk directly over to Chief Justice Elmsley and whisper at length in his ear.

*By night's end, Elmsley is sure to tell his wife. The friendship of the two women will be forever split asunder. And the whore will find herself a social pariah without a person in this little world to speak to.*

His mission accomplished, White does not wait to have a slice of Susannah's good pie. He takes another drink and downs it as he leaves the ballroom. It has been a successful evening. He doesn't even mind the headache that has come on from snorting the snuff in that box he borrowed from Peter Russell.

He heads for home, savouring the small comfort that comes from knowing that he has vindicated his wife.

*Silly as she is, she has deserved a better husband than I have been.*

# Chapter Forty-Seven

*January 1, 1800*

It is mid-afternoon. With Charles and William out on the ice no doubt yelling "Hoicks, hoicks!" and Susannah's little girls having their nap, John White decides to take advantage of the solitude and force himself to face an unpleasant task. At his desk in the withdrawing room, he pulls a stack of bills from a compartment and leafs through them. Berczy's bill of forty-four pounds for "fixes" around the house and Mrs. Page's cabin can be put aside until the man comes back from England. But look at the rest of them: Abner Miles, shopkeeper, forty-eight pounds; the German tailor, one hundred and fifty-five pounds; the garrison tally, fifty-one pounds; Dr. William Warren Baldwin, ten pounds; the schoolmaster William Cooper, ninety pounds—

He throws the lot on the floor. It's hopeless.

What is he to do? As Attorney-General, a position to which he once aspired, he now has no influence. He remembers how he helped the Gov draft the slave bill; how he made the circuits with his friend Osgoode; how he set up the Law Society of Upper Canada and laid out the governing rules for the certification of lawyers.

But Peter Hunter, the infamous Governor Poobah, wants no help from him. And Elmsley runs the whole show in the courts of the province. There are rumours that Elmsley may go to Lower Canada soon, but White knows now that there is no hope for his own advancement to Chief Justice. All that's left to him of any import is the drafting of the land grants, and that brings only the daily squabbles, accusations, and insults from Jarvis.

The special friends he has in this small world—Peter and Eliza Russell—seem almost as despairing as he is. He can do nothing to help them, nor can they offer him respite.

He has heard nothing from Marianne or Ellen. What would they have to say to him anyway, if they could bring themselves to put quill to paper? They hate him. He did write one letter to Ellen and then threw it into the hearth. It's hopeless to try to explain the inexplicable.

There can be no future with Susannah. If they could ever marry—the most unlikely of events—how could he take on the expenses of her two little girls?

"Moping melancholy" is the phrase that pops into his mind now to describe his woes. Looking back on his time in Upper Canada, he can trace a slope downwards into despair. Did he not once complain to William Osgoode of his unhappiness? Did he not even use that term "moping melancholy"? He seems to remember that his friend laughed at the phrase and tried to cheer him by encouraging him to think his efforts would be rewarded with promotion to Chief Justice. But that hope—indeed, all his hopes—are gone, gone, gone. "Moping melancholy," yes, a pretentious phrase perhaps, but one that exactly sums up his present state in the pit of the inferno.

He pours the rest of the sherry from the decanter into his glass. His head pounds, and the blood from his nose trickles down onto his upper lip. He wipes it away with a napkin that lies beside the decanter.

There is a frenzy of knocking on his front door. Mrs. Page is in the kitchen making supper. As he listens to her footsteps moving towards the door, he tries to scoop up the bills from the floor and throw them behind the sofa.

"Where is he?" he hears a male voice say.

*Oh, oh.*

John Small bursts into the withdrawing room. "A word with you, sir," he says, coming so close to White's chair that he has no room to stand. A tall man, Small looms over him, one of his hands extended in a fist.

"You are upset, Small. Please sit down."

"Ah, sir, those words tell me a good deal. You know why I have come today."

"I have no idea. But let us converse like reasonable gentlemen. I cannot talk to you while you are standing over me. Please, sit." White gestures to a chair.

Small sits down, then scrapes the chair across the floor so that it faces White's. They are so close now their knees are almost touching.

Susannah hovers in the doorway of the withdrawing room, obviously wondering what she should do. She twists her hands into her apron.

"Please leave us to talk, Mrs. Page, but in a few minutes you might bring us some wine."

"No wine for me, woman. I want simply to have a few minutes alone with your master."

Susannah leaves. White takes a deep breath and waits.

"Well?"

"You have said things to that bastard Smith about my wife."

"I may have. What are you implying?"

"He has been very liberal in certain scurrilous communications to the Elmsleys. They have passed on this communication to others, particularly to the Powells. Now the whole town is talking about my wife."

Small bobs his head from side to side as he says this, and the wig he wears slips to one side. He tears it off with one hand and places it on his knee. He runs his other hand through his mess of black hair. He is wearing a frock coat with silver buttons, one that seems too grand for his lowly station as Clerk of the Executive Council. But White notes the stains down the front of his waistcoat as if he had risen suddenly from his dinner table and upset a glass of grog over himself.

"What are you staring at, White? Does it give you pleasure to see me in this state?"

"I stare merely because I have no idea why you have come here today and why, having done so, you are telling me about your wife."

"I demand that you publicly deny the venomous gossip that Smith has spread."

"How can I deny it when I have no idea what exactly he said? Why do you not talk with him? He, according to you, is the man who has spread the gossip."

"The bastard has flown the coop, and no one knows when he will come home to roost. But does it matter? You are the one who started the rumours. He spoke directly to Elmsley and repeated, word by word, phrase by phrase, what you told him at the goddamn subscription ball. Out with it, White." Small raises his fist and whacks it down on the arm of the chair. "What did you say?"

"It is possible that he may have said more or less than I told him. If you will kindly repeat the exact tale which he communicated to the Chief Justice, then I will know whether there is anything to deny or not."

*Oh, I relish these words.*

Small stands up. He trembles from head to foot. Tears run down his cheeks, and his face becomes so purple that for a moment White worries that he will drop into an apoplectic fit.

"Sir, you are insolent. I will stay no longer in your accursed presence. Mr friend Alexander Macdonnell will call on you tomorrow morning."

He claps his wig back on his head, searches into the pocket of his frock coat and extracts his gloves.

He throws one of them down on the floor in front of White's chair. Then he runs from the room knocking into Susannah who has just come through the doorway carrying a tray. The bottle of wine smashes onto the floor spattering blood-red stains on the stray bills that he did not manage to hide. The front door opens, then smashes shut.

Susannah sees the glove. She screams.

"Hush, my dear," he says, "please, please . . ."

"You know what that glove means, John?"

"Yes."

"But you cannot . . . you must not . . ."

"Accept the challenge? I do not know what to do. Leave me, please."

236

She stoops down and tries to pick up the shards of glass with her fingers, putting the broken bits onto the tray. He bends over her and pulls her to her feet. "Leave it all for now, Susannah. I must be alone. Please."

She does as she is told. As she closes the withdrawing-room door behind her, he drops onto the sofa and shuts his eyes, trying to block out the horror of the afternoon.

He hears the patter of the boys' feet in the hallway and Susannah's shushing of them. The moments pass. What to do?

He remembers the character Edgar in *King Lear*, a production he once saw in Haymarket before he married Marianne. What was it that Edgar said? Something so pertinent to his present situation . . . Now he remembers, not the exact words probably, but something like this: "We are reconciled to death by the changes and chances of this mortal life which make us hate it."

He looks at the jagged neck of the wine bottle lying beside the sofa. He picks it up, brings it towards the pulsing blue vein of his left wrist. It would be easy, so easy to end this mortal life . . .

# Chapter Forty-Eight

*January 2, 1800*

White is still on the sofa in the withdrawing room. He has moved only once or twice in the night to find a chamberpot and to get a bottle of sherry from the kitchen cupboard. It is now mid-morning, a snowy, frosty day from what he has observed through the window behind the sofa. Susannah has been in to clean up the mess of spilled wine and broken glass. She spoke to him, but he lay with his eyes shut, pretending not to hear. Now that she has gone back to the hearth, he raises himself just enough to grasp the sherry bottle from the Pembroke table by the sofa. He splashes some of it into his glass, drinks it in one swallow, and prays for oblivion.

But he is unable to shut out the basic question that plagues him. What is he to say to Macdonnell when he comes with Small's formal challenge to a duel? He remembers how often in the past he has condemned duels: in newspapers, at dinners and parties in Niagara and York, and in the court houses of Upper Canada while Osgoode, not heeding a word, imposed token fines on murderers.

He has himself been able to avoid two challenges: one from William Jarvis in Niagara—thanks to Russell—and the other more recently from the Glengarry Fencible.

A gentle knock on the withdrawing-room door: "John, John, I must speak with you, please."

"Come in, Susannah."

She wears a starched dimity cotton dress in a becoming pale blue shade and a clean, ironed apron. She has pulled her blonde hair back into a neat braid, but strands of curls have slipped over her ears.

"You are a vision in the midst of the squalor of this room," he says, suddenly aware of his uncombed locks and unwashed face and the stink of wine from the carpet by the sofa.

She appears to read his mind. "I must take this mat and hang it on the line. I shall throw some snow on it and give it a good whacking with the broom. And you, John, will you not come into your bedchamber where I have put some hot water into a pitcher for you to wash yourself? It is near ten o'clock."

"Got to get myself in hand, you're right. Macdonnell is coming soon. Perhaps he is already on his way. But if he comes while I am still indisposed, pray take the message and deliver it to me." He swings his legs off the sofa and tries to stand up.

Susannah gives him a tug and gets him upright. She tilts her chin and looks into his eyes. "I will take no message, nor will I deliver one." Her voice is fierce. He has never heard her speak this way before.

"Well then . . . what am I to do if the man comes knocking while I am still—"

"I hope you will not accept the challenge, John. But if you do, I must have no part of it. I will not contaminate myself with the unspeakable horror of duels . . ." As her voice trails into silence, she raises her fist as if she would strike him.

"Whoa, Susannah, what is this all about?"

"I told you once that my husband died of a gunshot wound . . ."

"In a duel, is that what you are telling me?"

"Yes, in Kingston. When my man was appointed Clerk of the Legislative Council, a captain in the 25th Regiment of Foot wanted his position, and my husband was angry. He lost his temper and challenged —"

"My God, I know this story. Your husband was Peter Clark. His opponent was David Sutherland who killed him, and I—"

"You made a brave defence, sir. But Chief Justice Osgoode let the murderer go free with a fine. I remember the amount to this day. Thirteen shillings and fourpence. My husband's life was valued at thirteen shillings and fourpence, think of that, thirteen shillings and—"

White pulls her to him and puts his arms around her. "You were in the courtroom, my dear?"

"Yes, I heard it all. I suffered it all." She is sobbing now. He feels her tears wet against his cheek.

*But her name is Susannah Page. Her husband's surname was Clark. What . . .?*

He says nothing aloud, simply holds her tight and hopes that she feels some comfort from the close embrace.

Finally she says, "You must have wondered how I came into service. My little girls were born almost nine months after my husband's murder. I changed my name back to Page, my maiden name, got on a packet boat with my babes and settled here. Made a fresh start, I did, though times were hard until I found you, sir . . ." More sobs.

There comes the knock on the front door, that dreaded knock they have both anticipated. White holds Susannah tight and moves her carefully to the sofa where he sets her gently down and pulls her feet up on the cushions so that she is resting, he hopes, comfortably.

The knock has become louder, more insistent. "I shall go," White says. "Stay here and rest. I understand your pain. Perhaps in time you can understand mine."

Alexander Macdonnell's round cheeks are red, whether from anger or cold, White knows not. "I shall not sully myself by crossing your threshold," the man says, thrusting a folded, sealed note into White's hand. "Read it, and give me an answer."

*Meet me behind the Parliament Buildings at daybreak tomorrow. Bring a pistol and a man to act as your second. Tell no one of this meeting.*

*"I love the name of honour more than I fear death."*
*John Small*

White scrunches the note in his fist. He laughs. "Those last lines, I know them. They are the words of Brutus, a traitor and a murderer."

240

"What has Brutus to do with it? What answer do I give Small?"

Macdonnell has a walleye. White finds it difficult to know if the man is looking at him or over his shoulder into the hallway. He hopes Susannah has decided to stay in the withdrawing room.

"I find it a strange irony that you, a magistrate of this town, a man specifically appointed to keep the peace, should be standing at my front door issuing a challenge to a duel."

The man's lips purse in a muttered oath. "Shut up. Give me an answer."

"Very well. I answer in the words of Julius Caesar: 'Death, a necessary end, will come when it will come.' Tell your damned friend Brutus that I accept the challenge."

# Chapter Forty-Nine

*Later, January 2, 1800*

From hours of sloth and torpor, White now finds himself thrust into a frenzy of activity in preparation for the morrow. His first thought is who to ask to be his second, and the answer comes fast. Baron de Hoen, of course. Has the man not bragged about his fine duelling pistols and lamented his thwarted wish for a duel with the Yankee Reesor who cheated him of a bridle for his horse? He must get a message to the Baron at once.

*But first, remember the adage: two birds with one stone.* It's one of his Canadian expressions. The farmers use it when they bring down two passenger pigeons with one missile.

So he puts his blue velvet frock coat and lace-trimmed cravat into a portmanteau and sets forth.

As he goes out onto the path in front of his house, he hears pistol shots from Small's lot. *Should I walk over to the man and tell him it is considered ungentlemanly to practise beforehand? Remind him of those words of Brutus that he had the effrontery to write on that note? But I don't care, really.*

He walks first to the tavern on Queen Street where he hopes to find one of Berczy's German immigrant friends on his usual stool quaffing back a cup of whisky punch. The man knows the Baron—they live in the settlement called Markham—and he will carry a message in return for a shilling or two. But when White arrives at the tavern, the man is not there.

But Abner Miles's shop is close by, and he takes his portmanteau there and dumps its contents onto the counter.

242

"What's this all about?" Miles asks him, a sneer on his face as he looks over the frock coat and cravat.

"What will you give me for it?"

Miles runs this thick, grimy fingers over the material. "You owe me plenty, you know. So I'll give you four pounds for the lot here, take half of it back for that bill, and give you two pounds for your binge at the garrison."

*And how does the bugger know about my nights at the garrison? Not that I'm exactly surprised.*

"Highway robbery, man. I've worn this frock coat and lace cravat twice. Is that the best you can do?"

"You nobs think the working classes must bow down before you? Take it or leave it. It's of no matter to me."

White ponders a moment, thinking of what a fine figure he cut in that velvet coat with the lace cravat. He remembers how he stood in front of his pier glass admiring himself and how Susannah came in, unannounced, how they had laughed together, how they had danced . . . It had been the first moment of a new romance.

But into his mind now come unbidden some lines that make him smile:

> *The grave's a fine and private place*
> *But none, I think, do there wear lace.*

So he takes the money and leaves the store. On the path outside, he meets Dr. Baldwin. The young man is wearing leather breeches like a common labourer, and his knee-length woollen topcoat is shabby.

"A two-pound payment down on the money I owe you, sir," White says, pushing the coins towards Baldwin. "I apologize for the delay. I will ever be grateful to you for saving my boy's life." *And it is possible that I may never be able to give you the full amount that you so richly deserve.*

"Thank you, White." Baldwin tucks the coins into one of his worn leather gloves as if he must hold them close and feel the comfort of the metal against his skin.

*What to do next? There's a chance that the Baron may be at the garrison. It's his favourite place. But this early in the day?*

He goes back home then to put on the stock that dear Ellen knitted for him and the fur hat with ear flaps that the explorer Mackenzie gave him. Fortified against the chill of the west wind, he sets off then along the margin of the lake to the garrison.

He takes the familiar route to the Officers' Mess, and lo, there is the Baron sitting at his favourite table. Fortunately, he is alone, his only adjuncts being the bowl of rum punch in front of him and the ceremonial sword laid across the oak boards of the table. In a minute, White has made his request, and the Baron has accepted.

"I shall arrive in plenty of time so that we may have a little target practice before Small and his man arrive. Not that target practice exactly complies with the rules."

"No practice, thank you. I do not fear death. What will be will be."

"Have you fired a pistol before?"

"No, but I think it does not require a great deal of intellect to pull a trigger. Just keep the matter to yourself, please, and I thank you for your service."

They part then. White makes his way back home. The wind is at his back now, and he makes good time. He has one more errand to carry out.

# Chapter Fifty

*Still later, January 2, 1800*

It is late afternoon when he arrives at the Russells' grand house, feeling thankful he has not had to meet anyone familiar en route. The snow has fortunately kept most people indoors.

Miss Russell answers the front door herself. "Mr. White, you be a-coming just in time to enjoy some fine brandy shrub that Job has made. Dear Peter, as you may know, is absent today in Markham firming up some land grants that be gone awry."

*Well yes, I did know that. It's the very reason I took this hour to call.*

As they walk through the hallway to the warmth of the kitchen, he sees the servant Peggy sitting at the head of the dining-room table, hands folded. When she catches sight of them, she grabs the feather duster in front of her and makes a swooping motion with it across the top of the table. Miss Russell observes it all and sighs.

In the kitchen, White lets Job serve him the shrub in a glass. Its vinegar flavour is sharp but it does not overpower the cherry syrup and brandy, and he nods approval at the servant.

Remembering then the import of his visit, he adds, "I must speak to you alone for a few minutes, Miss Russell."

Job leaves, closing the kitchen door that leads into the hallway. They are now safe from Peggy's ears. White holds his drink up in front of him. "It is strange that I am enjoying this so much, Miss Russell. It may be my last glass of shrub."

"What in tarnation are you saying?"

"I have agreed to fight a duel with John Small at daybreak tomorrow behind the Parliament Buildings. He has heard the gossip I spread at the subscription ball about his wife, and he intends to teach me a lesson, a serious lesson, perhaps with a bullet lodged in my heart."

She, who seldom drinks liquor, now pours herself a large glass of shrub and takes it down at a gulp. "I am quite undone by this news, sir. You . . . you . . . have always spoke out against such stupidity. I know not what to do or say." The shrub appears to come back up into her throat and she belches and wipes her face.

"Dear Miss Russell, I beg you will listen to me and try to understand. I am struggling myself to understand my motives for this stupidity, as you rightly call it. Perhaps if I can talk to you I can sort it out. I have no one but you who will listen, no one but you who can offer solace, you surely know that."

She pushes the punch bowl of shrub away and folds her hands on her lap. "Forgive me, please. If you be the better for speaking, then speak."

He scarcely knows where to begin. He cannot remember how much his friend knows. He sits in silence, trying to find a means of unravelling it all to her. He looks down at his glass of shrub, afraid to meet her gaze.

But her quiet voice gives him an opening. "For certain, Mr. Small knew the story of his wife's amours long before he came to this new world. Did not the English lord pay him to take her away? For certain, it is not to defend her honour that he be issuing this challenge."

"You are right, of course. But why, then, did he do it?"

"That be the question, sir."

"Perhaps to make *himself* look honourable. 'I love the name of honour more than I fear death.' That was what he wrote on the challenge."

"And all the big wigs in this place will be mighty impressed with a man who stands by his woman, no matter how much she has put him to the blush."

"That's it, of course. Whatever the outcome, there will be a trial and Mrs. Small's liaisons, far and wide, will be the principal subject of that trial, but she will not signify. It will be *he* who will receive the accolades of an honourable man."

"And you, Mr. White, you will bear the brunt of it. You will be the villain."

"Yes. In telling that sordid gossip to Smith, I had hoped only to get back at the bitch for the nasty things she said to my wife. Now it seems I have played into Small's hands, given him an opportunity to show himself as an honourable man."

*One more failure in this life of mine. One more reason to put an end to it all.*

"I can scarce understand, sir, why you be saying 'yes' to this fight."

"Because . . . because I . . . want to cross from Life into Death." *There, I've said the words that have been in my heart and soul for these last few hours.*

He waits for her reproof, but she says nothing. The clock above the hearth mantel punctuates the silence with its relentless ticks. He stares at the dregs in his glass.

Then comes her gentle voice. "I understand, sir, how a body can wish for an end to this life. I too looked to cross that river after Mary died. I wanted to fly with her to a new world. But she left me behind. And gradual-like, I come to realize I must be a-staying here to look after my dear Peter."

"Yes, your brother needs you. But I have no one . . ."

"Your little boys . . ."

"Yes, I worry about them. But I have started them on their path. They must go on without me. But I intend to leave this world in the right way so that they feel no guilt about my leaving them. Last night, as I sat on the sofa drinking myself stupid, I thought how easily I might end my life: a slash of an artery; an overdose from a medicine bottle; oh, a hundred ways there are to leave this world, to cross the river as you put it. And then came Macdonnell to the door with the challenge to the duel. I believe I have often said that duellists are the worst and most worthless of men upon this earth. But many people feel that duels are an honourable way to die. I want William and Charles to think that I ended my life . . . if not honourably, at least with courage and dignity."

It is a long speech, and his voice breaks as he finishes. Miss Russell comes around the table to sit by him. He takes the second glass of brandy shrub that she pours for him. Now she puts her hand on his arm and speaks into his ear. "I shall say nothing to Peter. For certain he would try to stop things. Your secret be safe with me, sir."

"I have done nothing to deserve a friend like you, Miss Russell."

"You be keeping secrets for me all these long days and months, thank the Lord. For *your* friendship, dear Mr. White, I am ever grateful."

He kisses her hand. Tears blind his eyes. He stumbles out the back door into the drifts of snow.

# Chapter Fifty-One

*Midnight, January 2, 1800*
John White settles himself at his desk in the withdrawing room and writes a note to Peter Russell.

*My dear Russell:*
*Being obliged to meet John Small tomorrow, and in the event of my demise, I implore your protection for my sons. Until the means can be found of returning William and Charles to my brother-in-law in England, may I entreat you and your sister to take them into your household and watch over them.*

*I beg you also to give support to Mrs. Page and her two little girls. Mrs. Page is an admirable housekeeper who can, I hope, find employment with you. She and her daughters live at present in a cabin at the back of my park lot, and this accommodation, if given over to her, would ensure her privacy and yours.*

*I can give no excuse for my part in this reprehensible affair with Small. I need merely to say that I have always nourished for you and your dear sister the deepest affection. Without your support, I should not have been able to endure these recent months. I do not fear death. It comes as a release from my woes.*
*Your friend,*
*John White*

He folds the page and seals it, leaving it in plain view on his desk. If by chance he does not return to this room tomorrow, someone will find the missive and deliver it.

Darkness has swallowed the house. He takes the candle from his desk and tiptoes down the hallway to the children's bedchamber. Since his illness, William seems to have become a much older boy. He no longer wants the trundle bed, and he has moved into Charles's bed. It's a narrow space, but the two of them have worked it out harmoniously. Although Charles has said nothing openly, White sees that his small brother's near-death has awakened in the lad a tender concern for his well-being. They sleep on their sides, one body tucked into the other. He leans over them, careful not to kick the large pail of water beside the bed. It contains a fish they caught yesterday from a hole in the ice of the lake. They intend to show it to Russell and get him to explain how it breathes.

For a moment he stands there, smiling down at their smooth faces, pink from their adventures on the bay. He has procured three hundred acres for each for them, and perhaps one day—when this wretched little town grows into a metropolis—the land will have value. *May they always care for each other. May they grow up happy and prosperous and find peace in their married lives and families. And dearest Ellen . . .*

Of Marianne and Ellen, he has heard nothing since that dreadful day in Quebec. They have gone from his life. Will they care if he dies tomorrow? The question is not one he can bear to contemplate. At any rate, they have acreage here that may bring them money. When they first came to York, he acquired for Ellen two hundred acres, and for Marianne, one thousand.

It now remains only to say goodbye to Susannah. He has waited until the dead of night, hoping that she will be asleep and that he will not have to confront her anger and tears. From the back door of his house, he follows the trail beaten through the snowdrifts to her cabin in the wooded area at the rear of his park lot. An owl hoots from a nearby pine tree.

There is no sound as he enters the small timber structure that Berczy built for her when she and her girls joined their household. It has only one room, but it seems warm and cosy tonight, and the embers are still glowing in the hearth.

In a shadowy corner of the room, separated from the main space by a blanket hung from the rafters, he finds, as he had hoped, Susannah sound asleep in her bed. One small daughter sleeps with her, and the other lies in a trundle bed beside them. Their deep breathing, gentle snores, and the crackling of the embers are the only sounds he hears.

Glad is he not to have to disturb their peaceful slumbers. On the table in the centre of the room, he places his gold pocket watch, two signet rings, and a note saying goodbye. Even that bastard Abner Miles will surely give her a few pounds for the gold, enough to keep her and her daughters for several months.

Having heard both Peter and Eliza Russell's complaints about their servant Peggy, and having seen the slattern's ways himself, he is confident that his friends will welcome Susannah and offer her a position in their house.

Back in his own bedchamber, he puts on his nightshirt and tries to settle. But he cannot sleep. It is now only a few hours until daybreak. He gets up from his bed, dons a new frock coat, walks downstairs to the withdrawing room, stirs the fire in the hearth, and sits down in an armchair to wait.

# Chapter Fifty-Two

*January 3, 1800*

John White stands at his front window, anxious to intercept Baron de Hoen before he bangs on the door knocker and awakens the boys. He does not have to wait long. Striding down the pathway in the pale light of early morning comes the Baron. White opens the door and motions him in.

He is wearing a sky-blue military greatcoat and a bearskin hat with a ridiculous red plume. He carries a fine wooden case containing no doubt the duelling pistols.

White puts his fingers to his lips and they talk in whispers.

"Rotten cold morning," the Baron says. "Wear your heaviest."

What White has planned is not necessarily his "heaviest." It's what he wants to look best in, though he cannot tell the Baron this. He takes from the coat stand what his German tailor calls a carrick coat, a voluminous greatcoat in dark grey with five shoulder capes and a turned-up collar.

He flips onto his head the dark top hat with rolled brim. "Not that one, my friend," the Baron says. "Your ears will freeze." White ignores him. If he is to die, he wants to go out in style.

They move out into the quiet of dawn and turn their steps towards the Parliament Buildings. Piles of snow lie everywhere, and they sometimes have to leap over drifts in order to move forward. There is no wind, and the smoke from a dozen chimneys rises straight into the sky. It is utterly quiet, thank God, except for the occasional barking dog and the plop of falling snow from an overladen pine branch. Even the roosters have not yet awakened to herald the day.

"Thank the Lord for the silence," the Baron says. "I hope we shall be able to enact this affair without interference from some bloody do-gooder."

They arrive at the grove of woods behind the Parliament Buildings. Beyond that grove lies the bay, that bay he has grown to love so much. Small is waiting in front of the grove, a tall figure barely visible in the dim light. Beside him is Macdonnell, magistrate of the town, dressed in a drab greatcoat.

"Good day to you both," White says, relishing the irony of those words. Macdonnell makes a gagging noise in his throat, and White feels his ire rising. "Glad to see you here, sir. No doubt as magistrate you have dealt only with minor offences: drunkenness, selling spirits without a licence, and the like. You will no doubt be happy now to oversee and encourage a murder."

Baron de Hoen tugs on his sleeve. "Leave it. What is the point of this sarcasm?"

Small, he sees now, has his pistol already in hand. The Baron notices the weapon at the same time. "Hold on, hold on," he says to Macdonnell. "Does Mr. Small have an equivalent pistol for Mr. White?"

Macdonnell looks confused. "What do you mean?"

"Both opponents must have equivalent pistols so that one man does not have an advantage over the other. Produce that second pistol now, sir."

"But we have only one," Macdonnell says. "It's Mr. Small's. He has been practising with—" He breaks off, evidently realizing he has said too much.

"Quite so," the Baron says, "and exactly what I would expect from a man who has not the slightest notion of gentlemanly conduct." He walks up to Small, takes another look at his pistol, and then another, more intense look. "Good Lord," he says, his voice rising. "This pistol has a rifled barrel. Another disgusting breach of etiquette. Have you not read the *Code Duello of 1777* which sets forth twenty-six provisions for proper duelling? Give over your weapon to me this instant, sir, or throw it into that snowbank." He turns to White. "Can you believe such duplicity?"

White has no idea what breach Small has committed with this rifled barrel, nor does he have any idea what code the Baron is blathering on about, but he does not want to reveal his utter ignorance in front of his adversary, so he merely shakes his head.

The Baron opens his mahogany case. It is lined with velvet and contains, as White expected, a pair of duelling pistols. He thrusts the case towards Small and Macdonnell. "Choose one of these. They are true flintlock duelling pistols. None of those dastardly grooves in the barrel that you have tried to get away with."

They are long, slender pistols, engraved in silver with floral designs that recall the wayside flowers of England White once loved. It is hard to believe that such beautifully crafted objects could be weapons for killing. He watches as his opponent, obviously impressed, puts out his hand to draw out one of the pistols.

"Beautiful, beautiful, are they not?" The Baron actually licks his lips, savouring the moment. "On them were lavished the best of the talents of woodcarver, metal worker, engraver, and silversmith. I have treasured these pistols for more than twenty-five years."

True, perhaps, but White cannot bring himself to touch them. The Baron waits for a second or two, then draws out the second pistol. "Now," he says to Macdonnell, "the assailants must wait while we load the weapons. They must watch to ensure that we follow prescribed procedures."

As soon as the Baron draws forth the black gunpowder from its copper container and measures it, White feels his head begin to pound. He looks away, out at the bay which he can just see through a gap in the woods. Far off is the figure of a man on snowshoes. It may be his Indian friend. *Goodbye, Abel. Perhaps as you reset your traps today, you will come upon blood on the snow just as I once did all those months ago in Niagara. Goodbye, Yvette, I pray that by now you have a living babe and a loving husband to nurture with your dandelion wine and whitefish stew . . .*

The Baron thrusts the pistol into his hand, giving him a jab in the ribs at the same time. "Wake up, sir. Time to get on with it. The town will be alive in a few minutes." He raises his voice in command. "We will now mark out ten paces from this point. You, Mr. White, walk in that direction; and you, Mr. Small, in that one. When you have done that, turn so that you are facing each other, and I will set forth the rules for what follows."

White and Small do as they are told, obedient children before a stern master.

"Now, face each other square on. No side presentation. On command, you shall then raise your pistols. I will ask the question, 'Are you ready?' and wait for your answer. Then I will say, 'Fire!' You must fire within three seconds of the command at most. There must be no taking of time to aim carefully. These are the rules of the *Code Duello.* Do you understand what I have said?"

Both White and Small nod their heads, but before the command to raise their pistols comes, there is a loud cry from Macdonnell who runs towards the Baron and tugs at his arm. "Wait a moment, you blackguard! Your man has surely infringed these bloody rules you're going on about. Look at that greatcoat he is wearing. *Five* bloody capes! How is my friend to take aim if he cannot see the man's body? The coat must come off. Now!"

Clearly, Macdonnell is getting back at the Baron for usurping his authority. White waits, wondering what his second will do.

"Very well, sir," the Baron says. He turns to White. "Remove your greatcoat."

White throws his coat into the snow.

"Raise your pistols!"

White stands in his frock coat shivering uncontrollably. His arms are freezing, and the pistol shakes in his hand. He tries steadying it with both hands. But his gloves are too tight and he cannot seem to grip the thing. *Nevertheless I must not turn back now.*

255

"Are you ready?"

"Yes!"

"Yes!"

"Fire!"

His hand fumbles. There's a puff of smoke and a blast from somewhere. A huge giant punches him in the abdomen. He crumples into the snow. But snow is white, this is red . . . why . . . Someone is yelling . . . "Get him to Russell". . .

# Chapter Fifty-Three

*January 4, 1800*

Eliza Russell has sat by Mr. White's side since three men carried him to the house yestermorn on a stretcher made from his greatcoat. During the long hours, she has moved in and out of sleep. Now as she sees a new day's light through the window pane, she knows she has weathered the night. Has he?

She looks at him. His eyes are closed, but his mouth is open and blood trickles down his chin. "Internal bleeding," Dr. Baldwin told her and Peter. "He will not last the night." She holds a glass in front of his face and sees the mist upon it. Still alive.

Job tiptoes in with a good hot cup of tea and a buttered scone. But what she needs most at this moment is the chamber pot. She motions to Job to take her place. Past her brother's room she goes, listens to his snores, glad she sent him to bed, and that he has had some rest. In her own room, she relieves herself and washes her face, readying herself for the coming hours of the death watch.

Little William and Charles must not see their Papa in this state, that she knows for certain. She dips a quill in the inkwell on the table by her bookcase and writes a note to Mrs. Page telling her to be a-keeping an eye on their to-ings and fro-ings this day. Last night Mrs. Page brought over a sealed note from Mr. White which she had found in the withdrawing room. Later Peter read it to her as they sat together beside their friend's bed.

As she goes back to the death watch, she sees that the trail of blood on the hallway floor is still there. If any good can come from this wretched duel, it will be to have Mrs.

Page in this house in the place of the slattern Peggy. And the children, yes, the children. She smiles to think of childish laughter in their midst once again.

She gives her note to Job. He looks at Mrs. Page's name on the outside, nods, and indicates that he will deliver it as he is bid.

Mr. White is in a sort of coma from what she can tell. His breath comes in moans. She sits in the chair by his bed a-wondering what can be done to ease his passing. She must not look at his naked body. No.

The minutes tick by . . . The Lord forgive her, she must know the worst. She pulls aside the cotton sheet and the blankets they have covered him with and sees the bandage Dr. Baldwin wrapped around his abdomen. *Lordy, Lordy.* His whole lower body is seized up with a-shivering and a-shaking that will not stop. The bandage itself is soaked in brown-red blood, a dark contrast to the bright red blood that comes a-leaking from his mouth. She cannot look at it, cannot bear to think of what that body must be enduring. She pulls the sheet and blankets back over to cover the worst. *Dear Lord, let this end.*

\* \* \*

The sun has long ago moved out of the window. It is late afternoon. Peter comes in, touches her shoulder, looks at their dying friend, and sighs. "May it all be over with soon," he says.

At the sound of her brother's voice, Mr. White opens his eyes. They are glassy and unfocused, but he seems to be trying to communicate in some way. She and her brother lean in towards him. "Dear, dear friend," she says.

Peter looks at her. "Perhaps there are miracles after all," he says.

Mr. White struggles to speak, but the sound that comes from his throat, along with a bloody spume, they cannot understand. He is looking at them, that is for certain, and he reaches out a trembling hand towards them. She and Peter grasp it. It goes slack in their grip.

Moments pass. They look at the still, silent figure before them. "You must rest now, sister," Peter says at last. "Go and sleep. I shall see to the arrangements."

But she cannot rest. After her brother leaves, she sits beside her friend, unwilling to leave his body unattended. She thinks of the day she came upon him and his cook Yvette during the little funeral in the spring garden. How she stood with them as they sang "Joy to the World" with the words about the wonders of God's love. And she remembers how her friend sat with her and comforted her during those long night hours when her heart near broke over her daughter's death.

"I think of the wonders of *your* love, my friend," she says aloud. Then she leans forward and kisses the pale face streaked with blood.

"May you find peace, dear Mr. White." She remembers the words he spoke to comfort her after Mary's death. "Fly to another world now, a world free of pain."

The End

Ann Birch is a long-time historical researcher and an award-winning Head of English in several Toronto high schools. She has a Master of Arts degree in CanLit and is currently a fiction writer, editor, lecturer, and workshop facilitator. This is her third novel.